JOHN JEREMIAH SULLIVAN

BLOOD HORSES

Notes of a Sportswriter's Son

YELLOW JERSEY PRESS
LONDON

Published by Yellow Jersey Press 2013

2 4 6 8 10 9 7 5 3 1

Copyright © John Jeremiah Sullivan 2013

John Jeremiah Sullivan has asserted his right under the Copyright, Designs
and Patents Act 1988 to be identified as the author of this work

First published in Great Britain in 2012 by
Yellow Jersey Press
Random House, 20 Vauxhall Bridge Road,
London SW1V 2SA

www.vintage-books.co.uk

Addresses for companies within The Random House Group Limited can be found at:
www.randomhouse.co.uk/offices.htm

The Random House Group Limited Reg. No. 954009

A CIP catalogue record for this book
is available from the British Library

ISBN 9780224091862

The Random House Group Limited supports The Forest
Stewardship Council (FSC®), the leading international forest certification
organisation. Our books carrying the FSC label are printed on FSC®
certified paper. FSC is the only forest certification scheme endorsed by
the leading environmental organisations, including Greenpeace.
Our paper procurement policy can be found at:
www.randomhouse.co.uk/environment

Printed and bound by CPI Group (UK) Ltd, Croydon, CR0 4YY

M.W.S., 1945–2000

H.P.B.M., 1917–2000

He had a sincere awe of the beasts around us,
and he considered himself essentially on the
same level with them, very closely related—
not through evolution, that poor man's religion,
but through common destiny.
  —Joachin Seyppl, *The Animal Theme*
    and Totemism in Franz Kafka, 1954

BLOOD HORSES

THE KID

It was in the month of May, three years ago, by a hospital bed in Columbus, Ohio, where my father was recovering from what was supposed to have been a quintuple bypass operation but became, on the surgeon's actually seeing the heart, a sextuple. His face, my father's face, was pale. He was thinner than I had seen him in years. A stuffed bear that the nurses had loaned him lay crooked in his lap; they told him to hug it whenever he stood or sat down, to keep the stitches in his chest from tearing. I complimented him on the bear when I walked in, and he gave me one of his looks, dropping his jaw and crossing his eyes as he rolled them back in their sockets. It was a look he assumed in all kinds of situations but that always meant the same thing: *Can you believe this?*

Riverside Methodist Hospital (the river being the Olentangy): my family had a tidy little history there, or at least my father and I had one. It was to Riverside that I had been rushed from a Little League football game when I was twelve, both of my lower right leg bones broken at the shin in such a way that when the whistle was blown and I sat up on the field, after my first time carrying the ball all season, I looked down to find my toes pointing a perfect 180 degrees from the direction they should have been pointing in, at which sight I went into mild shock on the grass at the fifty-yard line and lay back to admire the clouds. Only the referee's face obstructed my view. He kept saying, "Watch your language, son," which seemed comical, since as far as I knew I had not said a word.

I seem to remember, or may have deduced, that my father walked in slowly from the sidelines then with the exceptionally calm demeanor he showed during emergencies, and put his hand on my arm, and said something encouraging, doubtless a little shocked himself at the disposition of my foot—a little regretful too, it could be, since he, a professional sports-writer who had been a superb all-around athlete into his twenties and a Little League coach at various times, must have known that I should never have been on the field at all. Running back was the only viable position for me, in fact, given that when the coach had tried me at other places on the line, I had tended nonetheless to move away from the other players. My lone resource was my speed; I still had a prepubescent track runner's build and was the fastest player on the team. The coach had noticed that I tended to win the sprints and thought he saw an opportunity. But what both of us failed to understand was that a running back must not only outrun the guards—typically an option on only the most flawlessly executed plays—but often force his way past them, knock them aside. Such was never going to happen.

In fairness, the coach had many other things to worry about. Our team, which had no name, lacked both talent and what he called "go." In the car headed home from our first two games, I could tell by the way my father avoided all mention of what had taken place on the field that we were pathetic—not Bad News Bears pathetic, for we never cut up or "wanted it" or gave our all. At practice a lot of the other players displayed an indifference to the coach's advice that suggested they might have been there on community service.

The coach's son, Kyle, was our starting quarterback. When

practice was not going Kyle's way, that is, when he was either not on the field, having been taken off in favor of the second-stringer, who was excellent, or when he was on the field and throwing poorly, Kyle would begin to cry. He cried not childish tears, which might have made me wonder about his life at home with the coach and even feel for him a little, but bitter tears, too bitter by far for a twelve-year-old. Kyle would then do a singular thing: he would fling down his helmet and run, about forty yards, to the coach's car, a beige Cadillac El Dorado, which was always parked in the adjacent soccer field. He would get into the car, start the engine, roll down all four windows, and—still crying, I presumed, maybe even sobbing now in the privacy of his father's automobile—play Aerosmith tapes at volumes beyond what the El Dorado's system was designed to sustain. The speakers made crunching sounds. The coach would put up a show of ignoring these antics for five or ten minutes, shouting more loudly at us, as if to imply that such things happened in the sport of football. But before long Kyle, exasperated, would resort to the horn, first honking it and then holding it down. Then he would hold his fist out the driver's-side window, middle finger extended. The coach would leave at that point and walk, very slowly, to the car. While the rest of us stood on the field, he and Kyle would talk. Soon the engine would go silent. When the two of them returned, practice resumed, with Kyle at quarterback.

None of this seemed remarkable to me at the time. We were new to Columbus, having just moved there from Louisville (our house had been right across the river, in the knobs above New Albany, Indiana), and I needed friends. So I watched it all happen with a kind of dumb, animal acceptance, sensing that it could come to no good. And suddenly it was that final Saturday, and Kyle had given me the ball, and something very brief and violent had happened, and I was watching a tall, brawny man-child bolt up and away from my body, as though he had woken up next to a rattlesnake. I can still see his eyes as they took in my leg. He was black, and he had an afro that sprung outward when he ripped off his helmet. He looked genuinely confused about how easily I had broken. As the paramedics were loading me onto the stretcher, he came over and said he was sorry.

At Riverside they set my leg wrong. An X ray taken two weeks later revealed that I would walk with a limp for the rest of my life if the leg were not rebroken and reset. For this I was sent to a doctor named Moyer, a specialist whom other hospitals would fly in to sew farmers' hands back on, that sort of thing. He was kind and reassuring. But for reasons I have never been able to fit back together, I was not put all the way under for the resetting procedure. They gave me shots of a tranquilizer, a fairly weak one, to judge by how acutely conscious I was when Dr. Moyer gripped my calf with one hand and my heel with the other and said, "John, the bones have already started to knit back together a little bit, so this is probably going to hurt." My father was outside smoking in the parking lot at that moment, and said later he could hear my screams quite clearly. That was my first month in Ohio.

Two years after the injury had healed, I was upstairs in my bedroom at our house on the northwest side of Columbus when I heard a single, fading "Oh!" from the first-floor hallway. My father and I were the only ones home at the time, and I took the staircase in a bound, terrified. Turning the corner, I almost tripped over his head. He was on his back on the floor, unconscious, stretched out halfway into the hall, his feet and legs extending into the bathroom. Blood was everywhere, but although I felt all over his head I couldn't find a source. I got him onto his feet and onto the couch and called the paramedics, who poked at him and said that his blood pressure was "all over the place." So they manhandled him onto a stretcher and took him to Riverside.

It turned out that he had simply passed out while pissing, something, we were told, that happens to men in their forties (he was at the time forty-five). The blood had all gushed from his nose, which he had smashed against the sink while falling, Still, the incident scared him enough to make him try again to quit smoking—to make him want to quit, anyway, one of countless doomed resolutions.

My father was desperately addicted to cigarettes. It is hard for me to think about him, to remember him, without a ghostly neural whiff of tobacco smoke registering in my nostrils, and when I have trouble seeing him clearly I can bring him into focus by summoning the yellowed skin on the middle and index fingers of his left hand, or the way the hairs of his reddish brown mustache would brush the filter of the cigarette as he drew it in to inhale, or the way he pursed his lips and tucked in his chin when exhaling down through his nose, which he made a point of doing in company. Once, in the mid-nineties, he lit up in the rest room during an international flight (a felony, I believe). A stewardess called ahead to alert the authorities, and he was nearly arrested after landing at the airport, but the coach of the team he was traveling with helped him grovel his way out of it. There were other little humiliations: places we were asked to leave, inappropriate moments at which he would suddenly disappear. He was absentminded, a trait that did not mix well with the constant presence of fire. Every so often I came home from school to find another small black hole burned into the chair where he sat. And there was the time a garbage bag into which he had tossed the contents of an ashtray caught fire in our garage, forcing my mother to point out to him again, with a look half earnest and half hopeless, that he was putting us all in danger.

About once a year he would decide to stop, but it was rare that he could go a full day without a "puff," and as long as he was sneaking puffs, the abyss of total regression was only a black mood away. He tried to keep his failures a secret, even allowing us to congratulate him for having gone two days or a week without smoking when in fact the campaign had ended within hours, as I realize now with adulthood's slightly less gullible eye: the long walks, "to relax," from which he would come back chewing gum, or the thing he would be stuffing into his pocket as he left the store. Sooner or later he would tire of the effort involved in these shams and simply pull out a pack while we sat in the living room, all of us, and there would be a moment, which grew familiar over time, when we would be watching him sidelong, looks of disappointment barely contained in our faces, and he would be staring ahead at the television, a look of shame barely contained in his, and then, just as the tension neared the point of someone speaking, he would light the cigarette, and that would be it. We would go back to our books.

The trip to the hospital—or rather the vow he made, when he got home, that enough was finally enough—seemed different. Before that afternoon his body had been weirdly impervious to insult. This was a man who never got a cold, and who was told by a radiologist, after thirty years of constant, heavy smoking, that his lungs were "pink," which almost made my mother cry with frustration. But now the whole neighborhood had seen him being loaded into the ambulance, and the enforced silence surrounding the question of his health—which, if it could only be maintained, would keep consequence at bay—had been broken.

He lasted four or five days. I assume so, anyway. My mother found him hiding in the garage, the "patch" on his arm and in his mouth a Kool Super-Long (his cigarette of choice from the age of fourteen—he liked to say that he was the last white man in America to smoke Kools). This doubling up on the nicotine, we had been warned, could quickly lead to a heart attack, so he threw out the patches and went back to smoking a little over two packs a day.

The thing they say about a man like my father, and a great many sportswriters match the description, is that he "did not take care of himself." I cannot think of more than one or

- 8 -

two conventionally healthy things that he did in my lifetime, unless I were to count prodigious napping and laughter (his high, sirenlike laugh that went *HEEE Hee hee hee, HEEE Hee hee hee* could frighten children, and was so loud that entire crowds in movie theaters would turn from the screen to watch him, which excruciated the rest of the family). In addition to the chain-smoking, he drank a lot, rarely ordering beer except by the pitcher and keeping an oft-replaced bottle of whiskey on top of the fridge, though he showed its effects— when he showed them at all—in only the most good-natured way. Like many people with Irish genes, he had first to decide that he wanted to be drunk before he could feel drunk, and that happened rarely. Still, the alcohol must have hastened his slide from the fitness he had enjoyed in his youth. He also ate badly and was heavy, at times very heavy, though strangely, especially taking into consideration a total lack of exercise, he retained all his life the thin legs and powerful calves of a runner. He was one of those people who are not meant to be fat, and I think it took him by surprise when his body at last began to give down: it had served him so well.

Anyone with a mother or father who possesses fatalistic habits knows that the children of such parents endure a special torture during their school years, when the teachers unspool those horror stories of what neglect of the body can do; it is a kind of child abuse, almost, this fear. I recall as a boy of five or six creeping into my parents' room on Sunday mornings, when he would sleep late, and standing by the bed, staring at his shape under the sheets for the longest time to be sure he was breathing; a few times, or more than a few times, I dreamt that he was dead and went running in, convinced it was true. One night I lay in my own bed and concentrated as hard as I could, believing, under the influence of some forgotten work of popular pseudoscience, that if I did so the age at which he would die would be revealed to me: six and three were the numerals that floated before my eyelids. That seemed far enough into the future and, strange to say, until the day he died, eight years short of the magic number, it held a certain comfort.

We pleaded with him, of course, to treat himself better— though always with trepidation, since the subject annoyed him and, if pressed, could send him into a rage. Most of the time we did not even get to the subject, he was so adept at heading it off with a joke: when a man who is quite visibly at risk for heart attack, stroke, and cancer crushes out what is left of a six-inch-long mentholated cigarette before getting to work on a lethal fried meal ("a hearty repast," as he would have called it), clinks his knife and fork together, winks at you, and says, with a brogue, "Heart smart!" you are disarmed. I have a letter from him, written less than a month before he died, in response to my having asked him about an exercise regimen that his doctor had prescribed. In typically epithetic style (it was his weakness), he wrote, "Three days ago didst I most stylishly drive these plucky limbs once around the 1.2-mile girth of Antrum Lake—and wasn't it a lark watching the repellently 'buff' exercise cultists scatter and cower in fear as I gunned the Toyota around the turns!"

And still we would ask him to cut back, to come for a walk, to order the salad. I asked him, my brother and sisters asked him, my mother practically begged him until they divorced. His own father had died young, of a heart attack; his mother had died of lung cancer when I was a child. But it was no use. He had his destiny. He had his habits, no matter how suicidal, and that he change them was not among the things we had a right to ask.

It hardly helped that his job kept him on the road for months out of the year, making any routine but the most compulsive almost impossible, or that the work was built around deadlines and nervous tension, banging out the story between the fourteenth inning, the second overtime, whatever it was, and the appointed hour. Among my most vivid childhood memories are the nights when I was allowed to sit up with my father in the press box at Cardinal Stadium after Louisville Redbirds home games (the Redbirds were the St. Louis Cardinals' triple-A farm team, but for a brief stretch the local fans got behind them as if they were major league, breaking the season attendance record for the division in 1985). While the game was in progress, I had a seat beside him, and I watched with fascination as he and the other reporters filled in their scorebooks with the arcane markings known to true aficionados, a letter or number or shape for even the most inconsequential event on the field. Every so often a foul ball would come flying in through the window, barely missing our heads, and my father would stand and wave his ever-present white cloth handkerchief out the window, drawing a murmur from the crowd.

My regular presence up there likely grated on the other sportswriters, but they put up with me because of my father. Every few months, I get a letter from one of his old colleagues saying how much less fun the job is without him. Last year I came across an article in *Louisville Magazine* by John Hughes, who worked with him at the *Courier-Journal* "Things happened in those newsrooms that are no longer possible in this journalistically correct era," Hughes remembered. "The New Year's night, for instance, when former *C-J* sportswriter Mike Sullivan made a hat out of a paper bag from my beer run and wore it while writing about the tackle that ended Woody Hayes's coaching career." This was typical. Once, when I was with my father on the floor at the newspaper office—I was probably five—he saw that I was excited by the pneumatic tubes that the separate departments used to communicate back then, so he started encouraging me to put my shoes and, eventually, my socks into the canisters and shoot them to various friends of his. When a voice came over the intercom saying, *"Whoever keeps sending this shit through the tubes, stop it!"* we had to bend over to keep from hooting and giving ourselves away. In the press box, he would trot me out to tell jokes I had learned. One of these involved the word "obese," and when I got to that part, I paused and asked, out of politeness, "Do all of you know what obese means?" The room exploded. For him, this was like having his child win the national spelling bee.

It had to have dismayed my father somewhat that the games themselves were lost on me. How many men would love to give their red-blooded American sons the sort of exposure to big-time sports that I took as the way of things? It was a wasted gift, in most respects. I remember meeting Pee Wee Reese in the Redbirds press box. His son Mark worked with my father at the *Courier-Journal*, and Pee Wee had come up to say hello. My father, sitting beside *his* father, had watched Reese play shortstop for the Brooklyn Dodgers at Ebbets Field in the mid-fifties, and he introduced me to the man as if he

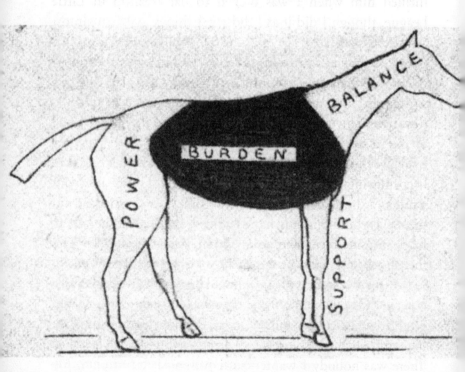

were presenting me to a monarch. I was embarrassed more than anything and turned away after shaking his hand. This scene repeated itself, with various sports legends playing the part of Reese, into my adolescence.

As an athlete, too, I was a disappointment. I made use of the natural ability that my father had passed on to me, but my concentration would flicker on and off. I could never master the complexities. A referee actually blew the whistle and stopped one of my sixth-grade basketball games to explain the three-second rule to me. He was tired of calling me on the violation. He put his hands on my hips and moved me in and out of the key, telling me where it was and how long one was allowed to stay there, while the crowd and the other players watched in silence. I had no idea what he was talking about and was quickly taken out of the game.

I was better at baseball, my father's favorite sport. It thrilled him when I was picked to bat cleanup in Little League, though I did it as I did most things, with an almost autistic hyperfocus: *The ball is there. Swing now.* I routinely homered, but still I would stand on the base with the ball in my glove when I was supposed to tag the runner, or forget to "tag up" after a caught foul and slide with gusto into the next base, only to be leisurely tapped on the shoulder by one of the in-fielders. Soccer I actively hated. But it lasted only a few weeks, until I figured out that if you were too tired to keep playing, or if you had a cramp, you could raise your hand and the coach would pull you out. So as soon as he put me on, I would raise my hand. Once I did this and he yelled, from the sidelines, "Come on, John, *goddamnit!*" Our eyes met. I kept my hand in the air.

My involvement with any kind of organized athletics ended at a tae kwon do studio in downtown Louisville. Why it was, given my particular handicap, that I chose a sport famed for its emphasis on absolute concentration, one has to wonder. There was nobody I wanted to fight, and I feared pain. My teacher, Master Gary, was a wiry-bearded veteran of the war in Vietnam, which had left him angrier than one who works with children should be. His lessons were governed by a constantly expanding set of rules and Korean words that left me paralyzed with confusion. I remember with an especially violent cringe the night I decided to practice my "form" during "meditation time." The other boys and girls were silent on their knees in perfect rows, hands folded, eyes closed. Master Gary faced them in an identical posture. At a certain point I inexplicably rose and went to the corner, where I began to flail away on the heavy bag. My father, who had arrived early to pick me up, finally hissed at me to stop. Master Gary never opened his eyes. Two weeks later I was leaning against the wall, trying to be invisible, when one of his sublieutenants, a mannish teenage girl with short dark hair and a slight mustache, swung into view before me. She screamed something, startling me so badly I had to ask her to repeat it. So she screamed it more loudly, *"We do not lean in this dojo!"*

If I was doing all this largely to please my father—and I can think of no other reason—he never made me feel that he cared very much how I performed. During games, he would cheer loudly, and torment me, no matter how hard I pleaded with him to stop, by using my nicknames: Prodge (short for progeny) and Beamish (from the Lewis Carroll poem: I got used to waving off my teammates when they would walk up and ask, *"What's* he calling you?"). I remember none of those clichéd angry silences after lost games, only a lightening, a sense of relief that at least it was done. And if all that professional baseball that I watched from on high, with that perfect view, seemed to me like modern dance—intriguing but in the end inscrutable—we were together. I was never bored when I was with my father.

The real joy for me came after the game; after I had followed him into the locker room, where he would dutifully get his quotes while I stood behind him, horrified by all the giant exposed phalli that were bobbing past me at eye level;

after the other sportswriters had gone back to their houses or hotels (he was the Redbirds' "beat," or all-season, writer, which meant that he often had to file two stories before packing it in); after he had settled back into his seat and flipped open his notepad, the long, lined, narrow pages blue now with his swirly shorthand. That was when the stadium emptied out and the bums who had somehow found a way to evade the security guards would emerge from the shadows, like ragpickers, and move about in the diminished light, finishing off half-empty beers. Looking down at the stands, I marveled that a place so recently full of bodies and noise could in such a short time empty out and take on this tremendous, cathedral-like silence. I would cross the suspended metal walkway that led from the press box to the bleachers and play by myself in the stands, now and then getting into some awkward, upsetting conversation with one of the bums. After a few months I built up my nerve and started venturing onto the empty field, running the bases, pitching invisible balls to ghostly batters, calling up to my father, hundreds of feet above in the press box window, to check me out. He would wave. On one of these nights, when I was restless, I learned to pick the lock on the door to the press-box concession stand by sticking a straightened paper clip into the tumbler on the handle and wrapping it around the knob. From then on, after hours, it was unlimited Cracker Jacks for me, and unlimited six-packs for my father, in whose delight at my ingenuity I took bottomless pride. There he would sit, an open beer next to his PortaBubble (an early laptop computer that weighed as much as a four-year-old child), a burning cigarette in his fingers, pecking out strange, clever stories about inconsequential games. There was a mildly retarded janitor who took me up onto the roof of the "box" one night and taught me the constellations. As the sky got darker, armadas of giant green bugs would come in at the windows, which were left cracked on account of the smoke. I would roll up a program and do battle with these, rushing around smacking the walls while my father sat with his back to me, typing and smoking and typing and drinking.

I can still reenter the feeling of those nights: they were happy. My father and I hardly spoke to each other, or I would ask him something and he would not hear me, or else he would answer only after the twenty-second delay that was a private joke in our family, suddenly whipping his head around, after I had forgotten the question, to say, "Um, no," or "Sure, son." But for me this distance somehow increased the intimacy. This was no trip to the zoo. I was not being patronized or baby-sat. I was in his element, where he did his mysterious work, and this—being close like this—was better than being seen or heard.

When I got older, there was another kind of distance between us, one that we both noticed, and both minded. I was angry at him for years, at the way he had passively allowed his marriage to my mother to drift into dissolution, at the fact that he was visibly killing himself. That night, in his room at Riverside, there was a certain unspoken feeling of "Here we are" between us, which may explain the morbidity—one might say the audacity—of the question I found myself asking him, a man of only fifty-five. There had, in the preceding year, already been the aneurysm surgery then the surgery (unsuccessful) to repair the massive hernia caused by the aneurysm surgery. For almost a year he had walked around with a thing about the size and shape of a cannonball protruding from his stomach. "My succession of infirmities," as he put it to me in a letter, "has tended finally to confront me with blunt intimations of mortality." Otherwise, however, it was not a morbid scene. This last operation had gone well, and he seemed to be feeling better than he had any right to. The waning sedative and, I suppose, twenty-four hours without cigarettes had left him edgy, but he was happy to talk, which we did in whispers because the old man with whom he was sharing a room had already gone to sleep.

I asked him to tell me what he remembered from all those years of writing about sports, for he had seen some things in his time, had covered Michael Jordan at North Carolina, a teenage John McEnroe, Bear Bryant, Muhammad Ali. He had followed the Big Red Machine in Cincinnati and was on the Cleveland Indians beat in the nineties when the Tribe inexplicably shook off its forty-year slump and began to win. He had won awards and reported on scandals. A few years ago, when my job put me into a room with Fay Vincent, the former commissioner of baseball, Vincent asked me who my father was, and when he heard, said, "Oh, yeah. I remember he was very fair about the Rose thing." I had to turn to my friend, a baseball expert, to put together that Vincent meant the story about Pete Rose betting on his own games in 1989, when Rose was managing the Reds.

Back home we rarely heard about any of this stuff. I had those idyllic nights with him at the park in Louisville, but that was triple-A ball, small-time city (which, in retrospect, was the reason I got to come along). My father's position was that to talk about work was the same as being at work, and there was already plenty of that. A sportswriter gets used to people coming up to him in restaurants or at PTA meetings and taking issue with something he said in his column or on some call-in show. But my father was sensitive to the slightest criticism—really the slightest mention—of his writing, almost to the point of wincing, I think because he came to the job somewhat backward. As opposed to the typical sportswriter, who has a passion for the subject and can put together a sentence, my father's ambition had been to Write (poetry, no less), and sports were what he knew, so he sort of stumbled onto making his living that way. His articles were dense and allusive and saddled, at times, with what could be called pedantic humor. They were also *good*, as I realized after he was gone—I seldom read them when he was alive.

His ambition, always, was to generate interesting copy, no

matter how far from the topic he had to stray. Some of his readers loved him for it, but others—and it is hard to hold it against them—wrote angry letters wanting to know why the paper refused to hire someone who would tell them the score, not use big words, and be done with it. Years of getting such letters in his mailbox at work had embittered my father, though never enough to silence his muse. When the *Other Paper*, the alternative weekly in Columbus, started running a regular column entitled "The Sully," in which they would select and expand upon what they they felt to be his most bizarre sentence from the previous week (e.g., "'Second base is still an undefined area that we haven't wrapped our arms around,' Tribe general manager John Hart said, sounding very much like a man about to have his face savagely bitten"), we were baffled by my father's pained reaction. The compliment behind the teasing would have been plain to anyone else, but he would not have the thing in the house.

On top of the touchiness, which, senseless to deny, had more than a tinge of pride to it, my father was self-effacing about his knowledge of sports (staggering even for a baseball writer, that living repository of statistical arcana), and this in turn made him quiet when faced with the ubiquitous "sports nut," his enthusiasms and his impassioned theories. The reaction could be painful to see, because the sports nut— with his team cap, powerful breath, and willingness to repeat nine times that Henderson was a moron to throw to third with two outs—often wants nothing more than affirmation. Few people understand, however, that the sportswriter, the true sportswriter, is never a fan. His passion for the game is more abstract. He has to be there, after all, until midnight, whether his team wins or loses, and his team is a shifting entity, one that wears many colors. He considers the game— or the race or the match or the meet—with a cooler eye; and for him there is no incentive to exaggerate or distort events. For the fan, the game is theater; it has heroes and villains, just or unjust outcomes. But however much the sportswriter tricks out his subject in the *language* of theater, it remains in his mind something else, a contest not between the more and less deserving but between the more and less skilled, or lucky. The contest, only the contest, endures, with its discrete components: the throw, the move, the play, their nearness to or distance from perfection.

I was never a fan. I was something else: an ignoramus. And in the end I think that was easier for my father. We had other things to talk about; the awkwardness of trying to bring "the job" over into civilian life never got in the way, since there was no question of my keeping up. The few times I tried—"So, quite a game last night," when by some chance I had seen it—he laughed me off, as if to commend the effort.

But now, this night, was different. I wanted to know, since the opportunities seemed to be slipping away. I wanted to hear what he remembered. This is what he told me:

I was at Secretariat's Derby, in '73, the year before you were born—I don't guess you were even conceived yet. That was . . . just beauty, you know? He started in last place, which he tended to do. I was covering the second-place horse, which wound up being Sham. It looked like Sham's race going into the last turn, I think. The thing you have to understand is that Sham was fast, a beautiful horse. *He* would have had the Triple Crown in another year. And it just didn't seem like there could *be* anything faster than that. Everybody was watching him. It was over, more or less. And all of a sudden there was this . . . like, just a disruption in the corner of your eye, in your peripheral vision. And then before you could make out what it was, here Secretariat came. And then Secretariat had passed him. No one had ever seen anything run like that—a lot of the old guys said the same thing. It was like he was some other animal out there. By the time he got to the Belmont, he was pretty much lapping them.

My father had never mentioned this before. In fact, my only real awareness of the Kentucky Derby, growing up within minutes of Churchill Downs, lay in noticing the new commemorative glass that appeared in the cupboard each May, to be dropped and broken, as often as not by me, before the next one arrived. I knew that he had attended the race every year for more than a decade, and that he sometimes took my older brother along, but he never said anything to me about it apart from asking, when I got old enough, which horse I would like him to bet on with my allotted two dollars.

I wrote down what he had told me when I got back to his apartment, where my sister and I were staying the night. He lived two more months, but that was the last time I saw him alive.

A year later I went to the New York Public Library and looked up the pieces he wrote for the *Courier-Journal* (then the *Courier-Journal & Times*) on that first Saturday in May 1973. There were rwo by "Mike Sullivan, Staff Writer": the procedural one, about Sham (including an interview with the jockey Laffitt Pincay in which Pincay predicts that although Secretariat had "ultimately pulled away" in what my father describes as a "magnificent, spine-tingling stretch drive," Sham would get him at the Preakness), and another, stranger piece, buried well into the section, which may be of interest to scholars of the newspaper business someday, if only because it shows how far into the provinces the New Journalism had penetrated by the early seventies. In it my father describes floating around Churchill Downs on the morning of the Derby, looking for something to write about.

Midway through the story "The Kid" appears, "loose-limbed . . . fitted out in old jeans and sneakers . . . slightly in need of a shave, he looked very much like a groom or stable boy." My father always wore a white linen suit to the Derby, à la his great hero, Mark Twain, though his colleague and friend the noted horsewriter Billy Reed once wrote that he looked more like a deranged Colonel Sanders, a look I imagine would have made him quite approachable to a lost hippie.

"Aren't you a groom or something?" my father asks, but The Kid replies, "No, I'm a—, uh, snuck in." The Kid says that he drove through the night to get to Louisville, and that he is on a mission to get Pincay's autograph for his "buddy" back home. Some weird post-sixties dialogue ensues. My father advises him not to go forward with his plan of impersonating a groom (the *man* might catch him) but instead to "wedge against the runway fence after the race" and try for the autograph there. The Kid is then given a meeting place for after the Derby. "At that time," my father wrote, "he would tell whether he'd gotten the autograph."

It was the next and last sentence that, for some reason, struck me as odd and oddly affecting, coming across it there in the hum and the mortuary light of the microfilm machine. It is: "If The Kid failed in his mission, this story will end here."

THE CHILD OF EUROPE

It was in Nuremberg, in the Unschlittplatz (Tallow Place, where the rendering vats had been in the seventeenth century); 26 May 1828—a Whit Monday—late afternoon. A boy aged about sixteen years and invariably described, in the written accounts, as "full-lipped," appears reeling down the hill. According to Michael Newton, the author of *Savage Girls and Wild Boys* (which includes the most thorough and readable telling of a story that has been told many times, always with conflicting details), the young man is "dressed like a stable boy," wearing "grey trousers that were far too wide for him," with "the first signs of a beard and moustache" on his face. He is approached by a couple of shoemakers who have noticed his strange appearance, but when they question him they find that he cannot speak except to repeat one sentence: "*Ein Reiter will ich werden, wie mein Vater einer war*": I want to be a rider, like my father before me. His feet are soft, "like a baby's," and torn, as if they have never been walked on before. In one hand he holds a letter addressed to "His Honour the Captain of the 4th Squadron of the Shwolishay Regiment, Nuremberg," and in the other, a book, which he cannot read, entitled *Spiritual Forget-Me-Nots*. The shoemakers try to get more information from the boy but succeed only in making him cry. He falls to the ground, exhausted, and is carried,

- 22 -

according to the Canadian historian Martin Kitchen, "to the stable where the stranger immediately threw himself down onto a pile of straw."

The captain arrives, but he has never seen or heard of the foundling, nor can he make sense of the incoherent letter, so the boy is given a pen, with which he writes the only thing he can: his name, "Kaspar Hauser." Again they try to get more out of him, and again he grows frustrated to the point of tears. Newton writes that the boy then began to repeat "the word 'Ross' (horse) over and over, pleadingly." The good burghers of Nuremberg, at a loss, lock Hauser in the prison tower for his own protection. There he lies on his bed and listens to the striking of the town clock. Years later, after he had been taught to write, he described what was going through his mind:

> I heard the same thing as I had heard at first, but I mean, however, that it was somewhat different, as I heard it much louder; it was not the same, but (instead) that the clock struck, it was become sounding. This I listened to a very long while; but when from time to time I heard it continually less and less, and when my attention was at an end, I said these words, *Dahi weis wo Brief highört*, by which I meant to say, he might also give me such a beautiful thing, and not always teaze me. . . . I began to weep again, and said the words which I had learned, by which I meant, Why are the horses so long without coming, and let me suffer so much?

"This passage offers us a strange insight into Hauser's mind," writes Newton. "Only the desire to possess beauty is coherently there, repeated over and over. . . ."

Over the next few days Hauser remained bewildered, though peaceable enough. Moved by his constant desire to see horses, one of the soldiers on guard made him the gift of a little wooden horse—probably fetched from one of the marvellous toy shops for which Nuremberg was then so famous. The boy's joy was so rapturous, and then his misery so excessive at being parted from his toy at bedtime, that several others were given to him the next day. From then on, Hauser played with his wooden horses endlessly, absorbedly, hardly noticing what else happened around him. . . .

Later, when Hauser had become famous throughout Europe and his ability with language had increased, he was able to tell the story of his youth, all of which—up until that afternoon in the Unschlittplatz—had been spent in a dark cell, with only wooden horses for companionship, "and such red ribbons with which I decorated the horses." There was a man who would bring him food and water, a man whose face he never saw. The reason for his being set free was as mysterious to him as the reason for his confinement. "The Child of Europe," as he came to be known, was passed from patron to patron, poked at and manipulated by homeopaths, journalists, priests, and aristocrats. He had wandered unknowingly into the West's ancient fascination with feral children (which, as Martin Kitchen points out, stretches back to the Greek myth of Neleus and Pelias, twins left by their mother on a mountainside, where they were found and adopted by a horse herder who let one of them—Pelias—be raised by a mare). Here, in Hauser, was a genuine tabula rasa, a perfect guinea pig for the testing of all sorts of theories of human nature. Newton writes that

he could not distinguish foreground from background in looking at a landscape; he thought of animals as having fully human intelligence; and he had no notion of the distinction between animate and inanimate. For this reason, he would grow anxious at the sight of crucifixes and plead that the suffering man might be taken down. His only skill was in riding horses, which he mastered easily and with enough success to astound his military instructors.

After ten years spent among human society, he was murdered. No one has been able to determine why or by whom. Suicide was mentioned, although if it was suicide, Hauser had stabbed himself in the heart. His epitaph is perhaps the only completely accurate thing ever written about him:

HERE LIES

KASPAR HAUSER

THE ENIGMA

OF HIS AGE

HIS BIRTH UNKNOWN

HIS DEATH A MYSTERY

1833

EIN REITER WILL ICH WERDEN

On a Saturday afternoon in July 1938, a half-starved teenager wandered into a bus station in Columbus, Ohio, appearing confused and disoriented. A policeman approached him and tried to speak with him, but the boy seemed not to know his own name. In his pockets the officer found $112, a bus ticket for Petersburg, Illinois, and documents that identified him as Thomas Dowell, an obscure local jockey. Seeing that Dowell was in profound distress, the officer took him to the police station, where a police surgeon sat with him and tried to find out what was wrong. Dowell remained mute but appeared deeply shaken. Concerned that the boy might get hurt if released, the doctor sat him down in a holding cell and left to telephone his mother.

While the officer was gone, Dowell slipped his belt off, coiled it around his neck, and hanged himself.

When word of the suicide made its way to the backstretch, no one seemed surprised. In his brief career Dowell had learned what . . . countless others had long since known. A jockey's life was nothing short of appalling. No athletes suffered more for their sport. The jockey lived hard and lean and tended to die young, trampled under the hooves of horses or imploding from the pressure of his vocation. For three years Dowell had known the singular strain of the jockey's job . . . waiting in vain for the "big horse" that would bear him from poverty and peril.

—Laura Hillenbrand, *Seabiscuit*

BEAUTY

For the last few years I have had on my computer screen three grainy little video clips that I got off the Internet. I click on them at the end of the day, when the blood sugar dips and aphasia sets in. They were bootlegged from some late-seventies TV sports documentary about Secretariat, and each of them shows him winning one of the legs of the '73 Triple Crown.

The quality is so poor that you hardly see anything beyond a bunch of pixilated brown masses, but the audio track includes the three calls by the race announcer Chick Anderson, which are for the ages. One of these—the last, from Belmont Park, which ends with Anderson holding back tears of disbelief as he shouts, 'it looks like he's opening. . . . The lead is increasing! . . . Secretariat is *widening* now! He is moving like a TREE-MENDOUS MA-SHEEN!"—is up there with Herbert Morrison's Hindenburg broadcast for sheer power of description and spontaneous verbal majesty. As my father remembered, Secretariat had a habit early in his career of starting races in last place; in fact, in the Derby call, you do not hear him mentioned (except in the early, obligatory rundown of the field) until the pack has almost reached the final turn, so that when the sound of his name bursts into the call, you can close your eyes and see him breaking through. Anderson's every word seems robed in magical, unsuspecting ignorance of what was about to happen that spring:

They're at the head of the stretch and Sham is the leader. He leads it by a length. Secretariat is in the center of the racetrack and driving. . . . Now at the head of the stretch its Secretariat! Secretariat on the outside, and he takes the lead! Sham holding at second! It's Secretariat moving away, and he *hasitbytwoandahalf!*

That represents about fifteen seconds of tape.

The drama is made only more perfect by the knowledge that, despite the oddsmakers' predictions, Secretariat had just lost the Wood Memorial, his final prep race for the Derby and one of only a few losses in his career (it was later revealed that the horse had been running with a troublesome abscess on his gum, which was spotted by the official track veterinarian when he lifted Secretariat's top lip to check his "tattoo number," the identifying tag given to all Thoroughbreds to ensure that trainers do not attempt to swap horses come race time). Many in the crowd on Derby day, including Secretariat's owner and trainer, were waiting to see if the horse was all hype. And the way he ran, it was as if he wanted to let them believe it as long as possible—for kicks—before he unveiled his greatness.

That afternoon he ran each of the last three quarters faster than the preceding one, after having spent the entire first quarter dead last. His official time, 1:59 and two-fifths seconds, is still the Kentucky Derby record, going on the thirty-first anniversary of his race. Sham also broke the previous Derby record that day, which should give you a sense of the field.

He is best described not as the greatest horse, nor as the greatest runner, nor even as the greatest athlete of the twentieth century, but as the greatest creature. The sight of him in motion is one of the things we can present to the aliens when they come in judgment asking why they should spare our world. He has a Boswell, or it might be truer to say a Homer, whose name is William Nack, the author of *Secretariat: The Making of a Champion* (1975). It is a masterpiece of the genre, possibly the only masterpiece of the genre. Writing a good horse book is no easy thing if you are writing for adults. Beasts do not make good protagonists, for the simple reason that unless you are younger than ten or have money riding on their success or failure, it is hard to identify with them fully. The literature of racing—from the dispatches filed by pioneer hacks like Joe H. Palmer and Red Smith, through the popular histories such as Edward Horaling's *Great Black Jockeys* and Alfred Cope's *Royal Cavalcade of the Turf* all the way up to Laura Hillenbrand's best-selling *Seabiscuit*—still is a wonderful place to spend time, probably because the sport, with its heavy subtext of history and symbolism, attracts the sort of writer who cares more about the story than the order of finish. But the horse books that succeed do so by spending most of their time with the human beings whose fates run more or less parallel to the track. There is plenty of that in Nack's book, too, but somehow he found a technique that allowed him to make his horse the central character without personifying it, without even indulging (more than once or twice) in the pathetic fallacy. The style is akin to art criticism. This is how he describes the last quarter of Secretariat's Derby. "Turcotte" is Ronnie Turcotte, the jockey who was "up" (i.e., chosen to ride) in all of Secretariat's best-known races:

> [At] the clubhouse turn . . . the colt was just beginning his move, if that was the word for it, for it had no definable limits, no distinctive beginning, and no distinctive end. It occurred gradually. Secretariat would . . . deliver up no spectacular cruncher that would power him to the lead. This was finer and rarer than that, a move artistic in scope and conception, relentless in the manner of its execution. And into the

turn it began, unspectacularly, with Turcotte sitting chilly. This was what he had been waiting for and now he let it unfold without interference, providing only guidance to the colt.

"Providing only guidance . . ." Turcotte himself has repeatedly said that the horse rarely needed even that. Often the jockey went as far as to keep his whip tucked into the back of his pants.

William Nack's description of Secretariat's Hopeful, a race for two-year-olds held every September at Saratoga in New York, perfectly captures a certain mystical quality that his races possessed, one that you notice when you watch the tapes: not that he was above the field—not a bully or a tedious domina-tor, in other words—but that he was *outside* of it:

> Secretariat moved to the field with a rush . . . bounding along as if independent of whatever momentum the race possessed, independent of its pace and tempo, independent of the shifting, slow-motion struggles unfolding within it, the small battles for position and advantage. [He] was not responding to any force the race was generating, but rather moving as though he'd evolved his own kinetic field beyond it, and Turcotte would recall sitting quietly and feeling awed.

Like any good work of aesthetics, Nack's book is heavy on detail. It begins (to the lasting chagrin of Kentuckians) in the area north of Richmond, Virginia, where in the small hours of the morning of March 30, 1970, Secretariat was foaled: Caroline County, a place Nack describes as "closer in spirit to Stephen Crane than Stephen Foster—a starker and less storybook Virginia than the mountains and the valleys." It is a place, or was thirty years ago, where the Civil War might just have moved through, so close to nonexistent was the recovery. Helen "Penny" Tweedy (née Chenery) had just taken over Meadow Stables, which had been in her family for generations. Her father, Christopher Chenery, had run the farm for decades. Now he was dying, and his daughter dreamed of "breeding champions, of saving The Meadow and restoring what the Civil War had interrupted" for the family.

Secretariat was "by" (as horse people say) Bold Ruler, his sire; he was "out of" a mare named Somethingroyal, his dam—her fourteenth foal, Nack tells us. He was a chestnut colt, his coat "like a new penny," with stockings of white on three of his feet and a white star between his eyes. For most of his life he would be called Big Red, his "stable name" (and that of Man o' War). He was given his racing name some months after his birth, as is the custom with Thoroughbreds. The rule book stipulates, among other criteria, that the name of a racehorse must be no more than eighteen characters—spaces included—and that it can be neither obscene nor already taken, whether by another horse or by a "notorious person." A Meadow Stables employee named Elizabeth Ham had been, before coming to the farm, the personal secretary of the Tennessean Norman H. Davis, Hoover's delegate to the General Disarmament Conference in Geneva, "the home of the League of Nations' secretariat." She suggested the word.

Disarmament: it is a nice detail that Secretariat had peace encoded in his name, given that the year of his magnificence found us still in Vietnam, with Nixon and Kissinger still in the White House. But then, everyone knows what came of the league's efforts in this direction. It was Norman Davis, in fact, who put forward the notorious, ostensibly conciliatory "reparations clause," which acknowledged Germany's inability to pay for the wreckage of World War I but reaffirmed its "guilt" in the matter, thus giving Hitler his longed-for excuse to withdraw from the conference in 1933 (leaders who have their minds bent on war quickly tire of diplomacy). The following

May, Davis made a speech in which he expressed his opinion—pitifully deluded, as it turned out—that the Germans could be lured back to the table if only the European powers would ease up. The Nazi Reich minister Constantin Freiherr von Neurath introduced that speech into his trial at Nuremberg, by way of explaining Germany's decision to go back to war.

EIGHTEEN HORSES IN ONE LINE

I had not seen so many units together since the days of Nuremberg in 1937 when I was in 3 squadron of the 13th Cavalry Regiment in Luneberg and we had been selected to march or trot past Hitler and his staff. Eighteen horses in one line to the music of our regimental march, played by no less than thirty bands at once. It was indeed a splendid occasion.
—Max Kuhnert, *Will We See Tomorrow?*, 1993

There is little natural standing water in central Kentucky. As in Tennessee to the south, the topography consists mainly of what geologists call karst: porous limestone that swallows rain and either moves it into the creeks and rivers or keeps it underground. For westward pioneers of the late eighteenth and early nineteenth centuries, this was considered a great selling point. Still waters bred plagues, and John Filson, whose *Discovery, Settlement and Present State of Kentucke* (1784) was the most popular of the early promotional texts describing the region, made sure to mention that it was "generally level, and abounding with limestone," and that "scarcely any such thing as a marsh or a swamp is to be found." (He also said that it was "in some parts, nearly level; in others not much so; in others again hilly," and that it was home to the "sugar-tree, which . . . furnishes every family with plenty of excellent sugar." But let that pass.)

To talk about the Bluegrass is always to go down to the limestone.* Everything an outsider associates with central Kentucky has to do with the rock beneath it: the subtle hills; Mammoth Cave; the Civil War (during which saltpeter was dug extensively from Mammoth); the spring water that goes into Bourbon whiskey; the slate walls that encircle the oldest horse farms; even the horses themselves, for some claim that the unusually rich calcium in the deposits that underlie Lexington finds its way into the bones of the foals that graze there (limestone is made of pre-historic bone, technically

---

*John Haywood's *Natural and Aboriginal History of Tennessee* (1823) includes the following tale: "In 1795, Joseph Ray was traveling from Holston in East Tennessee, to Sumner County in West Tennessee, Whilst he passed through the barrens in Kentucky leading a horse by his side, the one that he rode sunk suddenly thirty of forty feet below the surface. He leaped from the sinking horse, and saved himself from going to the bottom, with the other. He went to Sumner County and returned, and by means of assistance which he had obtained, he descended into the pit where his horse had sunk, and found running water at the bottom of the pit. The horse had walked about in the cavern, but was dead."

speaking, though the science on this circular alchemy is shaky). One could almost say that in Lexington's case, geology was destiny, and so it is essential to say a few words here about John Robert Shaw, the literary champion of the central Kentucky limestone, author of the explicitly titled *Narrative of the Life & Travels of John Robert Shaw, the Well-Digger, Now Resident in Lexington, Kentucky, Written by Himself, 1807*. It is a great and unknown American book, the only book, as far as I know, ever prefaced by its author with a claim to being "the production of a man almost totally illiterate."

A year before the *Narrative* came out, Shaw placed a teasing advertisement in the *Kentucky Gazette*. "In a few months," he wrote, "I shall present to the public a narrative of thirty years of my life and travels, five different times a soldier, three times shipwrecked, twelve months a prisoner of war, and four times blown up." The understatement of this description is staggering. Shaw's life was an endless series of those unspeakable horrors that in the nineteenth century went by the name of "misfortunes." Short of quoting at length, there is no way to indicate the deadpan and, at the same time, ever-so-slightly mystified tone in which Shaw relates this parade of hideousness. What follows is *one* of the chapter summaries:

—Our author is frost-bitten—gets his shoulder dislocated—is in danger of being drowned in the Susquehannah—goes to a still-house—drinks excessively—falls down as if dead—is carried to the barracks, where he conducts like a madman—jumps down the chimney and runs to the cliffs by the side of the river—leaps down from thence, and takes his seat on a cake of ice—floats down until he is taken out by some of his acquaintants.

Shaw was part of the wave of westward expansion into the Bluegrass that occurred in the first decade of the nineteenth century, after the roads had been cleared, and a tavern built, and the Indians killed or driven away. He was born in Yorkshire, in 1761, his father "by occupation a stuff-weaver." At fourteen he became a career alcoholic. One day a recruiter took him by the hand and said, "Come, my fine lad . . . I'll shew you the place where the streets are paved with pancakes," in which statement Shaw found no cause for skepticism. Although he did not know it, he was headed for America to fight against the colonials. He and four hundred of his fellow recruits were "deluded out under the pretence of doing duty in Portsmouth" and shipped to New Jersey instead.

Shaw arrived in Elizabethtown, understandably "in woful pickle." He witnessed the Tappan Massacre, and it provoked in him such a distate for the British army that he began to desert—or, in his phrase, "become prodigal"—at every opportunity, of which there were many. From New Jersey he took ship to Charleston, where he got sick "for the first and last time, that is, with common sickness; for I have been often times indisposed with the bottle-fever."

Shaw drank like he wanted to die. At some unspecified time, between desertions and days spent "punishing pints of grog" with his comrades (among whom were two good influences named "Curtis Grub and Peter Grub; the former of whom in one of his frolics jumped into the furnace in full blast; and the latter by putting a pistol into his mouth blew out his brains"), Shaw got his first taste of stonework, "and here was the first quarry I ever wrought in." On this very first job, he had "the misfortune to break three of my ribs," and knew that he had found his vocation.

Once the combination of working with unstable explosives and "taking a little more of the usquebaugh" was in place, Shaw's misfortunes began to gather momentum. He was "strucke . . . so violently in the mouth" by a tree he was trimming that he feared for his life. He "got groggy" with *another* man named Grub (no matter what place or circumstance Shaw found himself in, there was always a man named Grub around) and stumbled "into a well twenty feet deep, where I lay until I was drawn out by the assistance of major John M'Gaughey, now resident in Shelbyville, and fortunately received no damage."*

The situations in which Shaw habitually found himself were, in his way of putting it—and, indeed, in anyone's way of putting it—"deplorable." He broke his leg in another, different, stone quarry, then he injured his leg at the bottom of a well outside Philadelphia, when a rock he had left loose in the wall of the shaft came tumbling down on top of him and his employer, whom he had invited "to come down into the well and satisfy himself" with the quality of Shaw's work. "My leg was not much injured," Shaw reassures us, remembering at the last minute to include the fact that "Mr. Wilson will remain a cripple the residue of his days." Shortly after this episode, Shaw started off "to the country, resolved to take up my old trade of basket-making." This is the first mention of basket-making in the book.

It is also the last, for Shaw soon became a devoted

"The whole secret to Shaw's style may lie in the way he will stop to say, "now resident in Shelbyville," This was a rhetorical move at which British and Irish storytellers of the early nineteenth century excelled. Thackeray tried to put his finger on it in his *Irish Sketch Book*:

> A very curious tale is there [in Galway] concerning Manus O'Malaghan and the Fairies:—"In the parish of Algohill lived Manus O'Malaghan. As he was searching for a calf that had strayed, he heard many people talking. Drawing near, he distinctly heard them repeating, one after the other, 'Get me a horse, get me a horse'; and 'Get me a horse too,' says Manus. Manus was instantly mounted on a steed, surrounded with a vast crowd, who galloped off, taking poor Manus with them. In a short time they suddenly stopped in a large wide street, asking Manus if he knew where he was? 'Faith,' says he, 'I do not.' 'You are in Spain,' said they."

"The chronicler is careful to tell us that Manus went out searching for a calf," writes Thackeray, "and this positiveness prodigiously increases the reader's wonder at the subsequent events." *Indeed.*

practitioner of "Bletonism," or dowsing, delighting ignorant rustics with "the infallibility of the forked rod." He dowsed his way, by disasters, to the Bluegrass, where there was a great demand for his trade, the population growing daily and all the water being quite deep underground. The first thing he did in Lexington was befriend a man named M'Guire and go on a "hunting frolic" (there did not, in Shaw's universe, exist frolics and nonfrolics, only species of frolic). He and M'Guire were out for panthers. Shaw spotted one "on the limb of a large tree; calling out to M'Guire (and being entirely unacquainted with the different quadrupeds) yonder is a deer on the limb of that tree."

Next he got work digging a well for a man named Biswell, but a storm interrupted his progress before he could blast himself, so he returned "to my old trade of frolicing, the result as usual." Only this time the result was not quite as usual.

> Afflicted with [the bottle-fever], I was one night lying in the tavern before the fire, when I was disturbed by a parcel of ruffians, consisting of major Mastin Clay, lieutenant Spence, a Mr. Moss and Sow. They entered the house and had not been long there, before making inquiry of the landlord who I was? Answered, "old Shaw the well-digger, who is very sick." Damn him, observed Clay let us have a little fun with him. With that he laid a chunk of fire on my leg which burnt me severely. I jumped on my feet requesting of them to let me alone, saying I was then sick and no person to take my part, but even so, I would try the best of them singly: this exasperated them, and Clay being the greatest scoundrel among them, urged the rest to lay hold of me, which they did, compelling a negro who was in the house to butt me with his head and gouge me severely.

Shaw was never quite the same after the negro-head-butting frolic. He began to recover less quickly from his misfortunes, and when he fell off a horse on his way to Lexington (a pickle he would have laughed at a year before), he deemed it "a very narrow escape for my life." One almost begins to worry when he goes "out to Maxwell's spring" and drinks "a quantity of water," which occasions him to "vomit a quantity of blood." He even quit drinking for a while, but sobriety was of little comfort during his next well-digging adventure, in which he accidentally set off the blast "with about three quarters of a pound of powder in my hand, which consequently left me for dead in the bottom of the well."

It was not his fault, then, that he retreated back to the tavern and "got groggy" with acquaintances; nor can one blame him for the fact that when he left the tavern and was standing outside in the street, "a shop boy (Sam;. Combs) threw a handful of lime mortar into my eyes, by which means notwithstanding every remedy connected with the assistance of doctors was made use of, I lost my right eye."

This injury having healed (sort of), he

> commenced well-digging and dug nineteen that season, besides three more which I dug for Captain John Fowler, quarried stone and walled them in. In quarrying this stone I had the misfortune to be blown again; for whilst I was ramming, the blast went off, blew the hammer out of one hand and the rammer out of the other to a considerable distance. . . .

What is wonderful about John Robert Shaw is he never let go of his pluck. He went down into many wells during his ten years in Lexington, and he rarely left one on his own power; rather he was hauled to the surface, having maimed himself whilst ramming. In the process of "battleing with the lime-stone" he lost "no less than one eye, four fingers, one thumb

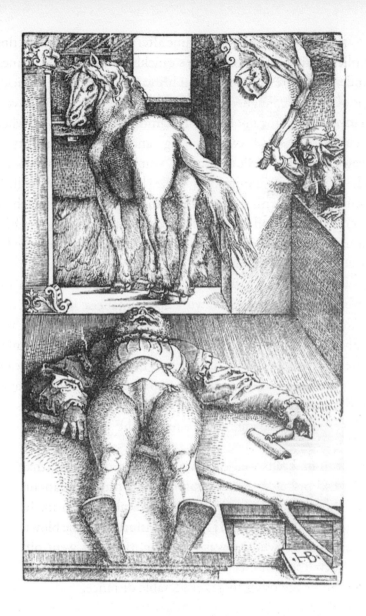

and seven toes." Yet he managed nonetheless to acquire five acres of land and to get "numerous progeny" on his unnamed wife.

By now the reader has concluded that Shaw's book is fiction disguised as a memoir, à la *Tom Jones* or *Gulliver's Travels*. I thought the same—until I read the account of Shaw's "last time of having been blown up while digging a well," this time "for Mr. Lewis Sanders of Lexington." So deplorable was this tale that Shaw, temporarily at a loss, turned the narrative over to a Dr. Fishback, his "then attending physician," whose existence can be verified independently of the *Narrative*. Fishback remembered:

> The 23d of August I was called upon to visit [Shaw], being informed that he had been blown up in a well for the fourth time. On approaching his mangled body, it presented a spectacle unparallelled by any thing which I have seen or known in the annals of man. The skull was fractured upon the frontal bone, a little to the right of its middle and just below the edge of the hair. . . . Having several years before lost the use of his right eye, but little hopes now remained, should he recover, of his ever enjoying the advantage of sight again, as the surface of the remaining eye ball was considerably bruised and torn by a number of small pieces of stone. In addition to the above, his face was enormously swelled and covered with blood, gun powder and dirt, so that it was utterly impossible to recognize the lineaments of John Robert Shaw. The impression produced on my mind, from seeing his body lacerated in every part, is easier to be conceived than described. . . .
>
> "JAS. FISHBACK."

"Here reader," Shaw adds helpfully, "picture to yourself my pitiable situation: a wife with a numerous progeny around my bed, bemoaning my sad condition."

It is not merely the added testimony of Dr. Fishback that reduces doubt concerning the fundamental accuracy of Shaw's *Narrative*. There is this obituary, which appeared in the *Kentucky Gazette* on July 25, 1806:

> SHAW, JOHN ROBERT—well digger of Lexington,
> killed Saturday August 17, 1806 by a blast being
> used in a well for Lewis Sanders near Lexington.

Suffice it to say, the editor who let that go to press knew little of the life and travels of John Robert Shaw, the well-digger, then resident in Lexington, Kentucky, 1806.

Seven years later another obituary appeared, and this one was sadly correct:

> SHAW, JOHN R.—well digger and stone quarrier of
> Lexington died Monday evening, September 6, 1813
> when blown up in a well he was digging for Robert
> Wilson. He was the author of the biography bearing
> his name.

He might have seen it coming. And perhaps he did. There is a strange passage, midway through the *Narrative*, in which Shaw appears to presage his end. It is the only moment of introspection, if it can be called that, in the book. After finishing a well and hurting his leg, he felt "anxious for a frolic" and headed to town. Upon "arriving at the sign of the White-horse," he and some acquaintances were "ordered to assist in conveying a madman to bedlam," which they happily agreed to do (it was a madman-conveying frolic).

> On our way we stopped at the sign of the Unicorn for
> refreshment, where I beheld a ghastly sight, a poor
> unfortunate man, who the day before fell into the
> fire in a fit, and burnt his eyes out, and his head to
> a cinder. The sight of these two unfortunate objects
> made such an impression on me, that I could not rest
> for several nights after. I thought I saw the madman
> grinning me in the face, and the unfortunate dead
> man following me with his ghastly appearance.

> He saw the plague enter the village on a white horse.
> It was a cancerous horseman, with a furnucle for a
> hat, that galloped the beast over grass and cobble and
> the coloured hill. Plague, plague, cried Tom Twp as
> the horse on the horizon, scenting the stars, lifted a
> white head.
>
> —Dylan Thomas, "The Horse's Ha"

HIS BIRTH UNKNOWN

May of 1833 was an unusually wet month in Lexington.
It rained so much that the streams broke their banks and
flooded the town. The weather then turned hot, creating
the ideal conditions for an epidemic. People began to die of
unknown causes, and finally, on the third of June, the first case
of "Asiatic cholera" was diagnosed. Unbeknownst to anyone
in Lexington, the disease had been moving toward them for
almost a decade. A pandemic had started in Southeast Asia in
1824 and raged across Persia, Egypt, and China, eventually
reaching Russia and, from there, cutting west across Europe. It
got to England in 1831; to the North American coast in 1832;
and now, a year later, it had arrived at the interior.

Within a week the disease was claiming fifty people a day,
including three physicians, of which the town had few. One
who survived, Dr. Short, wrote to his uncle, "I have en-
deavored to study [cholera's] inscrutable character, and to be

prepared with some degree of confidence to enter up in the conflict with it, but I must confess that its horrors have surpassed my conceptions." He then fled to the countryside. Left without even the dubious medical guidance of the day, the terrified citizens tried to treat the disease with brandy. Soon there were more patients than people to care for them. An early Lexington historian, George W. Ranck, wrote that "the streets were silent and deserted by everything but horses."

What no one could have known was that the unusually soluble limestone beneath central Kentucky, the very feature that helped make the territory such a desirable location in the first place, was also responsible for the unusual speed and proficiency with which the disease harrowed the population there. Bacteria, slopped into the backyard with the contents of the chamber pot, instantly found their way into the water table and wells. By the end of June, the "fell destroyer," as Ranck calls it, had killed so many that the cemeteries were choked. Victims were simply left at the gates by relatives or friends who unloaded them and hurried away. The historian J. S. March, in his *Conquest of Cholera*, writes that "the supply of good coffins" in Lexington "was soon exhausted."

At that point, the people turned in despair to the cabinet-maker Joseph Milward, who ran a thriving shop on Broadway (a few of his signed pieces survive in outlying Kentucky towns). Milward started making coffins—a lot of them, safe to say—and by 1838 his weekly advertisement in the *Lexington Observer and Reporter* included this nota bene: "I AM prepared with a HEARSE, and will attend to Funeral calls whether in the city or the country." Today the Milward Funeral Home is the oldest continuously operating business in Lexington, still on Broadway, still prepared with a hearse.

The cabinetmaker, my great-great-great-grandfather on my mother's side, had arrived in Lexington as an infant in 1805, not long after the place was settled. He came from Baltimore as part of "a rather unusual family group," according to Margaret Taylor Macdonald's *The Milward Family of Lexington, Kentucky, 1803–1969*. In the stagecoach on that unrecorded day were a middle-aged couple, Luke and Ann Adams Usher; Ann's daughter, Catherine Adams; and Catherine's three-year-old son, whom she had named Joseph Milward, though no record of her marriage to a Joseph Milward Sr., "respectable merchant of Baltimore," has ever been found. In any case, once she got to Lexington she immediately fobbed the baby off onto his grandparents and entered into her third marriage (there had been a husband before "Joseph Milward"). She was, at the time, nineteen.

Luke Usher, the patriarch of that unusual family group and the man who raised my ancestor, is described in a contemporary report as "of the Falstaffian model" with a "wife no less remarkable for size." He must have had some interest in things literary, since he is among the patrons thanked by John Robert Shaw for making possible the publication of the *Narrative*. He was also a thespian, after a fashion: he established the first professional theater in the state and staged the first Shakespeare production west of the Alleghenies (in Lexington you find many things that were the first of their kind west of the Alleghenies, owing to the fact that the town itself was one of the only things west of the Alleghenies for fifty years). Of greater interest is the fact that Luke Usher was the father of Noble Luke Usher, an actor who "touched the hem of fame" in Baltimore and was a close friend of David Poe, Edgar Allan's biological father. An early Poe biographer, Arthur Hobson Quinn, wrote that Usher's name "in all probability suggested the title" of the famous story, a claim that my family has perhaps wisely never made much of.

The Lexington Milwards split into two distinct lines after World War I, when my great-grandfather opened an insurance office in the city. He became ill toward the end of World War

II, and his son Hendree, my grandfather, was called home from bombadier training in New Mexico to take charge of the company, which he spent the rest of his life expanding. Today my twin uncles are the president and vice president of what grew into Powell Walton Milward, specialists in equine insurance, and when you drive in from rhe airport, one of the first things you see downtown is the giant yellow PWM sign on the side of a brick office building. This is my line: "the insurance Milwards," not the "funeral Milwards" ("the ones who have to pay when somebody dies rather than the ones who get paid," as the Lexington-born author Elizabeth Hardwick once put it). I often have to begin with that distinction when I meet a native.

I grew up spending weekends and school vacations and holidays in Lexington, and developed the sort of fascination with it that comes from being at once of and outside of a place. In comparison with Louisville, my only childhood reference, it seemed old, and Southern, and cultured. Partly this was a product of constantly moving back and forth between the middle-class tract house I was raised in, or the souped-up double-wides in which many of my best friends lived, and a more affluent milieu. I remember the ritual, before we would jam into the car for a visit, of putting on my khaki pants and navy blazer and tie and penny loafers, the timeless camouflage of the American *haute bourgeoisie*, which says, If we make ourselves as inconspicuous as possible, they may let us keep the money.

Most of my two or three childhood friends would have laughed at me, or else dispensed with laughter and pummeled me, had they caught me dressed like that on any day other than Sunday. Still, I had a yearning, very early on, to *belong* to Lexington, and when my geographical history became too convoluted to afford an obvious "hometown" (born in Louisville; childhood in southern Indiana; high school in Ohio; college in Tennessee), it was a great relief, in the end, just to be able to tell people, "I'm from Kentucky," a state in which I have never actually lived.

My grandparents built one of the first modern houses on the land that had been the grounds of Ashland, the estate of the Great Negotiator, Henry Clay, "Lexington's favorite son." A bachelor descendant of Clay's was still living in the old place when they moved into the neighborhood. Once in a while he would have his "man" drive him down—two hundred yards— to my grandparents' house. Their lights were the first he had ever seen from the mansion's back windows. When he moved out, Ashland was turned into an historical site. My sister and I took to going there Christmas Eve nights. We would trundle up the street in the snow and slip into the estate's walled garden, not to play but just to stand quietly in the dark among the weirdly white-blanketed hedges and trees.

Lexington has something of the walled city about it. New Circle Road, the bypass, surrounds it like a moat, barely holding back the more country element against which the town has always defined itself. Just beyond the circle, in almost any direction, are the horse farms, at once rural and refined, themselves bounded by the famous slate fences that were laid without mortar by slaves in the nineteenth century and are strong enough to withstand the drunk drivers who routinely smash into them. Where the stone walls end, the wooden slat fences take over—white for the most successful farms, according to local wisdom (since these have to be repainted more often), and black for the rest.

Lexington is, and has long been, the axis of American Thoroughbred culture. The *Kentucky Gazette* (first newspaper west of the Alleghenies) had not been in publication a year when an advertisement appeared for "The famous horse PILGARLICK of a beautiful chestnut colour . . . got by the noted imported horse, Janus, his dam by Silver-eye, and is the swiftest in the district of Kentucke. . . ." Locals will tell you, again, that it has to do with the limestone, that because of the high level of calcium in the grass, Kentucky horses are tougher than those raised elsewhere, but this was tacked on after the fact, as a boast or perhaps as an explanation for what had come to seem a part of nature, its contingent historical causes forgotten. Most of the unshakable horse-related myths in Lexington have this essentializing function in common: for example, that bluegrass itself—*Poa pratensis*—comes from the eastern European steppes, which happen to have been where horses were first domesticated; or that it was brought to the region by an Irish doctor, Redmon Barry, who also happens to have imported Barry's Grey Medley, an early, influential sire. In other words, that it was meant to be. But bluegrass has been known in western Europe, though not by that name, for centuries. It would have arrived on English ships and moved west in the wagons of settlers, along with honeysuckle and Chinese sumac and other "introduced species."

In reality, central Kentucky became synonymous with the horse by a combination of landscape and direct cultural inheritance, but mainly the latter. Simply put, the earliest Lexington elite were Virginians. The town's well-to-do will still go out of their way to let you know that their ancestors came from "the Old Dominion," and Lexingtonians who can trace themselves back to one of the FFVs—first families of Virginia—are known to do little but contemplate the fact.

It was there, in Virginia, that horse racing had first taken hold in this country, its growth unchecked by the Puritanism and general Dutch phlegm that stifled the sport in the North. The Virginia planters had imported their enthusiasm for racing—along with most of their favored leisure activities, as Thorstein Veblen later noted—from England, where horse racing in a recognizable form had been going on at least since the late twelfth century, when the monk William Fitzstephen, Thomas à Becket's amanuensis, recorded this scene at Smithfield:

Thither come, either to look or to buy, a great number of persons resident in the city—earls, barons, knights, and a swarm of citizens. When a race is to be run by this sort of horses, and perhaps by others, which also in their kind are strong and fleet, a shout is immediately raised, and the common horses are ordered to withdraw out of the way. Three jockies, sometimes only two, according as the match is made, prepare themselves for the contest (such as being used to ride know how to manage horses with judgment). The grand point is to prevent a competitor from getting there before them . . . You would think, according to Heraclitus, that all things were in motion.

In 1674 a tailor in York County, Virginia, was fined for having matched his horse against that of a physician: the sport was, in the words of the court, "only for gentlemen." This is the earliest known record of an organized horse race in the South—that is, one with spectators, not just two riders vying

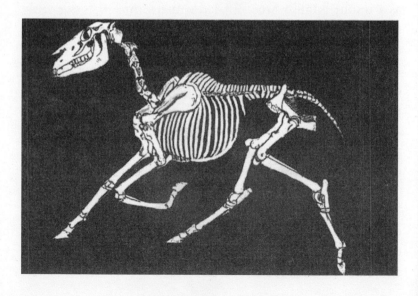

on a road (there had been sporadic racing in New York, on Long Island, since 1665, but it seems to have been less an amusement than a social responsibility, ordered from above by the governors for "the bettering of the breed of horses, which through neglect had been impaired").

By the mid-eighteenth century, wealthy Virginians were actively importing "racing horses" from England. They had already developed, in the century and a half that the colony had been in existence, an excellent native breed, and by as early as 1705 the feral population alone was so abundant that a contemporary observer mentions a "kind of sport, which the young people take great delight in, and that is, the hunting of wild horses; which they pursue sometimes with dogs and sometimes without." But the domestic horses were good only for so-called quarter racing: quick, quarter-mile sprints on a straight track, probably the sort of race Fitzstephen had been watching in London. In the centuries that had passed since that account, the English had turned to racing on oval or circular tracks, where the distance could be determined solely by preference, not by the difficulty of finding ever-longer stretches of flat, unobstructed ground; as a result, English breeders had come to prefer horses with greater endurance. Their colonial imitators were paying attention, but it was some time before enough of the land in the Southeast had been cleared to make the construction of such a course practical. In 1737 the first North American race on a round track was held in Hanover County, Virginia, and the importation of "thoroughly bred" horses, intended purely for use on the track or in the breeding shed, began in earnest.

In the context of modern animal husbandry, the word "Thoroughbred" refers to one of nearly a hundred classified equine breeds on the planet. Horse glossaries mention that it developed in England in the eighteenth century, that almost all true Thoroughbreds are descended from one of three "foundation sires"—Herod, Matchem, and Eclipse—and that these three horses in turn resulted from crossing Arab stallions (that is, stallions directly imported from the Middle East) with English mares.

It is unclear to what extent those "native" mares, the mothers of the first Thoroughbreds, were simply Arabs* that existed at a greater remove, in time, from Arabia, or to what extent they reflected the influence of the true English breeds: the hobby and palfrey et al., and the English "great horse" preferred by knights. Arab horses had been in the British Isles for more than six hundred years when the Foundation Sires were foaled—the first on record was imported by a Scottish king in 1121—and we can infer from how passionately the early Crusaders coveted their enemies' mounts that they were perceived, at once, to be utterly different from the horses back home: faster, lighter, and prettier, to begin with. No one knows, however, when the English first began to look at the Arab "type" as something that should be perpetuated through breeding, and to cross like with like.

The notion of a "breed" as something that could be identified and maintained is old in the West: Conrad Gesner, a Swiss naturalist of the mid-sixteenth century, was already able to reel off dozens of domestic canine breeds, many of which we would recognize. Presumably, after seven hundred years of prizing and acquiring Arab horses, the English would have produced plenty of mares that were genetic dead ringers for ones actually foaled in Arabia. None of the contemporary literature, nor any of the extant contemporary portraits, suggests that the "English" mares that gave birth to the first Thoroughbreds looked at all different from the "Arabian" stallions that sired them. James I (1603–25) even kept a stable

---

*Throughout "Arab" is used to mean simply "horse from Arabia," as opposed to "Arabian horse," which is now a distinct, official breed—membership determined, as with the Thoroughbred, by pedigree.

of what were known as Royal Mares, procured by his "master of horse" in the Middle East.

This is less revisionist history than a return to what was understood early on. In 1810, T. Hornby Morland, an English trainer and the author of *The Genealogy of the English Race Horse*, stated bluntly that "the English Race Horse is an admixture of the Arabian, Barbary, and Turkish horses, which have at different periods, during many centuries, been imported into this kingdom." He says nothing about "native" influence. But as time passed, and the English bred more and more of their own Arabian stock, and as the *exportation*, now, of this homegrown stock became more economically important, it became less desirable to hold up Arabia exclusively as the source of the finest horses. "If any proof were wanting of the superiority of the English breed of horses over that of every other country, it might be found in the avidity with which they are sought by foreigners," wrote James C. Whyte in *The History of the British Turf, From the Earliest Period to the Present Day*. The book was published in 1840, and it seems to have been around then that the "Arabian sires, English mares" theory hardened into conventional wisdom. Writers on the subject pointed—still point—to the fact that the Thoroughbred is slightly larger and thicker than the "pure" Arab horse, reasoning that the difference is due to the infusion of hardier English blood, via the Foundation Mares. But records suggest that this difference was less pronounced in the eighteenth century, when the two strains were splitting apart, and in any case there exists a pair of more likely, related explanations for it: first, that English breeders would have looked for exceptional size in the *individual* Arab stallions they acquired abroad, thus skewing the average height and weight of English foals; and second, that Thoroughbred owners have bred for size ever since. In the end, one would probably not be too far off in agreeing with Zeyd, the Bedouin in Charles Doughty's *Travels in Arabia Deserta*, who cries

down Doughty's claim that England has "the swiftest running horses," saying, "of horses thou canst have no knowledge, for they are of the Aarab." If all house cats speak ancient Egyptian, all Thoroughbreds speak classical Arabic.

The Arab horse is something of a scientific mystery. It emerges in the fossil record and in the art of the ancient Middle East looking exactly as it does today, and zoologists have had trouble linking it up with the rest of the family: "There are no intermediate types connecting them," writes the equine historian John L. Hervey. Perhaps because of this uniqueness, the Middle East's reputation for having the finest horses anywhere extends into deepest history. Three and a half thousand years ago, the pharaoh Thomtes II bragged in a papyrus of having brought an Arab racehorse back to Africa after his conquest of Mesopotamia. And the Arabs were recording pedigrees as early as A.D. 786, by which time they already had their own mythical "foundation site," Zad-el-Rakib.

It took over a thousand years for the English to draw even. In 1791 James Weatherby—a onetime Newcastle attorney who had become a sort of secretary to the Jockey Club in London—published the first edition of *The General Stud Book*, a fastidiously documented family tree that included all known Thoroughbreds in England, tracing them back to the Foundation Sires and beyond, to the Foundation Sires' sires, legendary Arab stallions called after their aristocratic owners: the Byerley Turk, the Darley Arabian, the Godolphin Arabian (whose name, back in the Middle East, had been Sham, Arabic for "sun"). From then on, to be an "accepted" Thoroughbred came to mean what it means today, namely, being in the *Stud Book* (or, rather, being included in the vast, computerized database, maintained in Lexington and London, which has taken over the role of the printed volumes).

One of the intriguing things about Weatherby's book is the question of where he got the idea for it. His stated motive for undertaking the massive amount of research it required was "to correct . . . the increasing evil of false and inaccurate pedigrees." But if his interest had really been so pragmatic, he would have needed to go back only two or three generations, the extent to which most professionals—including the original members of the Jockey Club, for whom he was unofficially working—have traditionally concerned themselves. (It is fascinating to think that your broodmare's far-distant ancestor is the Wrigglesworth Arabian, but if you want to win at the races in a few seasons, you had better worry about who her daddy was.) Weatherby's true innovation, apart from a systematic, proto-modern approach to gathering data, lay in the scope of his project. He wanted to go back to the *beginning*. Entries such as the following had little to do with "correcting evil":

> LORD CHEDWORTH'S SNAP—was got by Old Snap, his dam (called Young Bowes), was got by Dormouse, grand dam (called Little Bowes) by Mixbury, great grand dam (called Bowes) by Hurton's Barb, brought over by Mr. Marshall, great great grand dam by the Byerley Turk, out of a full sister to the Coffin Mare, whose sire was the Selaby Turk, and her dam a Place Mare—Mr. Place of Dimsdale, Stud Master to Oliver

Cromwell, stole this Mare out of the Stud, and kept her concealed in a cellar, till the search for her was over.

No one was urging Weatherby to go into this kind of detail, safe to say; and in England, at the time, there existed no example of such an ambitious tracing of animal descent for him to follow.

An example did exist, however, in Arabia. By the mid-eighteenth century, more and more Englishmen had begun going there expressly to procure horses, and these connoisseurs started bringing back stories of the Kohlâni, or "noble race"— the Arab Thoroughbred, recognized throughout Arabia as the flower of its species. A man who spent as much time as Weatherby did around racing stables could not have helped but hear stories like that included in the *Fragments* of the Reverend Stephen Weston (a noted Orientalist and a contemporary of Weatherby's). Weston mentions a Colonel Ainslie, who was shopping for Arabians in Egypt and ended up finding one that had around its neck "a leathern pouch," inside of which was a little scroll that read, in part:

> In the name of God . . . This is a high bred horse, and its colt's tooth is here in a bag about his neck, with his pedigree, and of undoubted authority, such as no infidel can refuse to believe. He is the son of Rabbaing, out of the dam Lahadah. . . .

And on and on, in language that would have been at home in Weatherby's book,

The question of the *Stud Book*'s overall accuracy is knotty. More than one writer, sensibly hostile to the whole idea of "pedigree" and the adoration of "blood," has dismissed Weatherby's ambition to create a complete blueprint of the Thoroughbred line, from the Darley Arabian to a horse foaled this morning, as fanciful, about as valid as those genealogies in the Old Testament. In a pamphlet published in Charleston, South Carolina, in 1857, an anonymous wiseass wrote: "No common horses, the sons and daughters of the famous something or other! Every proficient in equine pedigree knows that the genealogy of these wonderful beasts runs through a long list, that exists in a direct line, between them and the patriarchal pair that munched their corn in the Ark." But if the snobby philosophy behind Weatherby's endeavor makes us roll our eyes, the methodology was as rigorous as could have been expected in the centuries before any objective verification measures were available. Fraud certainly occurred; it was what Weatherby meant by "evil." Consider one scenario, which must have arisen pretty frequently: A breeder raises or buys an unusually fast animal whose parentage is not quite "pure." He sees that the animal could win him a lot of money at the track, but its ancestry does not entitle it to compete against Thoroughbreds (the sport is only for gentlemen). The incentive for such a breeder to claim a false sire or dam for such a horse, and perhaps even to pay the owner of that sire or dam to nod his head if anyone comes asking questions, would be high enough. And deception went the other way: a breeder might pass off his high-bred racer as having a less distinguished pedigree in order to encourage weaker competition. He could then bet on his own animal—the on-track version of pool-sharking.

Beyond outright cheating, though, there were honest ways for a pedigree to become flawed. Foals could be switched, for one. Broodmares were often kept together in the field, and sometimes, as with many mammals, they would unintentionally adopt one another's offspring. If the foals looked enough alike, the breeder might not notice the change. And mix-ups occurred even earlier, at conception. Before the advent of enzyme pregnancy testing, it was not uncommon for a mare whose ovum had already been fertilized to be bred again, to another stallion. The second stallion gets the credit in the *Stud Book,* though the first is the actual sire.

In the 1970s, the Thoroughbred "breed registries" responsible for maintaining the *Stud Book* began to implement blood testing, checking a foal's type to see if it matched what its reported sire and dam would have produced. This went a long way toward eliminating fresh mistakes. Then, in the mid-nineties, when DNA testing was introduced, it became possible not only to ensure with 99.99 percent accuracy that a foal's "immediate pedigree"—that is, going back one generation, to its sire and dam—was as claimed, but also to gauge how messed up the *Stud Book* had become in the course of the previous two hundred years.

In September of 2002 I spent an afternoon at the Gluck Equine Research Center in Lexington* with Gus Cothran, the director of "equine parentage testing" at the University of Kentucky's veterinary school. Cothran knew that I was there to hear tales of chicanery and the old switcheroo—he had seen a dozen like me—so he started off our conversation by assuring me that "it almost never happens anymore." But he pointed out that because of the way statistics behave in a closed set, small mistakes expand geometrically. To understand the math, he said, close your eyes and imagine a vertical pedigree chart: mother and father at the top, children underneath,

---

*My guide that afternoon at the Gluck Center was a charming, soft-spoken administrator named Roy Leach, who wore a maroon cardigan and a white street-sweeper mustache. Leach took me all through the facility, showing me the labs, where tall wooden display cases held rows of glass jars, each of which contained a different revolting equine parasite. In one, you could actually see the snake-sized worm—*Parascaris Equorum*—bursting through the small intestine of a foal. We ended our tour in the veterinary lecture hall. At the front, up by the blackboard, stood the rearticulated skeleton of "Spencerian (1956–74), Dam of Amberoid, winner of the Belmont Stakes 1966." There were still the dusty prints of horseshoes on the floor, where live animals had been led before that morning's class. Leach said, "You know what I love? Come over here." We bent down by the skeleton. "Look at the foreleg here," he said. "It's freestanding. It's actually *not connected by any bony structure to the body.*" Sure enough, there was a gap—about half an inch—between the spine and the frontal thighbone. I squinted through it, and saw Leach looking back at me from the other side, laughing. "Just muscle that holds it in place!" he said.

grandchildren underneath them, and so forth. The brackets get wider as they descend, which means that if the grandmother is "wrong," everything that comes after—in that particular line and in all the lines it spawns—is wrong. As the lines multiply, the mistakes multiply. And when you are dealing with a community that has been "closed" for two centuries, reproducing exclusively from within, the lines get monstrously intertwined.* A research lab in Ireland had done a study of Thoroughbreds' mitochondria, genetic information carried by the mother (the same sort of study that has traced all human beings back to a single woman who lived in Africa two hundred thousand years ago). The Irish lab found that prior to 1970 the *Stud Book* had been nearly 50 percent, as Cothran put it, "illegitimate." This means not that the *parentage* was wrong half the time, of course, but rather that if you were to try to determine the genetic makeup of an individual animal based on the book, you would as like as not come up with something that failed to jibe with the facts. Fifty percent seems not all that bad, considering. "But this is only the females," Cothran said. "The Y chromosome has yet to be done."

These figures undermine not the usefulness of the *Stud Book*, since a trainer is interested in tracing his horse back only so far as to some recent champions, but its romance. We like to look at the Derby winner and think, Therein runs the blood of Eclipse, in the same way that we like to claim descent from an FFV. But the book retains another sort of romance—even in its current, digitized form—that transcends its flaws and its antiquated pretense to totalism. What it really contains— what we are seeing when we squint at its original, tiny script— is a culture of obsessive attention to a certain kind of animal.

---

*Cothran said that "on average, Thoroughbreds have a 16 percent genetic relatedness— somewhere between first cousins and brother and sister." They are like one of those cousin-marrying Victorian clans—the Darwins, for example—that produce generation after generation of geniuses, tending, like most geniuses, to be a little neurotic.

It was handed down not as a set of objects or laws but in the form of living things passing from Arabia, to the British Isles, to Virginia.

It followed that when large numbers of Virginians began moving to central Kentucky in the late eighteenth century, they brought with them a tradition in which fast, impractically fine horses were idolized; more important, they brought the animals themselves. What they got in return was land that seemed to have been created for the Thoroughbred. As the Great Promoter John Filson had noted, it was—at least around Lexington—less heavily timbered than the landscape they had abandoned, with naturally occurring open expanses, gentler topography, more abundant streams, a more predictable inland climate, and, most important, widely available acreage. The horse people had found horse country.

The Revolution and the War of 1812 cut deeply into the blooded stock back in Virginia—at Elkhill, Jefferson's plantation on the James River, Cornwallis "carried off all the horses capable of service: of those too young for service he cut the throats"—which hastened the shift in focus to the west. Before the outbreak of the Civil War, there were at least seventy professionally organized racetracks in the South, and Kentucky had more than any other state (including a one-mile track on the present site of the Lexington Cemetery, where the Milwards are buried, not far from downtown). Central Kentucky had become fixed in the national mind as the place where first-rate American horses were born, and if in actuality any number of other places were as well suited for the cultivation of Thoroughbreds, believing made it so.*

---

*It was Hegel who noticed that when people accept something as true, the thing often functions in the world precisely as a fact would, and eventually—as the world weaves itself around assumption—it becomes indistinguishable from fact. Racing is full of tacitly agreed-upon fancies. The English horse writer Arthur Vernon said of the Kentucky Derby that it is "extraordinary chiefly because there is nothing sufficiently extraordinary to have raised it to the importance that it has since held." Just so. It became important because people wanted to win it; now people want to win it because it is important.

Once the Kentucky bloodlines were established as the most desirable to breed from, a culture and an economy grew up to support them. Local farmers began to cultivate the specialized, vitamin-rich grains that make up a mature Thoroughbred's diet; children of local families, having grown up around these expensive, high-strung, fragile creatures, became grooms and stable hands and trainers and jockeys who knew how to handle them; a local archive was established to keep the proliferating names straight; veterinarians developed a special knowledge of racehorse physiology. If you were a Thoroughbred owner who wanted to breed winners,* it made sense to stable your mares where the champion sires had been put to stud; and if you owned such a sire, you stood him where there would be a ready supply of people willing and able to pay the fees. This was not purely about convenience: long trips, whether by train, van, or, as is now most often the case, private jet, are risky when they involve animals whose every movement and bite of food and fluctuation in temperature is a cause for hand-wringing (the destabilizing effects of travel are often put forward as the reason that foreign horses do not win the Derby). The result of all this was that Lexington gradually made itself indispensable to those who wanted the best for their stock, present and future. That is why Queen Elizabeth keeps some of her horses there, visiting once a year to look into their well-being.

During the Civil War, the region paid a price for this dominance: both armies repeatedly raided the Lexington studs for mounts. Henry Clay himself was robbed of $25,000 worth of horses. None of the raiders was more notorious, or more effective, than the Confederate John Hunt Morgan, who knew exactly where the good horses were, having

---

* Breeding, not racing, has always been the real business of Thoroughbred owners: the latter makes money for the tracks and a few lucky winners, but the former drives an industry. Your horse can always lose, after all, no matter how fast he is, but if he has won a few times and enjoys active sperm, he is racing's closest thing to guaranteed income.

belonged, like Clay, to the Kentucky Jockey Club before the war. He began with the stated mission of rescuing his "native State from the hands of [its] oppressors," but when a majority of his fellow Kentuckians made clear their desire not to be rescued, he plundered it instead. A Union officer wrote a poem about it:

> John Morgan's foot is on thy shore
> > Kentucky! O Kentucky!
> His hand is on thy stable door,
> > Kentucky! O Kentucky!
> You'll see your good gray mare no more,
> > He'll ride her till her back is sore
> And leave her at some stranger's door,
> > Kentucky! O Kentucky!

In 1863 my great-great-grandmother, Kate Adams (but not, for clarity's sake, Catharine Adams, the promiscuous Founding Mare of my family), was driven from her home south of Lexington by the rumor of a Morgan raid. She had been warned that he was about to "come to our town and our home and destroy it." On her deathbed, she dictated an account of the experience, which had occurred when she was seventeen and which she described as one of the finest of her life. I found it folded up in my grandmother's bureau. "At ten o'clock," she wrote, "a bright moon-light night fortunately, our faithful colored man, Hiram, hitched up a two-horse wagon, put chairs in it and urged us to have seats, for he was going to take us to a safer place." They were on the road for sixteen days.

> One night we slept on the ground with our saddles for pillows, Another night we sat on our horses all night in the rear of the army, as John Morgan, of Southern fame, had felled trees and blocked the way.

We were eight hours cutting our way through two miles. At another time [we] were close enough to see a skirmish between our men and John Morgan's cavalry, no one killed, two wounded.

The last day of the sixteen, we rode in a pouring rain, a forlorn party to look upon, reached the Ohio River and made our horses swim across. We entered Portsmouth, Ohio, where we were well cared for, the hotel keeper refusing to take pay, as he was a Union man and glad to shelter refugees—as he called us.

All of the Milwards had declared themselves for the Union at the start of the war, though they were slave owners. The men and women they owned have a special page in the family Bible—Sally, Thomas, never any last names. The list of their birth and death dates continues right to the outbreak of the war. Kate Adams's family was particularly conflicted on this point: her father owned a hundred slaves, but both he and her brother fought for the Union, evidently without hesitation, as they were among the first in their largely Confederate town to enlist.

Hubbard Kavanaugh Milward, my great-great-grandfather, was the family's stab at a war hero. He had to be ordered off the battlefield at Chickamauga by the regimental surgeon after having been "run over by a horse, as to be unable to walk, mount, or dismount without great assistance." After the battle he was made colonel of his regiment and later marched with Sherman to the sea, during which total-war frolic he put one of the torches to Atlanta and paused to make such diary entries as:

Thursday, Nov. 24, Milledgeville, Georgia
Being in a church building, Adjt. Hamilton and I sang a few airs (religious), he playing on the

melodeon. Last night the State Arsenal was burned and tomorrow I am to blow up the magazine.*

When the war was over, enough horses had survived in Lexington to ensure the continuation of the bloodlines. There was not, however, enough money left in Kentucky for the natives to go on maintaining them. "To be a really big horseman, breeding and racing glamorous stake winners," wrote the unofficial state historian, Thomas D. Clark, "necessitates phenomenal expenditures of money," with the result that since the Civil War "fewer native sons have been able to stand the gaff." Most of the farms and tracks passed into Northern or Eastern industrialist hands, and the North came to control the sport, which remains the case, with exceptions made for the Irish, English, Japanese, and Arabs. The system amounts to a kind of absentee landlordism. With the exception of a few ungodly rich Kentuckians, the natives who work with the horses and on the farms are beholden to out-of-state or, as is more and more often the case, foreign owners. If the sport—as a spectacle and as a business—truly belonged to the Bluegrass, it would collapse in a day.

Yet it is also true that the business would collapse *without* the Bluegrass, for more than any other popular amusement, horse racing exists on mystique: If you want a sport of kings

---

*My grandparents once had a guest stand and announce that regretfully he was honor-bound to leave the house because my grandfather, who had just inherited a portrait of Col. Milward in the uniform of the aggressor, had decided to hang it in the living room. Kentucky has never entirely gotten over being divided against itself in the war ("brother against brother" was not just a saying there), and with white Lexingtonians who pride themselves on their Southern identity, the fact of the state's not having seceded can sit somewhat uncomfortably. This is not to imply that they lament the decision, but they sound at times as if they do not quite believe it, the way a left-leaning sixth-generation New Yorker might sound after learning that his great-great-grandfather left home in 1862 with all his brothers to fight for the rebs, just 'cause he believed in the cause. All of which may account for a tendency among many Lexingtonians to overcompensate in the mint-juleps-on-the-veranda-I-do-declare department.

in a democracy, you must somehow find a kingdom, and Lexington provides that. The place is horse-haunted. You cannot escape the totem animal there. Its cult obtains up and down the class ladder, from the calendars and ashtrays in diners and gas stations, through the Delacroix and Géricault and Stubbs prints on the walls of middle-class homes, to the odd original out on the "farms." Emblematic for me was the gold paperweight my grandfather Milward kept on his desk, a sort of medallion that revolved on a horizontal rod, each side bearing one half of a horse in bas-relief. When you spun it with your finger, the whole horse hovered before your eyes, there but not there, all four of its hooves tucked up like the trotter in those Muybridge photographs.

I remember the almost religious silence in the car when my grandfather drove me out one Sunday to the Kentucky Horse Park to see the life-size statue that stands over the tomb of the great Man o' War. My grandparents had been to visit the horse before he died. This became something of a pilgrimage for Lexingtonians in the thirties: to drive out to Faraway Farm, where he was at stud; to pat him; and to hear his groom, Will Harbut, deliver the cherished line: "He was the mostest horse." When Man o' War died, in 1937, he was embalmed— the first horse for which this was done—and lay in state for three days. Two thousand people filed past his coffin. His statue disturbed me: the massive, unseeing, all-seeing head, the muscles petrified in bronze. A child's nerves could feel the old idolatry in it.

And always, apart from the monuments and the bric-a-brac, there were the living horses themselves, out on the farms, the broodmares standing in the deep, blue-green, monotonous fields, behind the fences that run along the property lines, in the pasture set back from the two-lane roads, with a single ancient shade tree left standing scarecrow-like in the middle distance. I knew them only from the window of our car as it sped past on the way from Louisville to Lexington, cutting across their gaze. If they noticed the traffic at all, it was with that strange contempt of stillness for whatever is passing by. One would have liked to approach them, to touch them, but they were in another world. Thomas D. Clark mentions the irony that in the Bluegrass, more than in any other part of the South, the average citizen is cut off from horses. "There are few which inexperienced riders can handle, and no public bridle paths on which to ride."

My one real "personal" experience with a horse came in the summer I turned eleven. At that age I was spending all of my time in the woods across the street from our house in New Albany, dressed in camouflage, practicing fighting off the Russian invasion that television had convinced me was imminent. I must have gotten a reputation in the neighborhood for knowing my way around back there—or, more accurately, as the strange fat kid who knew his way around back there. I was not only going through a "husky" phase that year, but I had convinced myself that if I slicked my hair back flat to my head with water, it would make me look thinner, which meant that I constantly had to sneak into the rest room at school. On top of that, both of my top front teeth had fallen out, and only one had come back in, and that one was dramatically snaggled on the end. My smile at that age was more easily conceived than described, and not helpful at all was my habit of wearing a camouflage beret. My father, until the end of his life, carried my school photo from this period in his wallet. He said it cheered him up.

When the daughter of one of my father's colleagues lost her pony, Flicka, her mother called my mother and asked if I could look for it. I accepted the mission with pride and solemnity, perhaps even applying a little extra green paint to my face that afternoon. I tramped around in the woods for hours, ridiculously, looking in the leaves for signs. At one point, coming down a path that I often took, I looked up to see a red fox trotting toward me. It was the only wild animal I ever saw in those woods, which did not really deserve the name of "woods"—they were scrub lands between two subdivisions. The fox and I stared at each other for an instant that would have gone on indefinitely, or so it seemed, had neither of us moved, but something made me smack my stick against a nearby tree to drive the fox away.

By evening I was hungry and ready to cry. But then, just as I turned toward home, I spotted a bleached deer skull in a creek bed. Seizing it triumphantly, I ran with it all the way to the house of the bereaved girl, rehearsing the account of my discovery.

By the time I got there, they had already found the horse. It was twenty yards beyond the edge of their backyard. Somehow it had gotten free and gone running into the trees, but the rope that was still hanging from its bridle became entangled in the underbrush. The pony pulled and pulled till it broke its own neck, they said. It was half decomposed in a horrible way, the tissue showing through the skin in patches. I walked back to the woods, slowly, and threw the skull into a thicket.

I burned down "the woods" later that summer. I was camping back there with my friend Steven. Aspiring Commie-killers, we were given to frequenting "knife shows," if you know what I mean, and one of us had acquired a huge Rambo-style "survival knife" with "Strike Anywhere" matches hidden in the handle. We wanted to test the truth of that claim, so for an entire afternoon we ran around striking them everywhere, on the bark of trees, on stones, on our boots. With one of the lit matches, we started a small leaf fire, out of boredom, nothing dangerous. Unhappily it spread to a dry thicket of thornbushes, which went up crackling in every direction, like the unwound strands of a terrible fuse. Soon there were about fifteen small leaf fires, and then they were no longer small. And then the woods were on fire.

Steven was a very tough kid, and when I saw him crying, I started to cry. We decided between us that because he was faster, he should run back and have my mother call the fire department. After about half an hour—a span of time that seems, in memory, to take up half my childhood—the firemen showed up with their ancient gear: garden hoses attached to backpacks, which they filled from a pond. The fire had come to within about a hundred feet of some houses. I started back toward home, nauseated with fear and guilt, but halfway there I ran smack into my mother, who had come into the woods with the intention, I believe, of fighting the fire with her bare hands if that was what it took to save her child from the reformatory, When I saw her, I fell onto my back and said,

"Please just kill me!" which I think I meant at the time. I was starkers. I have no memory of what she said.

This little flirtation with delinquency could not have come at a worse time for our family. My father was mired in a full-on clinical depression. His mother had died just months before, on Christmas morning (the call came while we were opening our presents, and my mother sent us in, one by one, to the den, where we found him on the couch with his head in his hands). Then Gannett bought the *Courier-Journal*, ushering in a more streamlined corporate culture, one less amused by my father's unconventional style. A veteran reporter, he found himself spending nights on the copydesk, touching up other people's articles. He went into a kind of paralysis. For a time it seemed that he stopped speaking altogether. I remember passing him once on my bicycle, when he was out taking a walk, and saying hello to him only to have him look right through me.

The naps, always epic, got scarily long. The number of hours in front of the television grew. That was where my mother and I found him when we got back from the woods—in front of the television, watching sports, as if nothing at all were happening. I broke from my mother's arm and ran straight to my room at the far end of the house, but even from there I could hear the things she said to him, things no child wants to hear and that, I am sure, no adult wants to remember, Her anger was of course understandable—even understated, since she chose not to leave him—but from my perspective, I alone had caused it; I had committed the crime, and now my father was suffering for it; I had brought him down with me. And he was in no shape to tell me different.

There followed a few months—the only months I remember—of genuinely unhappy childhood: silence in the house or in the car, constant fear of my father's anger. But eventually he started seeing a psychiatrist, who, by her own account, did a double take when she looked at a chart of his brain chemistry.

She prescribed some pills, which got him over the hump. He was never that bad again.

Late in the afternoon of the fire my mother came into my room and said that she wanted to show me something. I was lying on the top bunk of my bunk beds, my face still black with soot, having essentially cried myself into catatonia. My mother sort of took me by the hand and led me back into the woods, down the path, toward the devastation. I could smell it before we even left the front yard. During this entire death march, which lasted about an hour, my mother spoke one sentence to me: "I want you to see what you've done." It was like something out of Job. My beloved woods! Blackened. I think at one point I actually dropped to my knees. My mother, capable as ever, went about kicking the smoking stumps to make sure none of them had reignited.

The next morning I woke up at five to start my paper route. I pushed open the screen door and dragged in the big lump of papers, bound in yellow plastic twine. With my Swiss Army knife—I owned, of course, the one with every available blade and tool—I cut the twine and began loading the papers into my canvas shoulder bag. It was not my habit to read the *New Albany Tribune* before I delivered it, but that morning I was curious—or I suppose it would be more honest to say, quavering with dread—to find out whether there would be any mention of the fire.

There was. On the front page, above the fold, in the center, with a five-by-seven-inch black-and-white image of a fireman in action. With sickness in my heart, I read the caption. It said, among other things, "The fire was apparently started by two youths playing with matches in a trash pile."

A few days later, I was sitting with my father in the den when the telephone rang. He leaned over and picked it up, and then he stood up, sort of nervously, and turned his back to me, which meant that it was a serious call. "Yes sir," he said (I can play back what he said like a tape, with long pauses), "I'm his father. . . . No. . . . No, I understand. Listen, he's . . . No, he's not a firebug or anything like that. . . . It was a *complete* accident. Yes, I . . . I really don't think that's necessary. . . . Really? . . . Oh, more an accident than arson, for sure. . . . Yes, we've talked to him. . . . No, I can promise you. . . . Thank you. . . . Thank you. . . . Bye."

At school, I found out that the cops had got onto Steven, who fingered me (but come on, he was eleven). My father said nothing about the call, a silence I was too grateful for, at the time, to find strange. I never did find out what he had saved me from.

MORNING WORKS

Keeneland comprises a racetrack, an auction hall, a clubhouse, a dining room, and a farm, but Lexingtonians always call it just "Keeneland." It is the Vatican of horse country, the place where the laypeople go to get close to the rarefied beast that has made their city famous. It was founded in 1936, when American racing had begun to thrive again after a series of blows. Concurrent with Prohibition, there had been movements across the country to ban gambling of all forms (though Kentucky and Maryland, true to their roots, had fended them off entirely*), and the Depression had dampened America's

---

*My great-great-grandfather the Right Reverend Lewis Burton helped to beat back one of these movements in 1910. He was the Episcopal bishop of Lexington at the time. When the racing authorities there moved to install pari-mutuel betting machines for the spring meet, he was able—presumably by calling on the well-known Episcopalian genius for acting as though a controversy does not exist—to get his more reform-minded Protestant friends to calm down. At the Church of the Good Shepherd (also known as the "horseman's chapel," because of how well represented the racing community was in its pews), a group of parishioners got together and presented him with a silver statuette of a jockey and his mount, as a token of thanks. I keep it on my desk.

interest in an amusement that usually requires the spectator to part with some cash. But now there were signs of recovery. In 1934 a record 14,261 races had been run in America. John Oliver "Jack" Keene, whose family had been on the land that is now Keeneland since just after the Revolution, undertook to create a place that would be a symbol of everything good about racing: an oasis from the businesslike atmosphere and general skeeviness that still cling to many American tracks. Although he quickly ran out of money, he sold the land to a group of investors who were sensitive to his vision. A year after the track was opened, a prominent trainer described it in tones of what reads almost like gratitude:

> In the cozy stands and on the green lawns of Keeneland are gathered every afternoon a people who know and love horses. . . . We all spoke the same language and the Thoroughbred was king. Nowhere was there any talk of fixed races and horses being pulled, as is heard on every hand where racing is new.

To this day, no American track can compete with Keeneland for sheer prettiness. It is situated on the outskirts of the city, across Versailles (pr. Ver-SAILS) Road from the airport, and the land beyond the course itself has been left undeveloped, so that when you are sitting in the stands, watching the horses run, you see nothing behind them but pastures to the horizon. If you were to clap your hands and be transported back to 1937, it is doubtful that many details apart from the electronic lights on the tote board would change.

The farm that you see in the foreground, its property adjacent to the track, belongs to John T. Ward, a Lexington native who works with the English owner John Oxley and who trained the 2000 Derby winner, Monarchos (in a glass display case on the wall of his office there is a hank of Monarchos's black mane, tied with two red ribbons). Keeneland is essentially

Ward's backyard, and his private exercise track. He takes his horses there in the morning for their workouts, or in the afternoons to race, and then walks them back home.

The racing world produces very few human beings, living or dead, who are famous in a way that even approximates other sports figures. You could probably count on your fingers the names a person on the street might find familiar. There are the legendary high-profile jockeys, such as Bill Shoemaker and Eddie Arcaro; and there are the top trainers, who these days would be Bob Baffert, D. Wayne Lukas, and John T. Ward. The trainers are known not because they outperform their competitors year-round (though in fact they do quite well) but because they have been consistently successful at winning recent Triple Crown races, the ones that get carried on network TV. Baffert is the flashy one, the one who shows up in the winner's circle wearing blue jeans and cowboy boots, the one who overemphasizes his regular-guyness and poses atop his cherry-red car and pisses off the bluebloods. Lukas is known mainly for being Baffert's rival. And Ward is known for being the anti-Baffert. He is a fourth-generation Kentucky horseman and a Lexington patriot who wears a bow tie in the winner's circle and rarely wastes an opportunity to talk about "tradition" or the "right way" of doing things, which racing adepts understand to mean, "not the way Baffert does them." This conflict does not necessarily exist (when I asked Ward about it, he said, no doubt truthfully, "We're all competitors, but we all run in the same business" . . . *zzzzzz*), and these thumbnail descriptions would hardly even be recognizable to many insiders, but that is the point: racing is desperate for human, as opposed to equine, stories, anything for potential fans to latch onto. Most of America tunes in when, say, Sammy Sosa is about to break the home-run record, but when your Sammy Sosa has four legs, cannot speak, and has, to all appearances, no idea what everyone is so worked up about, you have to work harder to generate narrative. So Baffert is talked about as "controversial" for doing and saying things that would not make the sixth page of the sports section if he were a football coach (in person he is friendly and solicitous in an almost gee-golly sort of way), and Ward becomes a kind of culture figure, a purist, a foil. If you are hearing about him here for the first time, you see what I mean.

I visited Ward's stable on a damp September morning, 6:15 sharp ("Happy to have you," he had said on the phone the night before. "Just don't bother us"). He looked to be in his mid-fifties, with silvery hair and deep-set, slightly watery cobalt eyes, narrowed in a way that suggested he was not yet fully awake. His manner was unaffected almost to the point of aloofness. He spoke quietly to his staff, with that trademark of someone who carries authority well: the ability not to seem rude while not saying thank you. Everyone in and around the barn was quiet, though nor reverentially so—an early morning atmosphere of not speaking unless you had to, and then keeping it short.

Ward took me around the stable, past the stalls. Most of the horses were standing with their heads poked into the walkway, in what looked like uncertain expectation, and we rubbed their noses—he warmly, the way you grab a dog's head and jiggle it a little; I nervously the way you touch a goat at a petting zoo (one of the horses put out its teeth and gently nipped the arm of my friend Chris, who had given me a ride to the farm. It left a saucer-sized bruise that over the next month moved through the color wheel, from red to blue to black to yellow to green).

When the first set of horses left the barn, we stood and watched them pass. The riders, men and women, were small but slightly larger than jockeys. I mentioned this to Ward, and he said, "It's like swinging two bats. The horse gets used to running with that many pounds, and when the jockeys are up, it feels light." The riders made eye contact with Ward as they went by in their windbreakers and black caps, patting the necks of their mounts; one guy was bent forward whispering into his horse's ear, "What you think? What you think, huh?"

As we shuffled along behind, on the way to the track, I tried to get Ward talking about his training regimen. The night before I had been up reading R. W. Collins's *Race Horse Training*, a rough and engaging little book, published in 1937 and out of print since the fifties. Collins was a Lexington trainer, a pretty successful one, and the book contains a year's worth of his diary entries, which had been carried by the *Blood Horse* magazine in '37. I found a used copy on Mercer Street in Manhattan and in a day learned more from it than from anything else I have read on the subject, though it is riddled with the sort of repugnant asides that one might expect from a man of Collins's time and upbringing (e.g., "Booze, niggers, and horses don't make a smooth mixture"; or, in a similar sociological mode, "[My new boy] Sammy is of Yiddish nationality. . . . I was amazed to hear him come to life when bargaining with a peddler for a pair of socks some days ago. Truly blood will tell").

Collins wrote as if he were speaking to a complete know-nothing, and the book's value lies precisely in that assumption. Thoroughbred training is like particle physics in the sense that the only people who *really* know anything about its byzantine mechanics are the people who do it, and they are always too busy or too put off by your apparent learning disability to explain anything to you. Or it may be more correct to say that, again like many scientists, trainers can have trouble believing that everyone else is not as wrapped up as they are in the particulars of their calling. These are people who rarely do anything else, bear in mind. The good trainers are there *every* morning, on call *every* night. The whole sport, winning and losing, revolves around infinitesimal fractions, and no one can afford to slack. Imagine a doctor who runs a hospital, and all of the patients are his sons and daughters, and they all have a rare bone condition, and you have some idea of the lifestyle. What usually happens when you ask a trainer a moderately recherché training-related question (as opposed to a racing-related question, which they *love* to answer) is that the trainer will assume you know exactly what you are talking about, and what he is talking about, and within seconds you are lost in the maze of one of the oldest, most superabundant idioms in the English language. More than once I have walked away from a ten-minute conversation in a trainer's trackside barn with my head down, staring at a page in my notebook that read something like, "Says colt 'ran his race.' Mentioned 'sesamoids.' Has large hands."

Collins writes about his daily professional concerns, dutifully gives you the specifics, then (and here is the uniqueness in his book) explains why these things matter to him in the first place. In a typical passage, he unravels the mystery of why a two-second difference in a horse's morning "work" (a timed practice run at a set distance—a horse is said, for instance, to have "worked five furlongs," or five-eighths of a mile, "in 59⅗") can send horsewriters running to the pay phones and move trainers to give somber, defensive interviews:

> Sent the colt and filly out to work, instructing the boys that I wanted to go a little faster, but not better than three-eighths in :36, and to allow them to gallop out a half in about :50. I was alarmed when my watch started off in :11⅖, quarter in :22⅗, and caught the three-eighths in :34⅕ for the colt, with the filly a length behind him, and then both galloped out and pulled up in :48⅖. Thus it is that one's boys can in a few seconds, by only a little mistake in judgment of pace, imperil all the work one had done, and even your investment. These young things have only done comparatively slow work, and I would not have asked them for speed approaching this for some

weeks yet. If this work does not cause them to knock off of their feed, buck their shins, or get speed-crazy, I am lucky indeed.

Ward grew up around men like Collins—his father would have known the man himself—so I was curious to hear him speak about how much his craft had changed, or if it had changed, in the decades since the book was written. So much else about racing, after all—most conspicuously how fast the average Thoroughbred moves—has stayed pretty much the same. The arrival of modern training techniques revolutionized the other ancient sports (the classic Olympic sports, essentially), but horse trainers, because their sport took on an organized, statistically quantifiable form at such an early stage, had already been honing their methods for hundreds of years, tinkering with questions of diet, schedule, exercise, race preparation, psychology. They had no laboratories in which to test this stuff until recently, of course, but they had hundreds of thousands of hours of collective man-to-animal exposure, which would have been just as effective in telling what worked and what was folklore. (The progress of breeding techniques seems to have been slower in coming, at least in England, where in 1658 Edward Topsell wrote, in *The History of Four-Footed Beasts*, "If the female refuse, take shrimpes beaten soft: with water, as thick as hone, therewithal touch the nature of the Mare in her purgation, and afterwards hold it to her nose; or else take Hens dung mixed with Rozen and Turpentine, and anoint the secrets of the Mare.")

Ward said, "It's true that horses for the last however many thousand years have been essentially the same. Our advancements in training methods are really minute. The trick—which has always been the trick—is you can't demoralize their minds. They remember everything."

We were passing through the field that separates Ward's

farm from the track. The sky was striped with pink by then, and the cuffs of my pants were soaked through with dew. Ward walked with his hands in the pockets of his jeans and never once took his eyes off the horses in front of him, their taut haunches sliding against each other as they moved downhill. A light clopping was the only sound. Ward would cross this field eight times before ten o'clock.

"A three-year-old horse at Derby time," he said, "is like a fifteen-year-old Olympic swimmer. They are strong and extremely athletic, and they don't know what defeat is yet. But once they experience defeat, they get smarter. You can tell a child to run as fast as he can and as far as he can, and he'll do it. You tell an adult, and he'll tell you to go . . . someplace else. Why do you think our military uses nineteen-, twenty-year-old soldiers? These horses are the Delta Forces."

I asked him how he kept them wanting to run.

"I like to give each horse his own individual educational program," he said. "It's like Montessori."

I really wanted to hear about his *care* of the horses. Collins's book is a virtual lexicon of arcane veterinary techniques that sound straight out of the eighteenth century, or straight off a snake oil salesman's cart. Every time I came across one, I flipped back to the flyleaf and jotted it down. The result was an accidental poem. When horses "get sloughed" or "cool out gimpy," when their legs get "puffed" or "filled," or their "shins are cold again," which is constantly, Collins and his boys will

"paint with silver blister"
or with "extra strong absorbent."
When painted, the shins "dry" and "harden."
"All the horses in my barn have their feet
packed with clay-mud every morning.
This keeps the feet moist and soft."
"Devil and Glow both stand in ice-water

for an hour daily, after which I paint
Devil's legs with iodine-absorbent paint.
When fever is out of Glow's ankle,
will begin either to paint or to blister it,
whichever then seems best."
Or else put "some linament on her throat."
"Gave Glow a physic ball."
"Blistered both Glow's ankles again
with mercury paint."
The knees of the horses are "fired"
or "punch fired" with a "firing iron."
"I again painted Light's tendon, Friendly's ankles,
and Village's tendon with mercury blister."
"Put a good sweat-lotion on her knees."
"In the meantime his leg had swollen round,
and I had it rubbed well with
Hagyard's Absorbent Lotion."
"Accordingly, I repainted it with Mac."
"The wound was painted with 'blue lotion.'"
"Poor General is still unable to bear
his weight on his injured right leg,
and I am wondering what it is doing under
its poltice of antiphlogistine."

I was wondering, too. I restrained myself from trying out the poem on Ward and just asked him about, you know, all the "painting." To my surprise, he said that many of these treatments are still in use, but not for the reasons one might think (God only knows what those would be). "For instance," he said, "they used to paint the horses' legs with iodine. Well, this tightens the skin and makes the joint look a little better. It's mostly cosmetic. But more importantly, it causes the workers to pay attention to the horse's legs every single day, so that problems are being noticed and identified early. So it has a benefit. Anything that brings attention, closer attention, has benefit. Anything I can do to get my people looking at the horses more closely, more often, I'll do it."

The silence of the track, when we got there, was startling. Every clink of a chain hung briefly in the air, small and distinct like a soap bubble. The first set was brought on to work, and Chris, who had come along, turned to me: "Do you hear that?" The horses were giving off a noise each time their front hooves hit the ground. But it seemed much too loud to be the sound of the hooves themselves. We cocked our heads. Chris, who grew up going to Keeneland every chance he got, said, "They're *snorting*. . . . God, that's loud." The compression of the lungs caused by the thousand-plus pounds they brought down after each stride was forcing blasts of air through their nostrils. They drew the air back in while gathering up their hooves. This is what a Thoroughbred sounds like, galloping. Neither of us had ever been able to hear it over the crowd.

To see them run singly like this, too—to see them just *run*, without the distraction of a race's unfolding outcome or the visual obstacle of other horses—was to gain a new appreciation for their power. Every one of them, as it went charging by, its eyes forward and its whole body rippling like a flag, was a Delacroix come to life.

Ward watched the works intently, quietly. At one point, after a horse and rider had gone by, he turned to his assistant, Patrick, and said, "That's not a good match." Patrick said, "Yep." I asked Ward what he meant. "That rider is overmatched," he said. "The horse is working *him*," Then he got up, and it was back to the stable for the next set.

There were four sets that day, each with four or five horses. The riders stayed up for the cooling period, after the horses had worked, which Ward said helps the animals stretch their backs. They stood in a field in front of the stables and were washed with pails of warm soapy water while drinking from pans that were placed in front of them. Then they were allowed to hang out for twenty minutes before being led back into their stalls, where they were immediately given feed.

The entire process, from their exiting the stalls to begin walking around the barn to their being put up again, had taken about two hours. I asked what must have seemed a foolish question: Was this the only time they were allowed out? "Two hours ten, two hours fifteen minutes," Ward said. "They're stalled for the rest of the time. Some organizations only keep their horses out for fifty-five minutes, but we like to let 'em stand around a little."

Collins writes that "way back when"—before his time, even—the racers had been allowed to stay in the field for a part of each day, which he thought toughened them up. But Ward said that the dangers were simply too great. These horses had cost millions of dollars to acquire, were costing millions of dollars to maintain, and had the potential (some of them) to earn millions of dollars on the track. One would not want to lose an investment like that by letting it step in a hole, or on a snake. They did not take an unplanned, unwatched step if he could help it.

Two is about 8.3 percent of twenty-four. Which means that these horses, from the time they were purchased as yearlings and for as long as their racing careers lasted, would spend 91.7 percent of their time in a stall. And that was with Ward's extra hour factored in. I had heard it said that they were treated like prima donnas, but it seems truer to say that they are treated like fighter planes, in the hangar when they are not in the sky.

I asked why their muscles did not get weak, spending so much time in a closed space, but Ward said, "It's more like weight-lifting than the way a runner trains." Short, extremely intense exertions, in other words, meant to tear down the muscles so that they can be rebuilt even stronger, which is presumably what is happening during all those hours in the stalls.

They had seemed content enough during our nose-rubbing tour. But surely they could smell the fields, and would know what to do were they to wake up one morning alone in one of them, without their riders or their regimen.* A strange fate for a beast: to be a symbol, one of the most lasting and potent, of everything wild and free, and yet spend all your time in a space just big enough to turn around in. It would be interesting to know if they mind. Trying to see inside their enormous heads is a game human beings have been playing since Job. Henry Adams thought that the colt "dies in harness, taking a new nature in becoming tame," though that seems a bit convenient for us, their tamers. It may be enough to say that their nature allows them to suffer our strange demands.

Back inside the barn, Ward is watching as two of his assistants try to shoe a difficult filly. She keeps kicking free of their grip, moving a few steps forward or back, and she has them dancing to stay clear of her hooves. Finally Ward steps in. He elbows the horse hard, in the ribs, sending her back against the wall. The blow looks more painful to him than to the horse, who can take it, though she does seem momentarily stunned, and allows her hoof to be held, her leg bent at the knee. The first two men come forward again with the mallet and the shoe.

---

*A wonderful fact of horse sociology (and they are, as the nature shows say, "intensely social animals") is that wherever domesticated and wild horses exist on the same range, as in the American West, the wild horses are known on occasion to "capture" the domesticated ones—taking them back home, as it were. And the opposite happens: a rancher will send out a trained stallion, known as a "Judas horse," to betray a wild band and deliver it into the corral.

When I left Ward, he was headed—across the road, in his case—to the Keeneland yearling sale. A few times a year, in the spring, summer, and fall, hundreds of the most carefully bred equine progeny on earth are led through the sales pavilion there, and in each sale a handful of horses—unproven, untrained, with only their pedigrees and their "conformation" to recommend them—go for millions of dollars apiece. The whole pageant of Thoroughbred racing swirls outward from these events, and from their Northern counterpart at Saratoga; they are a strange hybrid of a Sotheby's auction and an NBA drafting ceremony. Fates are decided: the fortunes of trainers and jockeys, owners' reputations, the outcomes of Triple Crown races.

All horses turn one on the first of January following their birth (New Year's Day being roughly when the new crop starts to appear). Given that the breeding season runs from February to June, and that a mare carries her foal for eleven months, a horse can be anywhere from eight to twelve months old when it becomes a yearling, which means that the animals for sale in September at Keeneland were between sixteen and nineteen months old. This may be when Thoroughbreds are at their most beautiful. They have just outgrown the awkward stiffness and knobby knees of the foal, and their muscles have begun to develop, rolling under their coats in waves as they walk.

A two-day sale was scheduled for September 10 and 11, 2001. I got there on the morning of the tenth, a day of immaculate weather, the low, overcast skies so often seen in central Kentucky replaced with brilliant blue and small clouds. At the door I was given my sale catalogue, a bound book that lists all the as yet nameless colts and fillies (each of which has a lot number affixed to its hip), with the names of their consignors or owners. The book also includes elaborate page-long pedigrees that note the amount of prize money won by each yearling's sire and dam. At the top of each page is a cranes-foot family tree going back three generations. Most of the people there had the catalogue in their hand, consulting it, scribbling in the margins. It is a kind of libretto for one of the most unusual pieces of theater in America.

The pavilion was all motion, people and horses making figure eights from one end to the other, assistants whispering on cell phones, race fans wandering aimlessly. There are so many things happening in so many different places at a year-ling sale (and in this it is utterly unlike a traditional auction) that I quickly got disoriented trying to put the picture together: it was like trying to learn economics by standing on the floor of the stock exchange. Conversations at these sales tend to be short and vague—everyone's eyes are continuously moving, taking in the parade of potential, not wanting to miss *the one*.

The elaborate process by which the individual horses are brought to the gavel begins in the week before the sale, when the trainers, owners, and others with serious intent to buy gather at the Keeneland stables, where the yearlings are kept on view. Each animal gets a thorough veterinary exam, the results of which will be broadcast on closed circuit just before it enters the bidding. Prospective buyers are informed if the horse is, for example, a "cribber" or "wind-sucker" (one that likes to gnaw on fences, which can lead to gastrointestinal problems) or a "ridgling" (a condition that includes both unilateral and bilateral cryptorchids—colts with either one or both testicles undescended, respectively—and the monorchids, which have only one testicle, period).

The trainers check them all over, do even deeper research into their pedigrees (there is a library on-site for this purpose, though the professionals carry most of the information in their heads), and watch them run around a bit. Sometimes a consignor will have sent around a videotape of the animal back on the farm, running around at its ease. Most of the hard decisions—about which horses a prospective buyer wants to bid on and how high he or she might be willing to go—are made before the public sale even begins.

The sale itself is about nerves, for those who plan to part with a lot of money, and spectacle for those who have come only to watch. The horses are led, one after another, on a circuitous route from the stables to the stage, beginning outside, moving slowly (always slowly) into the paddock, then through an oblong covered corral, stopping at various points along the way so that stressed-out trainers, about to gamble with millions of someone else's dollars, can get a last look. The grooms are brushing them the whole time, combing their manes and tails, whispering to calm their nerves, doing everything possible to make them look gorgeous and even-tempered. The amount of money that can be lost by a sudden unexpected movement, which could cause the horse to act up and look too high-strung in front of the bidders, is nonsensically large. People hang over the railings, watching them pass. Most conspicuous in the crowd are the Arabs, who move about trailed by pods of unsmiling bodyguards and assistants. Some of the horses notice the attention and tug against their bridles, as if it annoys them. The higher-profile trainers will often step into the corral with a horse that has caught their attention. They stand with arms folded, chewing their lips, their eyes moving deliberately over the animal's body, taking in every angle and sinew as they try to gauge the promise of a racehorse that has never run competitively in its life.

From the corral the horses arrive at a sort of backstage area, the last stop before the bidding starts. At this point people intending to bid on a yearling whose approach they have followed move into the amphitheater, where the auctioneer sits. As each hip number is called, a twenty-foot-high wooden door, like the entrance to a medieval castle, is pushed open, and a new handler, in a fancy green jacket and black pants, takes the shank and brings the yearling onto the wooden stage. Then the door is pushed closed again.

In the open paddock between the pavilion and the first of the rows of stables in which Keeneland's yearlings are kept, I find John Ward sitting on a bench under a shade tree, talking to some people who look like fans, to judge from the way they are keeping a distance. He has come into this sale with a celebrity aura, a native son who has just won the most prestigious horse race in the world, not to say in Kentucky. His bidding is done for the day ("One we got, and the other we didn't," he says*), but horses are still being led to the podium behind me, and every few minutes, when a nice one goes by, he will suddenly go silent mid-thought and stare past me with that fixed head and the darting, undistractable eyes, taking it in. You can almost hear the clicks as he compares the horse with the ten thousand others he has visually dissected in this way.

What has surprised me most, at the sale, has been realizing that the cultish emphasis placed on pedigree by many bettors and most racing journalists is shared, to an overwhelming extent, by the trainers themselves. Studies of the heritability factors involved in speed and endurance (or of the frequency, in plain English, with which these traits recur in offspring) find them "modest," and the argument has been made that even these figures can be largely accounted for by nurture, not nature. "What a racehorse may really 'inherit' from its ancestors," writes the biologist Stephen Budiansky in *The Nature of Horses*, "is not so much its genes as its price. . . .

---

*The one he got—a dark bay colt, hip number 92, by Pulpit out of Caress, "foaled in Kentucky," Secretariat being his great-grandfather on *both* sides—will be named Sky Mesa, and by a year from that day will have become the number one two-year-old Thoroughbred in the world. He will win each of his first three starts, including the Hopeful at Saratoga and the Breeder's Futurity at Keeneland, both important Derby-prep races. People will mention his name and the words "potential superhorse" in the same sentence. But he will be injured in Florida before the Triple Crown and sit out much of his three-year-old season, until he is finally retired to stud in September of 2003.

Nobody who pays $500,000 for a yearling is going to stint when it comes to care and training." It seemed to me, then, that the people actually bidding on these yearlings, the people whose own success depends on their having acquired talented animals, would have too much at stake, in financial and career terms, to adhere to a useless methodology because of some romantic attachment to "blood." I had expected to see the little man step out from behind the curtain and find that pedigree is the Thoroughbred world's version of astrology, whereas these people were doing astronomy. Or zoology, to be precise.

Ward shakes his head at the idea. He says that he studies the sale catalogue first, and only later goes to inspect the conformation of a yearling whose pedigree has attracted him. He does take into account certain practical considerations. For instance, he will look especially hard at the offspring of young sires, those who were born (in today's case) from roughly 1995 to 1997. But even here the underlying concern is with blood. "Early in a sire's career at stud," Ward says, "he's going to have the best broodmares brought to him, because he's still famous and in the forefront of everyone's mind."

He says that sometimes what trainers call a "nick" will appear on the breeding chart, an intersection of two lines that consistently produces winners. It is partly a question of what the horse will be expected to do. "We're looking for horses that are superior on the dirt," he says, "not on the grass. That's one of the givens. The strong majority of the time, their pedigrees will dictate their best surface. Tinker with that, and it will break you."

Why the preference for dirt? Is it the money? He laughs, "Aw, everybody wants to win the Kentucky Derby. That's still the big one. Even *Bob Baffert* will tell you that."

Ward comes off as pretty secular about it all, as any trainer must be who wants to win more than the sporadic lucky race. He acknowledges that winners "can come from anywhere." But when I ask him if he might not be making his own predictions come true simply by preparing his horses so well, he defaults to experience. "I've bought a Derby winner that somebody else trained," he says (meaning Fusaichi Pegasus, which won the Derby *last* year), "and I bought Monarchos, who I trained. Both of them were from families that had proven they could compete in the classics. You want to be sure there's somebody in there who's got a college education."

Still, I think there must be something in the yearlings themselves—in their bodies, that is, and not in their ancestry—that influences Ward's decisions. Otherwise what are he and his colleagues staring at so grimly? "Well," he says, and pauses, as if asking himself whether he really wants to get into the specifics of thigh length with a dilettante, "You're looking for reasons *not* to buy the horse. You're looking for animals you can't train. And we do hard vetting."

"But you would never just see an animal," I say, "and think that you had to have it?"

He shrugs. Then he points over my head at the stream of yearlings, each on its way to be sold, which has been flowing behind me the whole rime. "Look at 'em," he says. "They're *all* beautiful."

BLOOD

In *Stud*, the *New Yorker* writer Kevin Conley's book about horse breeding in central Kentucky, Conley makes the intriguing point that Weatherby's *Stud Book* preceded the first edition of Burke's *Peerage* by thirty-five years. There was, in other words, an official registry of equine aristocracy before there was one

for human beings. One could follow this trend—of looking to horse breeding as a model on which to pattern human reproductive affairs—both forward and backward in time. It begins with Theognis, a Greek poet of the sixth century B.C. who wrote that in "horses . . . we seek the thoroughbred, and a man is concerned therein to get him offspring of good stock; yet in marriage a good man thinketh not twice of wedding the bad daughter of a bad sire if the father give him many possessions."

Twenty-five hundred years later, this idea was picked up by Sir Francis Galton, Charles Darwin's first cousin. Galton is known as the father of eugenics ("good birth"), a term he opted for in favor of the less euphonious but more honest "human stirpiculture." In *Inquiries into Human Faculty and Its Development* (1883), he argued that governments of the future could take a page from horse trainers, who understood that "it is better economy, in the long run, to use the best mares as breeders than as workers." His logic was that horsemen, by ad hoc experimentation and a systematic (if intuitive) weeding out of undesirable traits, had developed a science by which "the more suitable races or strains of blood [have] a better chance of prevailing speedily over the less suitable." His work was greeted with great enthusiasm all over Europe and the United States, helped in part by how neatly it fit into preexisting Victorian theories of "good breeding."

In the twentieth century Galton's work was carried forward primarily by three men. One was an American, David Starr Jordan, the first president of Stanford University. The money for the school had come from a former governor of California, Leland Stanford, the owner of the Palo Alto farm and a respected breeder of trotting horses. (It was Stanford who had paid Muybridge to make those famous photographs, which were meant to settle a bet by clearing up the question of whether all four of a horse's hooves leave the ground at once when it runs—they do). One of the reasons that Stanford chose Jordan to run the school was that he trusted Jordan to pursue his theories of breeding and "heredity." As the historian Barbara Kimmelman has pointed out, in 1906 Jordan founded and presided over the "Eugenics Committee" of the American Breeders Association, a committee that Washington University biologist Garland Allen calls "the first organized eugenics group in the United States."

Another of these torchbearers was Charles Davenport, a promising biologist turned quack social engineer who wrote in *Heredity in Relation to Eugenics* (1911), "Man is an organism—an animal; and the laws of improvement of . . . race horses hold true for him also. Unless people accept this simple truth and let it influence marriage selection . . . progress will cease." Twelve years later he was even more emphatic, writing to his colleague Wickliffe Draper, the founder of the Nazi-loving Pioneer Fund (and a descendent of "Kentucky bluebloods," as he liked to remind people), that "the most progressive revolution in history could be achieved if in some way or other human matings could be placed on the same high plane as . . . horse breeding." Davenport inculcated the wife of the railroad tycoon E. H. Harriman with his ideas, and with her money (Rockefeller pitched in, too) he was able to establish the Cold Spring Harbor labs on Long Island, where researchers gathered to prove the necessity and feasibility of eliminating the "feebleminded" and other undesirables (read:

"Negroes") from the population. Dubious experiments were carried out, and the data were misrepresented effectively enough that several states adopted the policy of sterilizing "mental incompetents." Laboratory archives show that Davenport spent $75,000 (this was in the 1930s) acquiring "research in genetics of the Thoroughbred horse."

The other, and most successful, champion of eugenics in our time was, of course, Adolf Hitler. He hated horses, Hitler did. He could not ride well, and he resented the aristocratic arrogance of the cavalry officers, who were drawn—as was the case all over Europe—from the nobility. Hitler even tried to abolish the horse cavalry altogether, a sensible, if outspoken, move at the time, but the Wehrmacht found that horses were indispensable amid the mud and roadless wastes of the Russian theater.

In *Mein Kampf*, Hitler compares horses to Jews, whose "will to self-sacrifice," he wrote, "does not go beyond the individual's naked instinct of self-preservation. . . . The same is true of horses, which try to defend themselves against an assailant in a body, but scatter again as soon as the danger is past." He was as violently stupid about human affairs as he was about the behavior of Equus in the wild, which is in fact poignantly self-sacrificial: when danger is near, the strongest animals drive the weaker ones ahead, exposing themselves to attack. Rollo Springfield provides a haunting description of how this maneuver appears to the distant observer:

> If [a stallion] takes alarm, he flings up his croup, turns round, and with peculiarly shrill neighing warns the herd, which immediately turns round, and gallops off at an amazing rate, with the stallions in the rear, stopping and looking back repeatedly, while the mares and foals disappear as if by enchantment, because, with unerring tact, they select the first swell of ground, or ravine, to conceal them, until they re-appear at a great distance.

Hitler did find something to admire in the making of the Thoroughbred, if not in the animal itself, looking forward to the day when the "folkish philosophy of life" would "succeed in bringing about that nobler age in which men no longer are concerned with breeding dogs, horses, and cats, but in elevating man."

It is surprising how public and explicit this connection became quite early on—the connection, that is, between eugenics and the harmless old traditions of horse breeding. It was not merely a case of eugenicists making use of a convenient metaphor: they really wanted to treat us like horses. In 1921 George Adami, the vice chancellor of the University of Liverpool, gave a speech in which he called for a "human stud book." But we have to look to the Bluegrass to find the exact point of intersection: W. E. D. Stokes's *The Right to Be Well Born; or, Horse Breeding in Its Relation to Eugenics* (1917), written, by its author's own admission, during "the spare hours of my vacation." Moreover, Stokes boasted, he had "never so much as opened Mendel's Essay, 'Investigations into the Hybrids of Peas,'" for his intent was "to search out the truth of heredity, unbiased by other views." The result is a book that deserves a place beside John Robert Shaw's *Narrative* on the shelf of Lexington's literary oddities. Its colorful section titles—such as QUIT BREEDING DEFECTIVES!, and GRADE MEN BY THEIR LIFE GERMS!—suggest the tone (bear in mind that Stokes was serious—he ran for office).

Stokes was the president of Lexington's Patchen Wilkes Stock Farm, which is still in existence. He had raised champions in his time, among them the legendary stallion Peter Volo. One day, presumably during his vacation, Stokes decided that he could no longer in good conscience withhold from the world his accumulated wisdom on the subject of eugenics, "which means," in his opinion, "the breeding out of weaklings," for "the laws of heredity are just as inexorable when applied to man as when applied to the improvement of animals."

The Right to Be Well Born makes awkward reading, for it is often funny (one would have to be catatonic not to laugh at the august assuredness with which its patently insane claims are put forward), yet we read it now knowing how much suffering and death precisely this sort of mind would go on to cause in the twentieth century. Indeed, the book's tedious tone and diction eerily foreshadow the style of *Mein Kampf.* And its racism sickens. "The negro child appears very precocious during early life," Stokes writes, drawing on his long experience of subjecting the children of former slaves to backbreaking labor for just enough pay to maintain them in squalid housing that he himself owned, "but, when he reaches a certain stage, we find an impenetrable wall, beyond which there can be no further accomplishment."

On the other hand, there are unexpected moments of real insight, such as the passage in which Stokes points out that we need to QUIT LETTING JOCKEYS MARRY FAT WOMEN!:

> It is just as easy to produce a jockey of the right size, weight, and with it all, intelligence, as it it is to breed ponies or half-pound chickens and the like. The trouble is that a good ninety pound jockey invariably marries a one hundred fifty or one hundred sixty pound woman. . . . You see in their families one hundred sixty pound daughters and one hundred thirty pound sons, and you can better understand their bitter disappointment; how the extra twenty or thirty pounds their sons possess is their ruin.

The Right to be well born

by W. E. D. STOKES

AMONG THE YEARLINGS II

Seats in the amphitheater itself are reserved for high rollers (the total net worth of the crowd could be calculated in GDPs), but at any given time enough of them are out looking at upcoming lots that you can slip into their empty spots and watch the action. The auctioneer sits atop an enormous dais, at least ten feet above the stage. The horses themselves are so tall that he has to be up that high to see over them, and these through-the-looking-glass proportions make him seem like some indifferent judge in a Kafka tale. He uses the frenetic, twanging banter of the country fair—*"Ah got four hunnert 'n' fifty thousand now ken ah get four hunnert seventy fahv, four seventy fahv, ken ah get"*—rather than the somber drone of the art auction. (There is a wonderful unnecessity to this style; surely no horse would sell for a dollar less if he were simply to say, "I have a bid for four hundred and fifty thousand dollars. Would anyone like to bid four hundred and seventy-five?") The banter runs ceaselessly, from morning till evening, as the hip numbers are called in unbroken succession. When one auctioneer gets tired, another slides into his place, and when one horse exits stage left, another is poised to enter stage right, a carousel of every admixture of black, brown, white, red, and gray.

The auctioneer is flanked at the podium by two relay men. His calls are based not on what he sees but on what they whisper to him. They are watching the spotters, men who stand at the feet of the aisles and scan the crowd for that raised eyebrow or click of the pen that signals a higher bid. This conspicuous anonymity on the part of the wealthiest bidders has its uses, since for an unknown buyer there is cachet to be had in going head-to-head with one of the "names" on the floor, a sort of gamesmanship that can quickly grow expensive for all concerned. As an experiment, I take a seat in the front row and turn around to face the crowd, curious to see if I can spot the bids: I do not catch one. When the spotter registers someone willing to rise to the higher figure that the auctioneer is constantly dangling above them like a cat's toy, he spins on his heels with a "Hyah!" or a "Hey!" Each has his own trademark yell. The relay man writes down the new bid and repeats it, sotto voce, to the auctioneer, and suddenly—mysteriously, since the first event in the chain is almost totally imperceptible—the price goes up.

The yearlings themselves pace back and forth, occasionally rearing, their hooves clacking on the hardwood of the stage, their dark eyes roving crazily in their sockets, swallowing the crowd like the eyes of the panther in the Rilke poem. Somehow it is much, much stranger and more unsettling to be in the presence of a Thoroughbred than in the presence of, say, a giraffe, or some other novelty animal whose defining characteristic is its weirdness. These horses are mystical in their beauty; I cannot help noticing how much, despite their tails, they resemble enormous deer. Every motion of their limbs is a kind of flickering, so that one blinks and expects them to vanish. Many of them snort while they are being sold. Others are silent. One in ten will whinny, as if to protest being stared at so insolently, and the sound scissors through the room above the auctioneer's breathless tally. They shit prodigiously, and there is with them on the stage, apart from the groom, a uniformed sweep, who brushes the pile into a pan as soon as it hits the floor.

These two men are the only black people I see at the sale, which I have to remind myself to notice, having spent too much time down South to find it remarkable. It is sad, if not entirely fair, to note that if you were to trace backward through time the job of the man sitting atop the podium—the Keeneland auctioneer—you would eventually make your way to a man named Jerry Delph, said to be a model for the slave dealer in *Uncle Tom's Cabin*. Delph sold human beings and horses off the same block in the Cheapside district of Lexington, a neighborhood "still tainted," in the words of Thomas D. Clark, "by the indignities committed there against humanity."

It is something to see these animals looking back at all that Arab royalty and Irish aristocracy, the Japanese billionaires and the old Southern money and the New Economy arrivistes searching for a hobby, and at you. There is an innocence to these creatures; they are children, after all (seven-year-olds, if we were to reckon in lustra). Their pride is undeniable, too: they seem to know that the whole affair, the hundreds of millions changing hands every year, the roaring crowds, the vainglory, the tears, are about them, and are nothing without their power. Yet their power is ambiguous, for they have already accepted the halter. And just as they are the reason for this display, so all that money in the crowd, all that arrogance, is the reason for their existence, for the existence of their kind.

On my way out of the pavilion, I notice Bob Baffert and Prince Ahmed bin Salman bin Abdul Aziz of Saudi Arabia, the owner-trainer team behind the Thoroughbred Corporation, which in a short time has become one of the most successful breeding and racing concerns in the world. Baffert has solid white hair just long enough to call floppy, and he is wearing, here inside, his signature dark glasses (he is allergic to hay and uses the shades to hide the redness of his eyes). Bin Salman has a round, friendly face, with black hair he keeps oiled and a well-maintained mustache above his smile. Baffert is the most recognizable human face in the game, and bin Salman is arguably its most powerful player, yet together they are the antithesis of the old Kentucky horseman (Baffert lives in California and got his start as a jockey on déclassé quarter horses, and there is the matter of his *hay allergy)*, so Lexingtonians tend to love and hate them more strongly than everyone else loves and hates them.

It might be more correct, in the prince's case, to say that Lexington has never known quite what to make of him; unlike the Maktoums of Dubai, his foremost Arab rivals in the horse game, he does not own land in Central Kentucky, is not a "neighbor" (though he boards many of his horses here). Yet however skeptical the attitude toward him here, it is tempered with grudging respect. Back home, he controls the Saudi Research and Marketing Group, a media empire that publishes most of the kingdom's newspapers and magazines, and he belongs to the tiny pyramid-tip of Thoroughbred owners whose shopping whims can actually affect what sort of year the industry has. Today, for instance, he has already spent more than a million dollars on three colts. And this is after the first session of a week-long sale. And this sale is one of a dozen or so he attends each year, leaving aside any direct, individual owner-to-buyer.

In the back of the amphitheater, a little group of people— TV reporters and security men and gawkers—stands around listening to bin Salman extol the virtues of Officer, a colt he purchased last year. I insert myself between two sets of shoulders. The prince stands with his hands clasped behind his back. He wears jeans with a white Oxford shirt (if you mean to drop money at Keeneland, you want to spend time in the stalls, so the dress tends to be casual—for billionaires).

A few minutes in the prince's company are somehow enough to pick up the sense that he is good-natured and— strange to say it—unassuming. The moneyed South is full of people who act like royalty, so it is nice to brush up against a royal who acts like a person (there are thousands of princes in Saudi Arabia, granted, but bin Salman is King Fahd's nephew and the son of Prince Salman, the governor of Riyadh, which puts him rather close to the center of power). He makes eye contact with everyone, nodding in response to compliments.

On Baffert's advice, bin Salman has just bid five million dollars on hip number 203, a chestnut great-grandson of Secretariat.* But amazingly, the bid is not high enough. Sheikh Mohammed bin Rashid al-Maktoum, the defense minister and heir apparent of the United Arab Emirates, wins the auction at five and a half. (I later ask Rogers Beasley, the manager of the sales, whether the prince and the sheikh ever get competitive on the floor, going higher just to outdo the other. "Used to," he says. "They got smarter on us." He is not complaining: on

---

*For fun I try to count how many of the 573 horses for sale have Secretariat's blood in them but get bored at a hundred: the great champions sire armies of offspring.

this day alone, more than $60 million worth of horseflesh is sold.) Bin Salman, smiling and giving the palms-up "What can you do?" sign for the cameras, seems philosophical about having lost out, but Baffert is visibly disappointed. He was looking forward to training that horse, which is instantly led away, back to its stable, no doubt wondering why its time has just been wasted.

It will be allowed to get comfortable for a week or so in its new home on the sheikh's farm in Lexington, and then one day a trainer will walk up behind it, insouciantly but not stealthily, moving slowly, backing off each time it flinches or kicks and then reapproaching, chattering to it without a pause, keeping a hand on its rump, respecting its outrage but insisting, firmly though not forcefully, that the thing simply has to be done; and after as much of this as is necessary, when the horse has essentially been flustered into stillness, the trainer will strap a saddle onto its back. Within hours it will have felt for the first time the alien weight of another creature, an irritating two-legged thing that will add a hundred pounds to the half ton its muscles are already capable of carrying at full speed. Thousands of years of genetic predisposition to domesticity will tell it—without its understanding the directive but without its being able to resist—not to buck quite as furiously as its wilder cousins, not to hold on to its indignation quite as long, not to perceive this new presence as an enemy and so do whatever it takes, even injure or kill itself, to escape. By the time the bit is slipped into its mouth and it first tastes the whip, it will have come to see reality as a succession of such indignities, but perhaps not so awful, with excellent food that appears magically every morning and night, and a little herd of bipeds—reminiscent of the Presence, but taller—who seem to feel toward it almost the way its dam, if she is not forgotten, felt toward it. The existence for which it was destined—for which it was created, since it is a Thoroughbred— will have begun.

The Whisperer was now sent for. This mysterious horse-tamer soon arrived, was shut up with the horse all night, and in the morning exhibited the hitherto ferocious animal following him about the course like a dog—lying down at his command—suffering his mouth to be opened, and any person's hand to be introduced into it—in short, as quiet almost as a sheep. He came out the same meeting and won his race, and his docility continued satisfactory for a considerable period; but at the end of three years his vice returned, and then he is said to have killed a man, for which he was destroyed.

The man who effected the wonder we have just recounted was an awkward, ignorant rustic of the lowest class, of the name of Sullivan, but better known by the appellation of the Whisperer. His occupation was horse-breaking. The nickname he acquired from the vulgar notion of his being able to communicate to the animal what he wished by means of a whisper; and the singularity of his method seemed in some degree to justify the supposition. How his art was acquired, or in what it consisted, he never disclosed. He died about 1810. His son, who followed him in the same trade, possessed but a small portion of the art, having either never learned the true secret, or being incapable of putting it into practice.

—Rollo Springfield, *The Horse and His Rider*, 1847

ON TO THE FIELDS OF PRAISE

The trip to Lexington for the yearling sale was only the second time I had been back to the city since we had buried my father there one year before. The first, in the winter of 2000, had been to sit with my grandfather as he succumbed to a twenty-five-year struggle with Parkinson's disease.

My father's grave is at Calvary, a Catholic cemetery that lies directly across the road from Lexington Cemetery, where all of my mother's family back to Joseph Milward are buried. I went to the Milward plot first, and stood for a while at my grandfather's grave, the terse marker. He had an excellent name: Hendree Paine Brinton Milward. A classic thin man—with a resemblance, especially later in his life, to Samuel Beckett. He was a person of almost antiquated probity (I doubt, sentimentality aside, that there was anyone in the town who would have said differently). He had traveled only once, as a young man—had been in Germany on a sort of attentuated grand tour in '36, had seen the goose-steppers and the fear in the eyes. I saw the little diary he kept. For the days in which he was in Berlin, there was only one entry: "My German is awful, but there's no one here I'd want to talk to."

When the war started he was turned away from the service because of a game ring finger on one hand, the result of a childhood accident involving a milk bottle, which made it hard for him to hold a gun. So he went home and trained himself to grip the bad finger with the one next to it, imperceptibly, and to hold it down. When he went back to try again, the army doctor administering the test complimented him on the strength of his fist. He was sent to New Mexico, to learn to steer B-52s, taking with him my grandmother, to whom he would stay married for fifty-four years. One morning she woke up in Deming, New Mexico, and opened the blinds to find thousands of flakes of ash floating through the air and piling up against the side of the house, "like mayflies." The bomb had been tested at the Trinity site a few hours before.

His death had been well earned and peaceful, practically a sigh. He was buried next to his brother, who had been born in 1915, two years before my grandfather, and lived only twenty-six days. It was strange to think of the infant in the ground, always somehow older than the man.

The two graveyards, starkly separated from each other by the road and the traffic and the fences, with the rows of Anglo-Saxon names on the one side and the Micks and Macs and O's on the other, seemed at the time to sum up rather neatly how opposite my parents were in almost every way: he Catholic, she Protestant; she old Lexington, he a grandson of Irish immigrants, brought up in White Plains, New York, who moved to Lexington only as a teenager when his father, a construction supervisor, got a job overseeing the building of the IBM plant outside town; she a former cheerleader, he a former and unregenerate hippie; she a graduate student, he a college dropout; she a woman who is visibly affected by one glass of wine, he a man who was completely unaffected by punishing quantities of what he called "grog"; she partial to tennis, he a man who once joined a bowling league, and left me for hours on end in the bowling-lane nursery (such a place should not exist). It was a riddle to me how they stayed together for twenty years.

The headstone was not on the grave yet; the grass had not come in. It was late, and no one else was around. I had no flowers or anything else to leave and felt like a trespasser.

One of the most difficult things in dealing with my father's death—for many of the people he left behind, I think—is how totally inappropriate grief and mourning seem beside any memory of the man himself. He was a deeply funny person, a collector and disseminator of bawdy jokes and carefully clipped page-10 stories about insane trailer-park crimes. He had inherited some variant of that dark and antic strain of Irish humor that runs through Synge and Flann O'Brien, by which the worst imaginable situations, the worst outbursts of temper, will suddenly flower into a joke that makes everything bearable. It was often gross, this humor: in the press box at Jacobs Field, in Cleveland, where my father watched and wrote about so many Indians games, there is a plaque in his memory, the inscription on which reads, "Know it? I wrote it!"—the punch line of a joke that cannot be repeated around children, or touchy adults, a joke he loved to tell. He would freely discuss his near-constant digestive troubles, and remarked to me once that he had considered writing a book entited *Diarrhea: An Autobiography.*

The minutiae of his weirdness have taken on a strangely luminous quality for me since his death. I run through them sometimes, in my mind, when it seems that my memory of what he was *like* is getting fuzzy. He had strange, intensely loyal attachments to a closed set of brand-name products— Triscuits, Q-tips, V8 juice, Fig Newtons, Kool Super-Longs, Tab (which tasted like Coca-Cola left open overnight in a car and which he said he loved because "no one ever asks you for a sip")—and he would become depressed if he could not have these items around him. The first thing he would do on a road trip would be to run out and gather supplies.

His favorite invectives were "twit" and "clown." He harbored strange phobias, one of which involved birds. He had seen the Hitchcock movie as a child, and it had permanently messed with his head. I once came home from school—honest to God—and found him lying facedown on the floor behind the sofa, hands folded over his neck, tornado-drill style. A robin had gotten in through the chimney and was thrashing about in the fireplace. I opened all the doors and had just moved to open the grate when he screamed, "No, Johnny, he'll *peck our eyes out!*" Seagulls at the beach could send him running into the water, flapping his arms around his head.

He once put his hand over the receiver while giving a live radio interview from our basement—I was down there getting some laundry—and said, "Hey, Beamish, give me a good hillbilly name." I had no idea who was on the other end of the line. I shrugged.

"Come on, give me a good name. Like, I don't know, Jethro?"

"No," I said, "Enis is better."

"Thanks," he said, then got back on the phone in a Gomer Pyle accent—"Hey, it's Enis hyar"—and proceeded to comment on some Southern school's NCAA chances from the perspective of a toothless moonshiner (and still it hurt him that the public could find his journalism peculiar).

One of his oldest friends, Schley Cox, told me a story that gets at what it was like to be around him. This was in Louisville, in 1975. Cox had just had a hernia operation, and the doctor had said to him, "Go home. And whatever you do, don't laugh."

"So I called your dad," Cox told me. "I was at my mother-in-law's house. And I said, 'Sully, I want to see you, but I can't laugh. I mean, I really can't laugh. It hurts like hell. So you can come over, but no jokes. There can't be any laughing.' So your dad promised. No laughing. We would just talk. When he got to the front door, we stood there staring at each other for fifteen seconds—just staring at each other—and then we broke down into *peals* of laughter, and I was screaming it hurt so bad, but I couldn't stop."

My brothers and sisters and I trade stories of how he tormented us as children. There was a night when he took us to the drive-in (he loved the drive-in, loved all movies, even bad ones, though I once saw him stand in his theater seat at the end of some Hollywood remake of a European classic and loudly apologize, on behalf of the American people, to the original director). I remember what we were seeing that night—it was *The Man from Snowy River*. There is a scene in that film in which a herd of wild horses comes cascading down a nearly vertical hillside in slow motion, their bodies falling over themselves like that woman in the Duchamp painting, which looked beautiful outside, in the dark, on the giant screen. At a certain point my younger sister Beth fell dead asleep in the front passenger seat of the station wagon (we always had station wagons).

My father was sitting there, a tall glass of whiskey and water in his lap. With my mother at home and the youngest unconscious, he seized his opportunity to mess with the "yard apes," as he called all children, and began silently dipping his fingers into his drink then reaching his hand out the window, flicking whiskey at my older brother, Worth, who was a few feet away from the car, in a lawn chair. After each flick, my father would withdraw his hand, lightning quick. I was watching this from my seat on the roof of the car.

"Dad," my brother finally said, turning around, "I think its raining."

"No, I don't think so, son," my father said, as if he were inducting my brother into one of the world's great mysteries. "That's your *imagination*."

What a farce, and a gaucherie, even to try to tell the story of a life. A task for the novelist, on whom reality—not truth but reality—has a lighter claim. One chooses a mask, and can describe even that with pitiful inadequacy. My father's disappointments and sadnesses never quit him. His own father had died when he was only nineteen, dropping dead in harness, as it were, on the job at a construction site ("Four men came up to my mother at the funeral," he told me, "and claimed to be the one who caught him, which is how she knew that no one did"). He was devastated; he had worshipped the man. He dropped out of college, utterly lost for a while. In many ways I see now that he never got past it, that he was always, in some sense, a son. In one of his journals are his plans for a book that would tell his father's story, the story of "a great and unknown man." But he never wrote it. His temperament was not suited for the long commitment, for the artist's obliviousness to competing responsibilities, which necessitates a certain cruelty, let us admit. So he wrote his newspaper stories and wrote them well, downstairs at his green-leather-topped desk, on his creaking chair, in a haze of smoke, with the two things he kept in front of him for his entire writing life: a medieval globe and an ancient bottle of bourbon. On the wall was an unnerving hippie poster from the 1960s, a sepia-toned daguerreotype of a dead cowboy upright in his coffin, and underneath the coffin, in the typeface of an Old West wanted poster, a Christopher Logue poem:

> Be not too hard
> For life is short
> And nothing is given to man.

This was always behind him as he typed—or banged, rather, in the two-fingered style. The desk was vast, like the deck of a ship. It was accidentally lost during the settlement of his estate and is in a Salvation Army somewhere in Louisville now, or at the dump. It had one of those boards that you can slide in and out, and on this he would rest his coffee and his giant cut-glass ashtray. I used to stand down there in the room with him while he wrote, or did interviews on the phone. I am not sure why he tolerated me; it would have been no big thing, to either of us, if he had just told me to go away. But I liked to watch him. There was a crude square basement window in the wall that let through a perfect geometrical shaft of light where smoke and dust would swirl. We had an odd little game we would play. Part of the reason my father had remembered Secretariat's late charge at the Derby as such a mysterious, sudden event was that he was almost totally blind in his left eye—the side from which the horses would have been coming. He had contracted histoplasmosis (a real problem in the Ohio Valley, because of the extreme convection, which allows the fumes from bird droppings to build up in the atmosphere—at least that is how my father explained it to me). There was a tiny spot on his eye that the disease had left unaffected, a window through which he could see. I would step back about five feet from his chair, and he would take off his thick, nerdy glasses (which looked inexplicably hip with the thick mustache). He would cover his good eye with his right hand—we were very solemn about the whole thing. I would stick out my right arm like the hand of a clock and begin to move it in a circle around my head, by ticks, switching to the other arm when I got to twelve o'clock until we had isolated the spot. Here? No. Here? No. Here? That's it. We tried the game again many years later, at his apartment in Columbus, after a few drinks, but the spot was completely gone. He joked that he should take the left lens out of his glasses, "as a conversation starter." His—our—name means "the one eye" in Gaelic: Súileabháin.

He was raised Catholic, very Catholic, and always described himself as being at various stages of recovery from the experience (though like many Irish Catholics, for whom the affiliation is more ethnic than religious, he clung to little tics of the faith, always dropping his head and crossing himself, for instance, when the cross passed us going up the aisle, which drew looks at the decidedly low-Anglican church

we attended when I was a child). There was a peculiarity of his speech that he traced to one of the parochial schools he attended. As a boy, he had suffered from a mild stutter, which was made severe by a sadistic nun who would smack him with a ruler every time he got caught on a consonant. As a result, he picked up that habit common to people who learn all of their words from the page and never get a chance to speak them: private phonetics. I have somewhere a whole lexicon of words he would pronounce in his own way, stubbornly refusing to change no matter how many times you corrected him: ee-light for elite, fas-kist for fascist, skythe for scythe, sham-a-lawn for chameleon, ray-par-T for repartee (his stock phone message was, "Call me, boy, and let us have banter, badinage, and ray-par-T").

When the time came, his mother and father sent him to St. Joe Prep in Bardstown, Kentucky, a boarding school run by the Franciscan Brothers (now an historic site—my uncle Brien was in the last graduating class). Bardstown is the heart of Kentucky's Catholic country, an area overlapping two or three counties where in the mid-eighteenth century French missionaries were somehow able to displace the already well-ensconced Methodists. It is a curious little outpost of old Europe hard up against the culture—no less old, in its essence—of rural central Kentucky.

About ten miles from St. Joe lies the Abbey of Gethsemani, the monastery where Thomas Merton spent the greater part of his life. My father met him once. Seniors at St. Joe were required to do a weeklong retreat at the monastery: enforced silence, 3:00 a.m. vespers. There was a boy in my fathers class whose uncle had been a friend of Merton's family in France, and an audience was arranged. My father had read *The Seven Storey Mountain* and was already in awe of the man. A group of boys—the "literary types"—were assembled in a bare room. Merton came in swinging his arms and talking freely (they had not heard anyone speak in days). "You're from St. Joe?" he said. "Normally when St. Joe's here you can hear the beer barrels rolling down the halls!" That was the only thing my father, doubtless overwhelmed, could remember him saying.

St. Joe traditionally sent its students on to Bellarmine, a Franciscan college in Louisville, and that was where my father went in 1963. He shared a suite with two other Southern Catholic boys, who remained among his closest friends until he died. One of these was Schley Cox (he of the hernia story), and the other was Chris Wimmer, who is now the harbor master at Hilton Head. "We were three misfits who ran around together," Cox told me. "Wimmer was about six-five, a hundred twenty pounds. He and your dad liked to sit in their room and smoke and think thoughts." I called up both of them after my father died, when I suddenly realized, with a sort of panic, how little I really knew about my father's life before I came into it. His way of talking about the past was usually to recycle a set number of comfortable anecdotes. I could sense even as a child that there was pain there, isolated memories that would quickly open onto vistas of grief, and the few times I pressed, he became uncomfortable. But when I spoke with these two men, neither of them remembered any sadness, only strange behavior that struck me as deeply familiar.

Cox said that my father was obsessed with the University of Kentucky Wildcats back then. "This was one night in November," Cox told me, "and it was cold and rainy, and there was a basketball game. Mike was sitting at his desk there in the dorm room, where he did his writing. All the sudden he just jumps up, puts on his jacket, and says, 'I'm going to Lexington.' He had no car, but he was an accomplished hitchhiker. He gets out on I-64, and he's thumbing, trying to get a ride. And then from down the Interstate, here comes the Channel 11 wagon with Cawood Ledford in it." (Ledford was a legendary Kentucky sportscaster whose voice I grew up listening to in the dark on long car trips.) "So your dad starts doing this little pantomime, like he's shooting hoops. Cawood just whizzed on by."

Wimmer remembered my father as "hippie before there were hippies" (I have never been able to figure out how this transformation happened so quickly, in the summer between the last day of class at St. Joe, where he had a crew cut and wore a tie, and the first day of college, but my father was an impulsive creature). "Yeah," Wimmer said, "Schley introduced us. Your dad was wearing gabardine pants and Banlon shirts. He'd read 'Howl' and Ferlinghetti. He also hung out at Jack Fry's, the boxing bar, and could tell you off the top of the head who pitched every inning of the '56 World Series. I was trying to get the Beatnik look down, and he walked in looking like somebody's weird uncle. I thought, *Here's* an interesting guy."

My father was beginning his freshman year when his own father died. From everything I have heard, my grandfather, for whom I am named, was almost a god in the eyes of his eight children. Frequently he was away during the week, at a building site somewhere. When he would come home on the weekends, it was as though real life could begin. "Every one of us thought we were his favorite," my uncles always say.

When my father's parents married, in the early thirties, my grandfather was still a bricklayer (the men in the family had been stonemasons back in Ireland, and this trade seems to have evolved naturally into building work when they got to America in the 1890s). The boss on one of his jobs made him and another man compete to see who would be promoted to crew chief. The contest was sadistic: a factory was being built, of brick. The boss gave each man a wall and said, "Go to it. The first man who finishes gets the job." This took almost a week. My grandfather would come home at night unable to move, and my grandmother would spend hours massaging his back with rubbing alcohol so that he could hurl himself at the wall again the next morning. (He won the contest.) My father said that he remembered Saturdays when my grandfather and his friends would gather at a house in the neighborhood. One of their wives, as it usually went, would have said that she wanted a new kitchen, or a room added onto the back. So they would get together at dawn and start building. All of them were tradesmen, with different specialties. They would be drinking whiskey the whole time, and would become consumed with the project, working harder as the bottle got emptier, not stopping to eat, trying to outdo one another. The idea was to finish the work before midnight.

When my grandfather died, it occasioned some sort of rupture in my father's life. He quit the baseball team early in the season, after having worked hard to make the cut—a more serious decision, for him, than it may appear on the surface. His father had played semi-pro ball as a young man, and the sport, with all its loaded father-son traditions—oiling the glove, arguing over games—had been *theirs*. In a column that he wrote in the seventies, my father remembered a month they spent together—less than a year before my grandfather died—in Pawtucket, Rhode Island. It was the summer of 1963. My grandfather was supervising another building project and had given my father a laborer's job on the site. I assume the rest of the family stayed at home in Louisville:

> We drove to and from the job together every morning. As always, he had hunted up a church-league team that needed a first baseman. He drove me to every game, twice a week after work, in his blue 1955 Dodge. He watched every inning with a quiet absorption and a contentment unique to those who are, at once, baseball fans and fathers and old men.
>
> After the game we'd sit in the old Dodge and replay the game verbally, with long undemanding silences, as darkness settled in.
>
> Much as he detested it, he'd permit me my newfound vice of smoking. We sat in the front seat and shared the simple timeworn clichés of "percentage" baseball, the ancient and logical rules of the pastoral game.
>
> Then, driving home, he would pull off the road at least once to place a nitroglycerine pill under his tongue and wait until the pain in his chest went away.

My grandfather died the following February. And for my father, the game became hollow. He gave himself completely over to poetry, staying in his room, working and reworking his attempts on a gray manual typewriter that I remember seeing as a child. Cox said that the only reason my father even continued to attend classes, apart from English, was so that he could go back and write descriptions of the professors. He would come in from dates and immediately go to work on a set piece, describing what had happened—the girl, the restaurant, his digestive concerns. Cox said that he spent whole nights bent over the desk and would stand up in the morning having completed a single sentence. "And he was thrilled by that."

In his sophomore year—which turned out to be his last, at that or any other school—he was given an unusual term-paper assignment by his English teacher. She instructed the class to produce not a piece of original writing but a collage in which they were to reproduce as many examples of "beautiful language" as they could find.

Sometime during the seventies, my father entrusted the original of the paper to Wimmer, and Wimmer sent it to me. The thin sheets of typescript were coffee-stained and burn-marked, already starting to fox; they were penciled in my father's hand, at places where he had screwed up the page numbers, with apologetic marginalia: "Prime goof: two 13's"; "Skipped #15, sorry another goof"; "Another numerical muff." When I looked at it, I realized that my father had spoken to me about this paper once, in the car. I was about fourteen. He mentioned it with pride, as one of the best things he had ever written, which stuck out (he usually apologized for his newspaper articles, when he showed them to me, saying, "Remember, 'tis merely a squib"). Of course, he had not *written* the paper, not really. But what struck me, when I read it, was that almost all of the writers whose work my father was devoted to throughout his life—Faulkner, Bellow, Twain, Agee, Merton, Thomas Wolfe, Dylan Thomas—were there, and he had compiled it when he was twenty-one. Passages I had heard him rhapsodize about, such as the moment in *Huckleberry Finn* when Huck decides, "All right, then, I'll *go* to hell," or the "Caddy smells like trees" scene from *The Sound and the Fury*, or the passage in *The Adventures of Augie March* where Augie says that he wants to lick the inside of his dead father's ashtray—they were all represented.

In its way, the collage—entitled simply "Beautiful

Language"—*is* a little piece of brilliance: transcribed dialogue from *On the Waterfront* is juxtaposed with a verse from the Gospel According to St. Luke. A paragraph from André Schwarz-Bart's *The Last of the Just* leads into some lines from Dylan Thomas's "Fern Hill":

> So it must have been after the birth of the simple light
> In the first, spinning place, the spellbound horses walking
> warm
>> Out of the whinnying green stable
>> On to the fields of praise.

The paper is dated April of 1966, the year he dropped out; it would have been his last academic act.

He remained serious about poetry for five or six years after that. These were the years I heard barely a word about. Chris Wimmer was able to help me fill in some of the gaps, though he prefaced his recollection by saying, "It's a cliché, but it's true: if you remember the sixties, you weren't there." Survivors can tell you that if you wanted to have fun and get "turned on," you went to Haight-Ashbury, but if you wanted to get weird ("gross weird," as Terry Southern said in describing that point of freakiness beyond which you can never go back to mom's house), you went to Memphis. Robert Gordon, in his chronicle of the period, writes about a night at the Electric Circus on St. Mark's Place, in Manhattan. Allen Ginsberg and Timothy Leary were standing against the wall. Wimmer walked by with Jimmy Crosthwait, an experimental puppeteer who, like Wimmer, had grown up in Memphis in the fifties. As they passed, Ginsberg turned to Leary and said, "Watch out for those guys. They're nuts."

Wimmer told me that my father had been along on at least a couple of those trips to Manhattan. "Yeah," he said, "we packed it up in the '65 Rambler and put your dad in the back seat and came to New York. He stayed in Hoboken with some people he'd known in Memphis, a group called the Insect Trust."

In the house where I grew up, in New Albany, there had been a little cubbyhole under the shelf where my parents kept the stereo. When I was still small enough, I would drop the needle on one of their LPs and crawl inside, to listen to the music through the wooden boards: it was like being inside a speaker. One of these records was by the Insect Trust. The cover was black, with a sort of Hindu-inspired design. I played it once, and then never again: it sounded like a Chinese opera company had wandered in on a Howling Wolf rehearsal and was not pleasant to listen to in an enclosed space. I would probably like it now. The blues scholar Robert Palmer was in that band.

My father had lived with these people. "It was kind of a movable feast," Wimmer said. "We had Memphis apartments and New York apartments. Everybody was always there and everywhere." He reminded me that my father had come along on his first honeymoon, which I had known. But I had never imagined acid being part of the honeymoon experience, whereas the Insect Trust was definitely, definitely on acid. Wimmer gave me an "Ahhhh, you know" when I asked about my father's drug use, which I had suspected on some level, though it ended abruptly when he married my mother (largely at her insistence). I remember being with my father at a Bob Dylan concert at the Flats in Cleveland once. A petite, dark-haired woman sitting next to him volunteered that she had been following "Bob" for years and that she was sure tonight was the night she would succeed in smuggling her poetry collection, "Ages and Stages," into his dressing room. She and my father quickly struck up a conversation on the subject of Bob's genius. Suddenly she leaned over and offered us a joint. My father and I locked eyes, frozen, our brains echoing off of each other: He—probably—knows—that I— Then in perfect sync we turned and said, "No, thanks." That night, on the way home in the dark, I reminded him of the time when I was six or seven that I had asked him if he ever "smoked drugs." He had said to me then, very solemnly, "Once I tried it, son, but it made me sick." The memory made him laugh. "It did make me sick," he said, "about the two thousandth time."

In 1969 my father was failing to hold down several jobs in Louisville. He was ineligible for the draft, because of his blind eye, so he volunteered to work as an orderly at a VA mental hospital, which was then packed with young soldiers back from Vietnam, their brains thoroughly scattered. When guests would visit—local politicians and military officials and people like that—a few of the patients would run out and "masturbate at them," as my father put it. He said this made tackling them somewhat awkward. For a very few months he taught the fourth grade, but he was fired from that job when the principal talked to one of his kids and discovered that for the past two weeks the class had been spending most of every day listening to recordings of Hal Holbrook reading Mark Twain. I was at a restaurant with my father one night when his memory suddenly flashed on one of his students, a mildly retarded boy who had been unable to do the schoolwork but who loved words. Whenever my father would say, "Do you know what 'superlative' means?" or whatever it was, the boy would all but throw out his back straining to be called on, and always was. He kept a giant dictionary under his chair, which he would hoist onto the desk and flip through—while the class waited in silence—until he had found the word, at which point he would read the definition aloud. "He drowned not that long after I left the job," my father said, and as he said it tears sprang to his eyes.

One day, Wimmer said, my father showed up at his door in Memphis with a young woman, Donna, his next-door neighbor from back in Louisville. They were eloping. "We started going through the Yellow Pages, me and your dad, and calling all the churches in town. The Seventh-Day Adventist church said, 'Sure, we'll marry you.' So they did it there, with my mother and myself as witnesses." The marriage lasted just long enough to produce my half sisters, Lisa and Michelle. I never asked my father why he and his first wife eloped. Her parents may have disapproved. Pictures of him from the time support that theory.

In 1971 he was still in his mid-twenties, divorced with two children. He had hair down his back and a bushy, dark red mustache, always with the thick glasses. During some pause in the midst of all the frolicking—I have been unable to pinpoint the date—he had begun to write for the *Courier-Journal & Times*. He did a freelance piece for them, on spec, about a witch who lived near Bardstown. She was an old woman—she said she was a witch, everyone else said she was a witch. My father interviewed her and wrote a profile, which got picked up by the AP and printed across the country. An editor called him in and said, "What can you write about?" There were two things he could have said: beautiful language and sports. He said the one he thought would get him hired, and it decided his career for the next thirty years.

It was around then, I think, that my father relinquished his literary ambition. He told me the story of the moment he made up his mind, without mentioning when it had been. We were in Columbus when he told me, so I was in high school. I had just confessed to having looked at his papers. He kept all of his amateur writing stuffed away in a bunch of the leather satchels that Churchill Downs gives to the sportswriters every year before the Derby. One night I gave in to curiosity and spread the contents of one of them out on the floor. I had the nerve to tell him about it later only because I had found, in my snooping, that his poetry was actually pretty good, undeveloped (making no claims, here, for my right to judge— this was how it seemed), sloppily surrealistic in places, and marked here and there by his habitual word-mongering, but one did not have to search sympathetically to find the talent in it. A description of a bicycle wheel "unzipping puddles" comes to mind, and a piece that began:

> 30th and Round down west in white shanty town
> would slide on its dust into the river
> and cross to Indiana, a dead clown
> floating, if the trains did not shiver
> the house with their borderguard thunder.

Certainly it was better than some of the stuff we had heard from behind the podium at the Thurber House in Columbus, where we sometimes sat through poetry readings together, and I probably told him that I thought so. Sons often wander like sleepwalkers into their fathers' defeats.

He told me that at one point when he was in his twenties—1971 or '72, I assume—he was beating his head against a short story. It had been stuck in his typewriter for a month, never allowing itself to be pushed beyond the second page. "It was some Faulknerian thing," he said. "I was devouring Faulkner—everything he wrote, every word." One morning he woke up and pulled *A Portrait of the Artist as a Young Man* down from the shelf. He started to read. He read for hours, without looking up. "And then I came to a certain page, and I put down the book, and I thought, I will never, ever, *ever* be able to do that. And I was *insane* with jealousy. For weeks, just eaten up. I couldn't read anything. Everything I read, I got jealous. That was when I knew that I just had to let it go."

I said, "But wasn't Joyce, like, the best? Ever?" (I think I had read "Araby" by then, in a textbook.) "I mean, if everybody who couldn't write like James Joyce . . ."

"Yeah, I know," he said, "but I just couldn't. . . ." And he let it drop. He saw that it was not something I would understand. I was still at the age when I thought my doggerel *was* as good as Joyce, because of the world-altering fact that it had come out of my brain. My father had gotten past that. He had looked at himself in the mirror and said, "I will never be what I thought I was." In that moment—the moment of his telling me about it—he became much less sad in my eyes.

The reason why jealousy and not frustration or lack of nerve, would have been my father's breaking point is that the veneration of talent—other people's talent—lay at the center of who he was. This is what made him a good sportswriter, I think, for he was a failed athlete, too, and there could easily be an overdose of masochism in spending so much time watching others do what you grew up believing you were meant to do. It was a religion for him: the religion of the thing done well. Or not "well"—he was not the sort of man to stop and admire fine woodworking, or to clean the bathroom, for that matter—but surpassingly. When he called to read you a paragraph from a novel, or to describe something he had seen Chris Farley do on television (Farley, whom my father considered a poet, was a hero to both of us); or when he forced you to pay attention to a song in the car, or told you about some move he had seen a college player make on the basketball court ("It was like he was playing the game three seconds in the future"), the implication in his tone was not that he wanted you to agree with him about the thing itself—since its value was beyond doubt—but that he needed you to be with him for just a moment in marveling at the fact *that such people existed.* Resentment born of envy would have been a living hell for a man like that, and so he decided to turn away.

The decision freed him up to be a fanatical reader, and that is how I like to picture him, to hold him in my memory. We are at the beach in northern Michigan, where we used to spend a few weeks every summer. He has just come out of the lake, where his strange hard-kicking style sent up little explosions of water as he moved along parallel to the shore. Now he is in a lawn chair, feet bouncing, cigarette dangling, clip-on shades, the mustache. A can of Tab is resting on the shelf of his belly. His skin, still unscarred, is turning alarmingly red. He has the

glow of the health he was born to enjoy. And the paperback is propped against his chest. Every so often, without warning, he throws his head back in amazement and exclaims, *"Jesus!"* Then he says, "Listen to this. . . ."

A PILLAR OF CLOUD BY NIGHT

The next morning, the eleventh, a man rushed out of the managers office at Keeneland saying that New York was under attack by terrorists. Within minutes a voice came over the intercom: the sale was canceled until further notice. The announcement was timed so that a final round of bidding could be completed, and when the day's last yearling was led away, tossing its head, the doors were left closed.

The crowd seemed unsure of what to do. Most people were standing around, talking quietly to one another or on their cell phones. One of the sheikhs (the female groom I spoke with was unsure which) simply walked out of the stables, phone to his ear, and climbed into a black car that squealed away.

Bin Salman was still in his suite, having breakfast, when he heard about the attacks. His racing manager, Richard Mulhull, said that the prince immediately called him on his cell phone, distraught, asking, "Who in the world would do this? Who's crazy enough to do this?"

That afternoon, before it was known that fifteen of the nineteen hijackers had been Saudi nationals, the prince did a very shrewd thing. He granted an interview to the *Lexington Herald-Leader* in which he phrased his support for the United States in terms that Southerners could appreciate. "We gotta get them and get them big," he said. "And do like we do in Arabia: an eye for an eye."

Every reporter at Keeneland realized (cynically, perhaps) that a provincial side-story had just materialized. Here were these powerful Arabs, highly placed members of at least two ruling families, all stranded in Central Kentucky in the aftermath of radical Islam's first full-scale assault on U.S. soil. They must have been scared; there must have been unusual security concerns. Surely federal agents had descended, earpieces crackling. But the story was not to be had. Everyone knew where most of the Arabs were staying—at the Marriott Griffin Gate (if you grew up in a palace, Lexington does not exactly offer you an array of "suitable lodgings")—but the Southern Governors Association, to whom Cheney had just given a speech the day before, was ensconced there, too. Cheney himself had checked into the hotel briefly on the tenth, so the place was already guarded like a fort.

The following morning, the twelfth, the sale commenced (people had flown in from all over the planet to attend it, so there was little room for piety), and the mood in the pavilion was bizarrely unchanged. There was actually no discernible shift in the atmosphere, no tension, no decrease in volume either of sound or of cash flow. The bidding picked up precisely where it had left off, with the prince in his usual spot, Baffert beside him, even the other loaded, expressionless buyers watching them from the corners of their eyes. And the yearlings went around. The blip of a news story that had been this odd juxtaposition—powerful Saudis in Kentucky on 9/11—disappeared.

Or rather, almost disappeared. On October 5, the *Tampa Tribune* ran an article describing a Lear Jet that had taken off from Tampa, Florida, bound for Bluegrass Airport, on the afternoon of September 13, a time when private aviation was forbidden by the FAA and when the use of chartered aircraft, which would have included the Lear, was severely restricted.

The "Phantom Flight," as the atticle dubbed it, had been chartered—or at the very least facilitated—by Raytheon Airport Services in Tampa, a subsidiary of the Raytheon Corporation, which supplies arms to Saudi Arabia and numbers among its board members former director of the C.I.A. John Deutch, On board the jet were two private security men and three young Saudis, one of whom was Prince bin Salman's nephew and the grand-nephew of the Saudi defense minister. The three passengers were friends; they had been studying English in Tampa, not far from where some of the 9/11 hijackers had been taught to fly but not to take off or land, and presumably someone powerful feared for their safety.

The flight marked the beginning of the U.S. government's now notorious evacuation of wealthy Saudis, including many bin Ladens, after 9/11. A series of flights, lobbied for (as Craig Unger later reported in *Vanity Fair*) by the Saudi ambassador to the United States and Bush family friend Prince Bandar, began leaving the country very soon after the attacks. These international—as opposed to domestic—flights were not in any way illegal, though they occurred during a period when noncommercial aviation was still discouraged by the FAA.

But the "phantom" flight to Lexington was different. It should never have been in the air,* and several people with major security clearance would have had to go well out of their way to make it happen. The FAA, the F.B.I., the State Department, and the White House denied that it ever took place, but the fact that it did—on the day and time reported by the *Tampa Tribune*—could be verified with only a few phone calls.† The flight was on its way to meet bin Salman, who, at the time, was somewhat ambiguously confined at the Marriott,‡ with Baffert handling the bidding back at Keeneland. Skip Keyser, a customs agent at Bluegrass Airport, said there was pressure to get the Saudis out of town immediately. "I was

---

*An official at Bluegrass Airport told me that "the airspace here was not considered open until the fourteenth."

†The two bodyguards, who were on the plane, confirmed it twice; John Solomon, a criminal intelligence officer in Tampa who helped to arrange security for the flight, said, "The detectives assisting with that [operation] worked the job on the thirteenth, and the job ended with the flight taking off" (a statement corroborated by the Tampa police department's "special assignment" files); and records at Bluegrass Airport showed that a Lear jet was fueled there on the thirteenth,

‡Both Richard Mulhull, the prince's racing manager, and Jack Rusbridge, his private bodyguard, asserted that bin Salman's room was being guarded by F.B.I, agents, who had called immediately after the attacks "to express concern for his safety," but the F.B.I. denied this outright. "We were certainly aware that he was in town," said the bureau's Kentucky spokesperson, David Beyer, "but the F.B.I, did not provide security for any of the visiting Middle East people." When asked about this a second time, Rusbridge.—a twelve-year military man and longtime security specialist who understands the distinctions between law-enforcement agencies—insisted that the F.B.I. had been there, in the hallway outside the prince's room. "Absolutely, four or five of them." he told me. "There were Secret Service guys already on duty [because of the Southern Governors conference], and we had F.B.I., C.I.A., local marshals. No one moved from the horel."

getting phone calls from everywhere," he remembered. "They wanted these people gone. And everybody here was scared that some kook was gonna come out of the Eastern Kentucky hills and start shooting at those planes, with the Arabic letters [on the tails] and all. We couldn't hide 'em."

It took three more days for bin Salman to get out of Lexington. An airport official with access to that week's outbound manifests told me the prince flew to London on the sixteenth, aboard another chartered jet, along with the three young Saudis from Tampa and his standard retinue. Two federal agents were on the tarmac, checking passports.

Almost a week passed before I was able to get home to New York. When I finally got off the plane in Newark, the shuttle into which I was crammed with twenty other people crossed the George Washington Bridge in the dark. The plume was off to the right, and when we craned our necks to follow it into the sky, it rose beyond the reach of our sight, merging with the darkness.

At the ad hoc memorial that sprung up instantly in Union Square, someone wrote PEACE between the blind eyes of George Washington's charger and draped a white flag over Washington's outstretched, war-pointed arm.

A CERTAIN MYSTICAL QUALITY

Frederick the First of Prussia once demonstrated the horse's effectiveness in battle to the Duke of Marlborough—probably no less to his own surprise than to the Duke's. He selected a compact arena, put himself and his guests safely behind metal grating and had the doors of several pens surrounding the arena opened simultaneously. Out raced a lion, a bear, a bull, a tiger, a wolf—and a horse. The horse was in strange and slightly crushing company. The natural fury of the other beasts is several times greater than the horses. It must also be remembered that, save one, they were all carnivorous animals who could use one another for food, if nothing else excited an attack. At any rate, the five of them charged one another and tangled themselves up in a hopeless struggle, ripping at one another's throats, snorting and clawing. The horse meanwhile stood by and quietly watched them. Eventually the bear, battle-scarred and infuriated by the gory encounter, emerged victorious. The horse still stood by and watched him.

The climax came when, bleeding and frenzied, the bear discovered the horse. Without warning he launched a terrific charge. The hoofs of the horse caught him, nevertheless, with a fearful blow, and knocked him back. Again the bear, in a blind rage, attacked the horse and took a thunderous blow in the face. His mouth hung limply open, his jaw broken and the fatal power of his great teeth gone. The battle was over. And the horse was still standing, looking at the blood-stained heap of beasts. He didn't go near it.

—Arthur Vernon,
The History and Romance of the Horse, 1939

ICON

We have never been certain whether the horse means peace or war, death or life; it depends on what culture you consult,

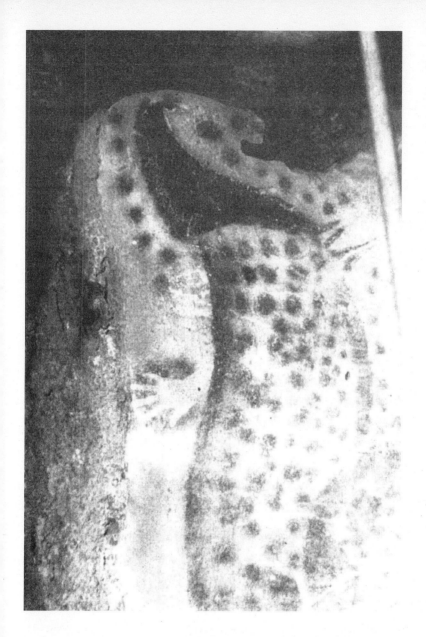

and down through time it wavers, like a compass at the pole. Symbols become more polysemous as they grow in familiarity: jade will always signify purity, but the apple can stand for anything. And nothing, until, say, 1913, when Ford began using interchangeable parts—or until now, on some parts of the planet—has been more familiar to us than the horse. It is not too much to say that a person today who knows horses, really knows them, understands more about what it meant in the past to be human than the most knowledgeable historian.

In most places—pretty much everywhere in the industrialized world—the horse has passed out of our common life. It is a pet, or a police horse; at most it carries an unregenerate cowboy. But thousands of years of symbiosis leave a trace. It shows up most clearly in the language, this deep familiarity, in all the excellent words. You can go mad noticing them. Beyond all the metaphors that have passed into our speech—all the pony-tails and tantivies, the horsebeans, horseleeches, and horselaughs (futile even trying to get through the "horse" listing in the OED), beyond all the junkies shooting horse and all the cutpurses hung from the "mare foaled of an acorn"—beyond that there is, most excellent of all, the terminology, the words we have evolved in order to live in such close association with these beings for such a long time, to be able to talk about them and what they do; piebald and roan, withers and farrier, crupper and martingale. A Martian, equipped only with time and a dictionary, could reconstruct the history of the human race by looking for these little proliferation-points of vocabulary, where the language suddenly explodes, signaling long intimacy, necessity. And yet, in an irony both strange and somehow perfect, when our Martian got to the word "horse" itself, he would find that white flag of lexicography: "origin unknown."

There is a theory that our language itself—our real language, Indo-European—is before all else the language of horsemen. Historical linguists have long wondered why in the West we speak a derivative of an obscure tongue that is thought to have developed six thousand years ago on the central Asian steppes rather than one of the many languages once dominant in Eurasia, of which today Basque is the only survivor. An archaeologist named David Anthony, at the Institute for Ancient Equestrian

Studies in New York, put this enigma together with the fact that the steppes are where he and other excavators have unearthed five-thousand-year-old horse skulls showing the world's earliest known signs of bit-wear, a discovery that pushes the advent of riding back a full millennium.

It would have taken thousands of years for the horse to go from being our meat, to being our milk, to being our legs. Our first awareness of them would have been as a spectacle, when they came thundering past on their seasonal migrations. Sandra L. Olsen, in an essay entitled "Horse Hunters of the Ice Age," says that the first people to eat them were the Neanderthal, who probably scavenged skulls from carcasses that the herd had left behind (other animals would have carried off the rest of the meat, but the Neanderthal alone were clever enough to crack open the bone and extract the nutrient-rich brain matter). Horse teeth, evidently made into necklace beads, begin showing up at habitation sites in the Middle Paleolithic; the tails, too, were brought back to the caves for use as thread. Next we tried to hunt them, but they are too fast and smart and, in their truly wild state, extremely fierce, so the Ice Age hunters began to corral the herds, positioning piles of stones in such a way as to block their route and diverting them into naturally enclosed spaces where they could safely be felled with spears (one of these kill-sites, at Roche de Solutré in Burgundy, was excavated to reveal a three-foot-thick layer of horse bones covering two acres).

The next stage—domestication—is perhaps the most mysterious of all. The only plausible theory researchers have been able to come up with is that of the biologist J. Clutton-Brock, who argues that somewhere, at some point, one of these hunters must have adopted a horse as a pet. We can see this Cro-Mag there in the grotto, slaughtering mares and stallions willy-nilly as his ancestors had already been doing for millennia, when suddenly he notices, at his feet, a petrified foal. He finds it sort of cute and takes it back to the cave, where he and the rest of his band discover that these terrifying animals, if captured young, are actually quite gentle. On his next expedition, he brings another one home, or his friends do. A thousand more years go by, and we have become horse herders, milking the mares, slaughtering and eating the adults, perhaps even strapping our belongings to their backs when the horrible winters drive us south, keeping them in pens just beyond the edge of our circle of huts. The oldest signs of this achieved domestication show up on the Eurasian steppes, about seven thousand years ago.

David Anthony's theory, simplified here in a way that he would not appreciate, is that on an unrecorded afternoon, people belonging to one of these steppe societies were standing around looking at their horses in a pen, and someone decided to climb on top. Anthony speculates that it may have been a child—a nice symmetry, given that it was probably a foal we first adopted. This was a notion that could have occurred in regard to only a few Old World animals (camels, elephants, and perhaps water buffalo being the others). Although Equus can be quite threatening when it needs to, it is alone among hooved quadrupeds in having no horns or antlers to hurt us, and its back is long and sturdy enough to accommodate our bodies, a biological affinity that Darwin noticed when he wrote, in *The Voyage of the Beagle*, "A naked man on a naked horse is a fine spectacle; I had no idea how well the two animals suited each other." Almost as if they were waiting for us.

The species—both species—never looked back; what had been separate destinies were woven together in a double helix. The horse was saved from the extinction it had been headed inexorably toward, and the people became riders. These riders, speaking their harsh proto-Indo-European, having climbed atop and learned to guide the beasts that everyone else was still using for meat or milk—or simply watching with admiration— were able not only to spread their culture at formerly unimaginable speeds but also to put the fear of

God (literally, perhaps) into whomever they met. Before long everyone spoke their tongue, worshipped their horse-headed deities, and rode horses.

Among our first conscious signs of ourselves, in the limestone caves of Spain and France, they are already there, prancing, stampeding, and evidence suggests that we had already begun to see them as something more than themselves. Books about Ice Age art mention the paradoxical fact that horses make up a significant number of the painted images even in caves where they are hardly to be found among the bones, undermining the "hunting magic" line of interpretation, and the historical zoologists Pat Rice and Ann Paterson found that when all of the artwork, in all of the prehistoric caves, was catalogued, "horses outnumbered every other group of animals." There is even what looks like an altar to the horse in the south of France, in a cave at a place called Landes, dating back fifteen thousand years, a "kneeling sandstone figure" of a mare amid skulls and horsehead figurines. Our awe in their presence—who has not felt it, just standing across the fence from one?—is as old as anything we can call ours.

They began in North America, in warm glades that are

now the Great Plains. The dinosaurs had vanished, and the mammals—tiny rodents living on the margins of the food chain—crept forth into the vacuum, where they flourished. By fifty-seven million years ago, one unassuming branch had become Eohippus, "Dawn Horse," the size of a small dog, with multiple clawed toes on its feet. There was a land bridge then—not the one we hear about, which connected Alaska to Siberia, but another one, going the other way, from Canada to Europe. Eohippus (or Hyracotherium—"shrew-beast"—as the scientists would now prefer that you call him) crossed this bridge, and spread over most of the planet. But at some point during the Miocene, maybe fifteen million years ago, something started happening to the little tapir-looking creature back in its aboriginal stomping grounds, in North America. In the rest of the world, it was spending most of its time in the forests, walking around, but here the evidence suggests that it preferred more open habitats, which rewarded speed. Its DNA responded (we are thinking, needless to say, in geological time). Its stubby legs, designed for scurrying, started to lengthen. Its claws, all but the central one—which had begun to bear more and more of its weight, for the same reason that a track runner puts more pressure on the ball of his foot than on the heel—started to shrink up into its legs, to become superfluous. The surface of its teeth grew more irregular and complex, better for grinding down grains than for plucking and chewing soft leaves.

A little under a million years ago, the old Atlantic land bridge having receded and a new one having formed over the Bering Strait, this thing, which was now a specimen we would recognize, found its way over—opposite to the way we came—and colonized Europe and Asia: herds of wild horses, alpha stallions with their harems of mares, "bachelor bands" of sub-dominant males, moving like wind patterns across the steppes and the plains. They had become ungulates— mono-toed, hooved—and they had become fast, faster than anything on the solid earth apart from the cats, and the cats could maintain their speed for only a few hundred yards or so, whereas this creature could run from morning to night. The entire genius of evolution had gone into crafting *asva*, as it was called in Sanskrit, this verb made flesh, this thing whose every atom wanted to run, from the giant nostrils, drawing huge drafts of air into the cavernous heart and lungs, to its long, powerful hindquarters (the horse essentially leaps when it gallops, like a tremendous hare).

They kept changing, growing bigger, even faster. They had developed those enormous eyes that seem always to see you no matter where you stand, like the eyes in old family portraits, which allowed them to watch the grass they were eating and the predators lurking in it at the same time. A few more hundred thousand years and a few more modifications (mainly of size) gave us *Equus caballus*, the one we know, the one that Solomon and Napoleon rode.

There still exist horses today that, to judge by the cave paintings, resemble the animals our distant ancestors worshiped and tamed: the Przewalski (pronounced psheh-VAHL-ski) steppe horses of Russia and central Mongolia, small and tan, thick-necked, with a stiff mane and a dorsal stripe, and the distended belly you see so clearly at Lascaux. They were named for a Colonel Przewalski, a Russian explorer who brought back the first specimen in 1881. The Mongolians, of course, had always known they were there; they called them *taki* and ate them when they could catch them. The Europeans had been cyclically forgetting and rediscovering them for centuries. John Bell, a Scottish physician who traveled from St. Petersburg to Peking in 1719 on a trade expedition under the auspices of Peter the Great, recorded the sight of these ponies:

> There is, besides, a number of wild horses, of a chestnut colour; which cannot be tamed, though they are catched when foals. These horses differ nothing from the common kind in shape, but are the most

watchful creatures alive. One of them waits always on
the heights, to give warning to the rest; and, upon the
least approach of danger, runs to the herd, making all
the noise it can; upon which all of them fly away, like
so many deer. . . . Notwithstanding this wonderful
sagacity, these animals are often surprised by the
Kalmucks; who ride in among them, well mounted
on swift horses, and kill them with broad lances.

They disappeared from the wild sometime in the 1970s—
this is the supposition, at least, as they were last spotted in the
late sixties, though the possibility remains of an isolated band,
constituting the world's only true wild horses, somewhere
deep into the interior. Where central Mongolia is concerned,
"gone" can mean only "not seen in a very long time," and in
any event the book on prehistoric-looking throwback ponies
is not yet closed: French explorers stumbled onto a previously
unknown subspecies in central Tibet only ten years ago. They
named it the "Riwoche horse," for the valley where it was
found. The Tibetans had known about it for longer than their
cultural memory stretched, and had been practicing a unique
form of catch-and-release, lassoing the ponies, using them as
pack animals, and turning them loose. (For Westerners to find
an unrecorded land mammal of that size, at this late date, is
not much less likely than a fisherman walking into the biology
department at St. Andrews with a dead Nessie.)
    In the nineties, Przewalskis bred from zoo stock were
reintroduced onto the steppe and appear to be multiplying.
But they are not "wild," not, in other words, independent
of human beings; neither are the "wild" horses of North
America—not the mustangs of the West or the ponies of the
Eastern sea islands. These are feral. People argue about when
they got loose, the more romantically minded holding out
that the mustangs come from horses brought to Texas in 1530
by the shipwrecked Spanish explorer Cabeza de Vaca, but they

descend nonetheless from domesticated stock. There have not been true wild horses in the Americas for ten thousand years. No one is certain why they died out after having succeeded here for so long. Humankind doubtless had something to do with it—this was before the revolution on the steppes, and the tribes who encountered these bands of horses would have thought only, *Meat*, or at most, *God, meat*—but disease and climate change may have been equally responsible. There is a hopelessly slim but tantalizing chance that somewhere, on a mammoth tusk or a fallen chunk of rock wall, maybe, there survives a painted image of one of these indigenous North American horses. What is certain is that when they were reintroduced—by Columbus (on his second voyage, which included thirty-four horses), by Cabeza de Vaca and Cortés, by Pizarro and de Soto (whose mount famously breathed right into Atahuallpa's face)—the natives had no idea what they were. The Conquest was among other things the confrontation of the horsed and horseless hemispheres. "Big dogs," said the Indians who met Columbus on the shore; "sacred dogs," said the Cherokee; "holy dogs," said the Lakota; "great elk dogs," said the Blackfoot. The Creek called them "great deer," and the Aztec said, "Their deer take them onto their backs," The Inca "thought the horse and rider were one creature," according to the official Conquest historian Bernal Díaz del Castillo, a confusion that Shakespeare may have been thinking of when he had King Claudius say of the Norman rider:

> He grew unto his seat;
> And to such wond'rous doing brought his horse,
> As he had been incorps'd and demy-natur'd
> With the brave beast.

The reaction was played out again and again over time and gives us a clear idea of what those earlier tribes must have felt when confronted with the sight of the steppe riders coming over the horizon. Darwin records an anecdote from an early voyage to Tahiti:

> When a horse was landing for Pomarre in 1817, the slings broke, and it fell into the water; immediately the natives jumped overboard, and by their cries and vain efforts at assistance almost drowned it. As soon, however, as it reached the shore, the whole population took to flight, and tried to hide themselves from the man-carrying pig, as they christened the horse.

Courtesy of del Castillo we actually have a list of the sixteen horses Cortés brought with him from Cuba to Mexico (the names and descriptions of the men on board were not as conscientiously recorded). These were the first horses to survive on either of the American continents, as Columbus's stock had been quickly devoured. Eight of Cortés's horses were wounded during his first skirmish in the New World, but they were "cured with grease from the dead Indians." Unhurt was El Arriero, the Muleteer, an "excellent dark stallion," according to del Castillo, "one of the good horses we brought in the fleet." Cortés tied this stallion to a tree and ordered that a mare be led slowly back and forth before its eyes. El Arriero went wild. "You and your people have angered the horses!" Cortés had his interpreter scream at the Indians, who prostrated themselves in fear.

"After God," del Castillo famously said, "we owed our victory to the horses." A passage from one of Cortés's *Relaciones* to Charles V suggests how clearly this debt was recognized at the time, not merely afterward, and gets at the admiration—almost reverence—the Spaniards felt for their mounts. The siege of Mexico had just begun:

> That day the people of our camp were in no danger, except that as those on horseback came out of their

ambush, a man fell from his mare. At once she galloped off towards the enemy, who wounded her with arrows. She, when she saw their wickedness, though badly wounded, came back to us. That night she died and though we felt her death, for the horses and the mares were our salvation, our grief was less, as she did not die in the power of the enemy. . . .

One of the strangest stories to emerge from the Conquest concerns the horse that Cortés chose for himself, El Morzillo (the word seems to have been both a description and a name, *morzillo* meaning black with a slight red sheen). El Morzillo injured his foot on the shore of Lake Petén Itza, in Mexico, in 1525. Cortés had grown attached to the animal and asked the chief of a friendly tribe to look out for it until he could return. "The chief promised to take care of him," Cortés wrote, "but I do not know that he will succeed."

It has not come down to us what the chief or his followers did immediately after the Spaniards left. Other anecdotes from the Conquest suggest that without instructions as to care they would have tried feeding the horse what they themselves liked most to eat: chicken and fruit and fish and corn-beer. They were probably terrified of the animal. Samuel Eliot Morrison writes that the Guaraní, when Cabeza de Vaca ran into them in 1541, begged him "to tell the horses not to be angry with them." Most of the tribes assumed that the creature was immortal, since it was clearly a god, and when an Aztec war party succeeded in felling the mare ridden by Pedro de Morón, a soldier under Cortés, her head was cut off and sent around with a runner to the nearby villages so the people would know that the new creatures could be killed.

Cortés never came back for El Morzillo, and it was 150 years before any Spaniard made his way back to Petén Itza. In 1697 a Franciscan named Ursua arrived there with two of his fellow friars. They had come to bring the gospel to a group of Indians who were "ignorant even of the knowledge of the true faith," having been brushed by the Conquest, and then left in peace.

As the three friars and their horses approached the island of Tayasal by raft, an Indian named Isquin appeared on the shore. He stood watching them as they got closer. In the *Historia de la Conquista de la Provincia de El Itza*, the Franciscan chronicler Juan de Villagutierre Soto-Mayor writes that when Isquin saw the horses, he

> almost ran mad with joy and with astonishment. Especially the jumps and bounds made by the animals moved him to admiration, and going down upon all fours he skipped about and neighed. When tired of the manifestation of his joy and his astonishment, he asked the Spanish name of the mysterious animals. When he heard it was *caballo*, he forthwith renounced his name, and from that day this silly infidel was known as Caballito. Then, when he had duly been baptized, he took the name of Pedro, and to his dying day was called Don Pedro Caballito, for he was born a chief.

The Spaniards thought little of this behavior at first: he was only a "silly infidel." But a few weeks later, as they were making their rounds of the islands in Petén Itza—smashing and burning idols, preaching "the Incarnation of the Eternal Word"—they entered a temple in which they had been told was "an idol much revered by the Indians." Inside they found a statue of a horse, carved out of stone and placed atop a six-foot-high wooden platform. The effigy was seated on its hindquarters like a man.

The friars were so astonished that for once they were moved to do a little anthropology. Asking questions of their guide and the islanders, they learned that "these barbarous infidels adored the abominable and monstrous beast under the name of Tziunchan, God of the Thunder and the Lightning, and paid reverence to him." The Indians remembered that a long time ago—"in the time of their grandfathers"—a warrior had brought them this sacred creature. Villagutierre surmises that they first tried to keep El Morzillo alive, and when they could not, carved a replacement, so that Cortés would not be angry on his return. "Their veneration grew by time," he writes, "and the abominable image became the chiefest of their gods."

After he heard this story one of the assistant friars took up a stone and smashed the idol. R. B. Cunninghame Graham, in his *Horses of the Conquest*, writes: "Thus was destroyed through an excess of that intemperate zeal, that Talleyrand so much deprecated, one of the most curious monuments of the New World, and a memento of the Conquest that should have been preserved as carefully as if Praxiteles himself had carved it with his own hands." Eighty-four years later, the last twinges of any resistance to the Spanish Conquest were ended in the plazas at Cuzco, in Peru, and at La Paz, in Bolivia. In Peru, an Indian named José Gabriel Condorcanqui, the grandson of the last Inca, Túpac Amaru, had begun calling himself after his grandfather and making trouble for the Spanish authorities. Inspired by his example, the Bolivian revolutionary Julian Apasa took the name Tupaj Katari: a transliteration, in his native dialect, of Túpac Amaru, "shining serpent" or "standing serpent." The Spanish had them both drawn and quartered in 1781. Four horses were tied to their bodies—one to each limb—and driven "toward the four compass points" while thousands of Indian witnesses stood wailing.

The horse has often meant doom to a culture, as the populations that lay in the way of the Mongols might attest if they could. There is that mysterious line in Herodotus, in *The Persian Wars*, when Croesus, king of the Lydians, wants to know what it means that all the horses in his kingdom have suddenly started acting funny, as if they were afraid. "Look for the entry of an army of foreign invaders," says the oracle, for the horse is "a warrior and a foreigner." And it was, which is why most of us have never heard of the Lydians. The association with war goes back to the very beginning, almost everywhere you look, from the Greeks with their horsetail helmets, to the Assyrians on their murderous chariots, to Job's warhorse, which "saith among the trumpets, Ha, ha."

Judaism has had an uneasy relationship with the horse, which Adam named *sus*. Deuteronomy includes the commandment that the king of Israel "shall not multiply horses to himself" (though Solomon later did just that, and David commanded cavalry). The antipathy seems strange until one considers how completely the ancient warhorse symbolized power and wealth, which tended to be in the hands of the Egyptians, the Babylonians, the Greeks and Romans—the oppressors. There are disturbing echoes of this old enmity: the fifteenth-century Roman festival of Campidoglio, which included the *palio degli ebrei*, a race in which Jews were made to run naked, carrying Christian jockeys on their backs; or Kobyla the Mare, a superintendent at the Majdanek concentration camp whose nickname referred to her pastime of stomping on women and children while wearing hobnailed boots.

Early Christianity inherited Judaism's sense of the horse as a creature too proud—too close, like the Tower of Babel, to God. *Equus asinus*, the donkey: this will be Jesus' mount. It leads him to safety when Herod orders the killing of all male children under two, it is standing there in the stable when he is born, and it carries him into Jerusalem. The New Testament, when you think about it, is an implicitly antihorse document. Mighty Saul, "breathing out threatenings" against the Christians, is knocked from his horse when Jesus appears before him on the road to Damascus (the text does not say that he is on horseback, but the Renaissance painters knew that it must be so). The whole significance of Jesus' arriving "meek, and sitting upon an ass," is that he is *not* sitting on a horse or in a chariot; and in the earliest depictions of the Entry he rides sidesaddle, a patently unhorsemanlike posture. This is not simply a textual, hermeneutical thing; people got it, got the symbology, early on. The earliest known crucifix in all of Christendom, a graffito on a Roman wall that dates to around A.D. 200, shows Jesus with the head of an ass. His was to be not cavalry, but Calvary; the horses must wait till the end, till the apocalypse, when all is perfected, and then they bring war. All of which was fine so long as the new religion remained the province of converted Jews. But when Christianity began to spread, touching cultures that had inherited, along with the language of those proto-Indo-European speakers, their formalized veneration of the horse, accommodation had to be made. That veneration ran deep, from a four-thousand-year-old grave in Russia that when excavated was found to contain the bones of a man who had been decapitated, his skull replaced with that of a stallion, to the elaborate horse sacrifices of the Indian Rig Veda, with their haunting liturgy: "You do not really die through this, nor are you harmed. You go to the gods on paths pleasant to walk on." The twelfth-century Welsh historian (some would say fabulist) Giraldus Cambrensis recorded the following during his travels at the other end of the Indo-European world, in Northern Ireland:

> There is in the northern part of Ulster, namely in Kenelcunell (Tyrconnel), a certain people which is accustomed to consecrate its king in a rite altogether

outlandish and abominable. When the people of that land had been gathered together in one place, a white mare is brought forward into the midst of the assembly. He who is to be inaugurated, not as chief but as beast, not as king but as an outlaw, embraces the animal before all, professing himself to be a beast also. The mare is then killed immediately, cut up in pieces and boiled in water. A bath is prepared for the man afterwards in the same water. He sits in the bath surrounded by all the people and all, they and he, eat of the meat which is brought to them. He quaffs and drinks of the broth in which he is bathed, not in any cup or using his hand but just dipping his mouth into it round about.

Giraldus means what you were hoping he did not mean by "embraces."

As Christianity absorbed the horse as a symbol, it endowed it with the ostensible virtues of the faith: mercy, suffering, peace. And in this regard, the horse is the perfect Christian icon, for it lays aside its own superiority in serving us ("If the horses knew their strength we should not ride anymore," wrote Twain in a notebook). With the Renaissance there comes a whole cadre of saints who always appear, in the paintings, on horseback, indicating not strength but succor, compassion. The face of the white horse in El Greco's *Saint Martin and the Beggar* is plainly the focus of the painting: we meet its eyes before we even think of turning to the two men represented. And if you were to go looking for the U.N. secretariat today, you would find yourself, at First Avenue and Forty-second Street in Manhattan, confronted with an enormous black-iron statue of St. George on horseback, slaying the dragon, which in this instance is made of two disarmed nuclear missiles donated by the Soviets in the eighties. St. George and his horse, which stands on the very belly of the beast, wear identical expressions: impassive, serene. They are not warriors; they are defeating war.

That old horse-religion is still alive in Europe. The most significant animal-related rite on the continent, and arguably the ritual practice with the greatest continuity and deepest provenance in all of European culture (apart from, say, *eating*), is the dance of the hobbyhorse, which St. Augustine was already complaining about in the third century A.D. ("If you ever hear of anyone carrying on that most filthy practice of dressing up like a Horse . . . punish him most severely"), and which you can find enacted now in many places in Europe. It is impossible to say just how far back it goes (certainly well beyond the written record), but two anonymous hobby dancers who were arrested by the Puritans in 1611 for perpetuating heathenism probably got it right when they said in their defense that "what they had donne, was done tyme out of mynde of man."

There is Shakespeare's famous and obscure line in *Hamlet*, evidently an allusion of some kind (perhaps to a popular song, as the same or a similar line appears in eleven other Elizabethan plays), though scholars have not been able to trace it. At a certain level, its meaning is perfectly clear. The prince has just been taken to task by Ophelia for being irrational in his grief:

> O heavens! die two months ago, and not forgotten yet? Then there's hope a great man's memory may outlive his life half a year: but, by 'r lady, he must build churches then; or else shall he suffer not thinking on, with the hobbyhorse, whose epitaph is, "For, O! for, O! the hobbyhorse is forgot."*

*This use of the hobbyhorse to stand for something beyond rationality, something we forget only at our peril, was picked up in 1916 by a group of European artists who named their movement Dada, French for "hobbyhorse," asserting absurdity, whim, and the authority of dream against all that technology and efficiency were wreaking in World War I. (If we accept that they chose the name, as one version has it, by inserting a paper knife into a French-German dictionary, this only shows that chance often conspires with truth.)

It typically happens on May Day, though in some places, such as Ste. Souline, in the Loire Valley, the people wait until Whitsunday (Pentecost)—in any case, in spring, when the crops are coming up and people are feeling spry. A team of men from the town is entrusted with the particulars: maintaining the costumes, appointing the actors, supplying the liquor. The costumes, some of which are quite old themselves, range from the "hooden horse," a horse skull on a pole with a sort of skirt around it which falls down and encircles whoever is holding it, to the more conventional horse-suit. The details of the actual custom vary, but the archetype goes like this: Old Hoss rides into the midst of the people. He is staggering and reeling. The people sing, "Poor . . . old . . . tired . . . horse." He falls to the ground. A pretty girl comes along. She sings, "Tee hee, tee hee." The horse takes notice. He sings, "Wee hee, wee hee." This goes on. Eventually he gets back up, and he and the girl run off together. When he comes back, he is fresh, reborn, and so is the year. In certain places, he then runs into the sea.

With the exception of the Puritans, Christianity did what it has always done when faced with such firmly entrenched pagan practice: it made room. The extant iconography includes at least one horse-headed saint, St. Alar (as the Bretons call St. Eligius), at the Church of Saint-Sylvestre in Kergazuel, France. And every fifty years or so, construction workers in Wales or somewhere tear up the floor of a medieval church and find a carefully placed horse skeleton. Ancient graves in which people and horses have been buried together are so common in Europe and Asia that archaeologists hardly even get excited about them anymore—many prehistoric cultures are thought to have believed that the horse led the soul to the afterlife. The scholar of folklore M. Oldfield Howey mentions "the well-known story of the old Irishwoman who killed her dead husband's horse, and when remonstrated with, replied, 'Do you think I would let my man go on foot to the next world?'"

The Welsh have a custom, Mari Lwyd (the Gray Mare,

their hobbyhorse), which they celebrate not in the spring but at Christmastime. In this case, the horse goes from house to house asking for hospitality, typically in the form of alcohol. It all goes back, by some accounts, to a Welsh tradition that on the night of the Nativity, a gray mare was put out of the stable in order to make room for the ass (folklore is so *correct*, sometimes), and she wanders the earth to this day, looking for shelter.

Non-European cultures had their hobbyhorses, too. No doubt some version of the dance existed wherever the horse was known. It comes naturally to us when we are young. Chinese children rode "lantern horses," wooden hobbies with lamps attached: it must have been lovely to see them circling in the dark. Who knows but that hobby riding did not precede horse riding—perhaps David Anthony's hypothetical steppe child, the first rider, had been practicing on a stick when the idea struck him to try the real thing. Doughty's *Travels in Arabia Deserta* includes a beautiful description of a Bedouin game that was probably older than God:

> Some moonlight evenings the children hied by us: boys and girls troop together from the mothers' *beyts*, and over the sand they leap to play at horses, till they find where they may climb upon some sand-hillock or rock. A chorus of the elder girls assemble hither, that with hand-clapping chant the same and ever the same refrain, of a single verse. . . . Every boy-horse has chosen a mate, his *fáras* or mare; they course hand in hand together, and away, away, every pair skipping after the other and are held themselves in chase in the moonlight wilderness. He kicks back to the horses which chevy after them so fast, and escapes again neighing. And this pastime of Aarab children, of pure race, is without strife of envious hearts, an angry voice is not heard, a blow is not struck among them.

FIRST FRIDAY IN MAY

Driving through the mountains of West Virginia, approaching the Kentucky border, I start picking up news of my native land on the radio. It is flooding in the Southeast, and people have been swept away. Two U.K. students have defenestrated themselves to death after wrestling their way to an open dorm-room window; "alcohol was involved." The political scene is uncertain: two candidates for sheriff in the eastern counties have been assassinated (*The New York Times* will later report that "local spin doctors may have staged the shootings to evoke a kind of perverse nostalgia, and thus voter sympathy"). But in Louisville no one cares. It is "Derby," as locals call this weekend, a combination, according to the city's own propaganda, of Christmas and Mardi Gras.

In the eight months since the yearling sale, I have been tracking the crop of two-year-olds, and now three-year-olds (the age of the horses that run in the Triple Crown), hoping to get lucky and to end up accidentally having followed a contender. I have won money on a sublime black colt named Mayakovsky, who placed, as I had bet he would, in the Hopeful at Saratoga, and I have lost all that money and more watching an Irish-trained horse, Johannesburg, sprint across the wire in the Breeders' Cup at Belmont Park. I have kept an eye on Bold Truth and Test of Time, horses that John T. Ward had spoken of as promising back in September, And I have tried to educate myself about the sport, becoming, in the process, a devoted reader of the *Daily Racing Form,* only dimly aware of world events beyond the two apologetic headlines printed in each day's issue under the heading of "News Briefs." These frequently make for strange juxtapositions: SIRWINSITALL BRUISES SHIN AT AQUEDUCT . . . 13,000 DIE IN TURKISH EARTHQUAKE . . . CRIST SAYS "DON'T COUNT ON CLASSY DAME." And if more than two wars break out on a Friday, the racing fan has to wait until Saturday to hear about the third.

I come into Louisville along the Ohio, which lies heavily in darkness. The streets are empty: it is two in the morning, and by now everyone is out in the backyard puking. After thirteen years away, the first thing I do is get radically lost, driving blocky figure eights until I happen to find the Galt House, the old hotel we used to pass on our way to my father's office.

Louisville occupies a strange place in the regional scheme of the United States. If one has never been there, one likely has *no* mental picture to associate with it. A "river town," it is most often called, as if any moment it might come unmoored and go floating off down the Ohio. A city that Northerners call the northernmost Southern city, and that Southerners call the southernmost Northern city, each fobbing it off on the other like an unwanted child. When Dickens came here, he admired his hotel (the Galt House), noticed some pigs, then wrote, "The city presenting no objects of sufficient interest to detain us on our way, we resolved to proceed next day." Visually, it is more reminiscent of Detroit than of Lexington, and it has none of Lexington's defensive insistence on its right to be Southern. People here are not really even Kentuckians, metaphysically speaking; they are Louisvillians, and seem fine with it. Which is its charm. There is plenty of there here.

Trent Apple, the only friend of my youth with whom I have stayed close, is waiting for me at a Derby party. He is married now; both he and his wife, Laura, whom I will be meeting for the first time, are attorneys in Louisville. Everyone at the party, when I find it, is an attorney, and everyone immediately extends a sort of instantaneous, uncomplicated *niceness* that is one of the things I miss most about this part of the country. The hostess hands me a plate of Derby pie with homemade whipped cream on top, promising, without any irony I can detect, that I will "never go back to Cool Whip."

These "country lawyers," as Trent introduces them, have been playing drinking games with hard liquor for an uncertain number of hours. Most of them will be at the race tomorrow. Earlier in the evening, they had discussed, argued over, and worked out their betting strategies, but now nobody remembers what they were. One curious and, I think, likable thing about many Louisvillians, as opposed to Kentuckians in general, is that they often make it a point not to be pedantic about the Derby. Here, "Derby" is something that happens to you. Your job is to be present and, if possible, avoid the police.

Back at Trent's house, we go to work on the wine, and the past starts floating up. Trent was my golf partner when we were eleven. We used to hump our bags a mile and a half to the nine-hole Fuzzy Zoeller Par-Three Golf Course in New Albany (Zoeller remains New Albany's only famous son). We were usually the only sober people on the course. It was run by an ancient man, tall and thin, who wore a khaki grounds-keeper's uniform and would tool around on the establishment's only golf cart shouting "Replace your divots!" at nobody. One day we showed up only to be informed by a sign that the course was "closed due to vandalism." An article the next morning in the *New Albany Tribune* reported that a gang of youths had carved satanic symbols into several of the greens—"using a potato fork," as the reporter helpfully added. Trent says that after I moved away, New Albany even garnered some supralocal press for its homegrown satanism. In 1995 a gang of teenage lesbians, one of them a "devil-worshiping dropout," murdered one of their friends by pouring gasoline on her and setting her on fire. Michael Quinlan, a reporter for the *Courier-Journal*, wrote a best-seller about it, entitled *Little Lost Angel*.

I always tell Trent, honestly if melodramatically, that he saved me when we were in school. Like many small towns, New Albany was not always kind to those who were "different," and it could lead the young into some rather grim social destinies. Trent was one of those kids who arrive in the world with their personalities fully formed. I remember the first time I met him, on the bus in third grade. He was wearing Indiana University basketball shoes, and a few of the older boys, Louisville fans, gave him grief. He was the new kid, he should have been intimidated, but he gave them the most cosmically indifferent shrug, as if to say, Are you guys into shoes? From that moment on, he never seemed to worry about respect, and he had the same shrug for me when I wanted to know why he was reading Gandhi's autobiography in the sixth grade. Under his influence I went from being a confused Rambo-loving arsonist to being possibly the youngest Kentuckian ever (if I may boast) to join the American Socialist Party—Trent and I mailed in our applications on the same afternoon.

My father loved him, and would ask him leading questions, knowing he could count on a good line. Once, in the parking lot at Scribner Junior High, where Trent and I both served out the seventh grade, my father, who was picking us up from school, noticed a real delinquent getting into one of the other cars. Scribner went up only to the eighth grade, but this kid could have grown a full beard in about twelve hours. My father said, "Hey, Trent, how *old* is that guy?" "Dunno," he shot back. "He pays taxes." My dad loved that. He would quote it.

It is good to hear Trent's memories of my father. He talks about the summer he came to northern Michigan with us, and my father decided that he would communicate with others only through the lyrics of Bob Dylan songs. He had a little crappy slimline Panasonic tape player, the same one he used to do interviews sometimes, and for an entire two days, if you asked him a question, he would reach into his plastic bag and pull out a Dylan tape. Then you had to wait a few minutes while he cued it up (needless to say, we were humoring him, partly to see if he could pull it off). Finally he would hold up the tape player and play whatever lyric he thought answered your question.

At four-thirty in the morning, the three of us—Trent, Laura, and me—are in the bar of the Brown Hotel, the only people there, trying to buy cigarettes, passing out on the couches. My last twinge of consciousness is the thought that I am going to have to learn what I can of the Derby from whatever the *Courier* prints the day after.

But at nine my hosts are up fresh, telling me to put on a tie. Trent's family arrives to take us to the Derby. At least I think they are taking us to the Derby, which is why I extend a shaky hand and offer them my shiny Churchill Downs parking pass, as if to say, Take it. It is all I have. But as it turns out, we are not going to Churchill Downs. We are going to a decommissioned railway switchyard on the northwest side of the city. Trent's wife and mother and sister are wearing fantastic hats that his mother has made herself. They are the biggest hats I have ever seen, so outré that they transcend garishness and achieve a certain startling flair (I am not questioning their taste: this is the tradition). Trent's dad wears a boater. He catches my eye in the rearview mirror, and I realize that my mouth is hanging open. Trent says, "Old saw: the louder you are on Derby Eve, the quieter you are on Derby Day."

At the switchyard, a line of refurbished vintage Southern Railroad train cars is standing on a stretch of vestigial track. By now I am thoroughly confused. Is this an intervention? Everyone can tell by looking that any effort to explain our itinerary would be wasted on me. It must have something to do with Trent's father's company, a perk.

We climb aboard the train, which is air-conditioned. There are dozens of men and women here, holding cocktails. The men are dressed sportily, pastel polo shirts under navy blue blazers; they have about them the strange boyishness that so many white Southern men hang on to all their lives. I am steadily trying—starting, failing, starting again—to make a cup of coffee connect with my mouth when it is announced that we will now get off the train and onto a bus, which pulls out with a police escort. At this point I still have no idea what is happening. But there is no question that we are now headed for Churchill Downs. A guy up front with a microphone is reading off the betting advice of the *Daily Racing Form* columnists. We roll through nice old solidly middle-class neighborhoods, a part of Louisville I do not remember. Sunlight. Kids in the yard. A mile away from the track, they are already holding up signs: "Parking. $2."

When the bus hisses to a stop in the actual parking lot, Trent's father asks me if I would like to ride home with them, too, on this bus. I say I will pass, that I might want to stick around after the meet and watch the cleanup, "to get, you know, some color." This will turn out to be a dreadful mistake.

I pass through the press entrance unmolested and head straight for the press box, where I know I can sit down and get coffee and vomit if necessary. But the air up there brings me around, and as I sit paging through the *Racing Form,* looking down on the track and the infield, where people have already started to gather, I catch a bit of the true turfwrirers' badinage:

"I had dinner with two beautiful women last night."

"Let me guess . . . your sister and your mother."

"No, my sister and my old girlfriend, Krystal. From Nashville."

"Oh, I remember her. Big-Face Girl!"

"What?"

"Oh, you *know* you know what I mean."

"But you said it out loud, man. You don't get to say it out loud."

Another scribe offers the opinion that, "quite frankly," all of this year's Derby horses "suck rubber donkey dong."

Outside, ranged along the edges of the roof, are shadowy men in dark vests and sunglasses. They carry sniper rifles. Security is said to be extra tight this year, owing partly to the presence of Prince bin Salman and the Makhtoums, representatives of the secular Arab regimes and as such some of the only people on earth the Islamic fundamentalists hate more than us and the Israelis. In order to get through the checkpoints, all of your food and beverages had to be in clear plastic. In just the forty-five seconds I spent at the gate I saw one woman get her chips taken away and a man forced to part with his false plastic binoculars, which were full of Bourbon,

Two old friends of mine from Lexington, Chris and Becky Johnson, and Chris's brothers, have seats just above track level, in front of the wire. When I find them, they are passing around clear plastic bags full of ham biscuits, a Kentucky delicacy, which they feed me. There is a blimp hovering overhead, and two propeller planes towing banners: "Merrill Lynch discriminates against women" and "Déjà Vu: Totally Nude Gentlemen's Club, SHOWGIRLS." The sun is getting bright. There is a guy in a Panama hat smoking a joint right next to a female army private in camouflage, and she is smiling. People are taking their picture.

Chris and his brothers, John and Patrick, run a flower business together, and they tell me a story about last year's Derby, when they decided they would have a close-up look at the traditional Derby wreath, a horseshoe-shaped mantle of roses that is placed around the neck of the winning horse. When they found it, a woman was standing there, entrusted with keeping it safe.

"Hey, where do those roses come from?" John asked her.

"Why, these are *special* roses," the woman said, "grown right here in Kentucky."

"Bullshit," he said, "those are Ecuadoran."

"Yeah, you're right," she said, "but don't tell anybody, okay?"

The "undercard," the term used to refer to all the nontelevised races run before the "big one," which (when there is a big one) always comes near the end of a day, is under way. My friends are arguing over their bets, but I have decided to hold on to my money until the Derby, which is the only race for which I have studied the field. One of the things I have spent the past eight months doing is working on a personal betting system, specifically geared to high-profile juvenile races, the ones I most often attend. It works *comme ça*: decent money, to place, on every horse between ten- and twenty-to-one. The Sullivan System was developed largely out of necessity—when I was at the track I was jogging around with a notepad, stepping in piles of dung and trying to figure out which horse was which, and had little time to study the sheets—but whether by accident or not, I have come out ahead with it.

Back at the paddock, the circular staging area where horses are held, saddled, and mounted before each race, people are crushed against the railing, not so much to see the horses as to see the celebrities, who are not there to see the horses, either, but to see one another, and to make sure that *USA Today* gets their good side. Sean "Puffy" Combs is here, in a white suit, along with 'N Sync's Joey Fatone, the one with the shoe-polish goatee; so is the Backstreet Boys' Kevin Richardson, the thin-faced one with the costume-shop goatee. Richardson is a Lexingtonian; I heard him sing "The Star-Spangled

Banner" before a Wildcats game, which he did with real pizzazz. Someone says, "Hey, is that Britney Spears?" But no, it is Jessica Simpson, another blond teenage pop singer. Ivana Trump is here, too, in a tasteful feathered hat.

It is not late in the day, but already on the ground at my feet has appeared that eternal symbol of undergraduate disgrace: the barefoot girl, unable to stand, plopped down in a pool of beer; her dress, too short even when she was standing, now opens to reveal her last remaining patch of unsunburnt skin. Her friends are standing about ten feet away. One asks the other, "Should we help her?" Neither moves.

A heavyset fraternity-looking guy in a white T-shirt and a white cap is screaming at Ivana, and people actually quiet down to enable him. "Ivana!" he bellows. She goes on chatting. "IVANA! We love you, Ivana!" She keeps her back turned ro him, but now it is clear to all that she is consciously keeping her back to him, which is fun to see. He has pierced the veil. Emboldened, he shouts, "Ivana! Why'd you keep your last name if you're divorced, Ivana?" which seems an oddly specific and unheckler-like question. Sensing the misstep, perhaps, he switches to Puffy, who has recently changed his name to P. Diddy. "P. Daddy! P. Daddy!" he cries.

Some people walk up and start talking to this fun-lover, wanting to know what he is all about. He tells them all proudly that he is from Illinois. It is seemingly the only piece of information about himself that he possesses. Then a woman walks up and starts patting him on the shoulder, giving him a good slap on the back every time he lets loose with one of his wild namings. She is almost motherly toward him, I think. Then I hear her refer to him, in conversation with another bystander, as "my son."

The behavior of this lunatic and his dam raises a question about the people inside the paddock, which is: What kind of person would voluntarily endure what is essentially a foodless outdoor cocktail party of strangers in heavy sun, in a prison-yard-style enclosure, wearing outlandish clothes and trying to appear relaxed while being gawked at and openly insulted by hundreds if not thousands of drunken hill people? It is sad to be reminded, once again, that all this horse racing business is about the rich, for the rich are hideous. There is nothing they cannot ruin. And if there is one other thing that horse racing is all about, it is people who do not have money—much less money to lose*—losing it.

So it is beautiful when the horses themselves appear, in their ignorance and their majesty, and assert their presence amid all this crappiness. "Oh Horse, Horse, Horse," wrote D. H. Lawrence in a letter, "when you kick your heels you shatter an enclosure every time," and finally I see what he means. Only those with souls most thoroughly hollowed out by fame fail to turn and watch the three-year-olds when they take their slow lap around the paddock. And the jockeys! Who could not love a sport with its own paid battalion of wee men, their bright, gay silks, their young faces, their ambiguous quasi-midgetry. They are perfect little people, shrunk down with a ray, surprisingly muscled. It is as if we have had to evolve a special breed of human being, so that the Thoroughbreds might have riders.

One of the blimps passes just overhead, causing a momentary eclipse of the sun, and I make up my mind to get inside the paddock itself, given that I have gone to the trouble of getting a press pass. But it is too close to Derby time.

---

*I was once in a cab in Manhattan, waiting for a light to change, when an extremely drunk guy, dressed in a navy workman's uniform—name tag, I swear to God: RICH—ran up to my window, which was open, and screamed at the driver, "WHAT'S THE FLAT RATE TO YONKERS RACETRACK, BUDDY?" The beer on his breath came clouding into the car; it was like someone had stuck a potato into the muffler. The driver got out a little book, flipped through it. "Forty-five dollars." The guy said, "Fuck that. Peace!" and staggered away. Spend enough time around racing and you will witness too many of these moments, passing scenes that illustrate the sport's dependence on working-class hopes and dollars. A common refrain at the end of a day's card (I first heard it at Monmouth, in New Jersey) goes, "I can't bet with these tickets. They're my only way home."

Although I get past the first security guard, another guy, in a newer uniform, puts his hand on my chest and says, "Only if you are with NBC." As he escorts me out, I spot Bob Baffert, shaking hands with one hand and patting his horse with the other. As of last night, he and bin Salman had two horses entered in the Derby, but one of them, Danthebluegrassman, has been scratched from the race this morning, and they are left with one horse only, a black colt with a white star between its eyes, War Emblem, which is tossing its head nervously. I had never heard of the horse until this morning, Baffert looks confident, despite having already received a beating in the press for entering Danthebluegrassman late, which kept another, Kentucky-based trainer out of the race altogether.

I have a cousin somewhere in the fabled "infield" (the track equivalent of the bleachers or the pit), so I go in search of her, thinking that I am sure to see some sights. But this, too, is a disappointment. The infield crowd is incredibly *well behaved* (all the papers will report on this the next morning—fewest crimes ever). The machine guns and the plastic-bag dictum seem to have done the trick. I expect at least to see titties and knife fights, but this is more like Slip-'n'-Slide and keg stands, men kissing women's bellies, that sort of thing, though the infield remains a wonderful place to see a certain kind of Kentucky face, one made obsolete in other parts of the world by dentistry and nutritional guidelines. One Southern stereotype that is not in the least exaggerated and that lends some support, perhaps, to the old canard about Appalachian people having held on to an English cultural inheritance squandered by the rest of the country, is the extraordinary state of many Kentuckians' teeth, which seem to fall or get knocked out in groups, rather than singly, lending a rather shocking aspect to their smiles.

I get to the seat my friends have saved for me just in time to see the horses being led to the post, their jockeys floating atop them, their coats shimmering in the perfect sun as if they were coated in lacquer. Each is accompanied by a gentle "lead pony" whose nerves are not so tweaked as those of the Thoroughbred, and each instinctively hides its face in the pony's neck as they near the gate, as if in fear of the crowd. A voice comes over the loudspeaker announcing that we will now sing "My Old Kentucky Home." Here and there, a hankie is unfurled, as some native son or daughter fails to suppress a tear. In the box directly in front of us, there is a group of men in their late twenties with the look of well-heeled WASPs who have not yet awoken to their homosexuality, a type found everywhere in the South. They are wearing bespoke poplin suits that sort of match, and shirts of the softest, softest pastels, and their arms are around one another. Each looks to his friends' faces as they sing and sway, as if for confirmation of the feeling they are feeling. When we get to the second line of the song—which was changed in the program notes only in 1972 from Stephen Foster's "'Tis summer, the darkies are gay" to the line I learned in school, "'Tis summer, the people are gay"—the boys smile broadly and emphasize the original word.

The singing of this line is a somewhat charged moment in the history of the Derby. Whites fought hard against the change even at that late date—bear in mind that the track was segregated well into the 1950s: separate entrances, separate grandstand, separate rest rooms, everything, this for a sport with a history not only of devoted and skillful black grooms, which fit easily enough into the old white Southern vision of "their place," but of outstanding black jockeys as well. There is a good book on this subject by Edward Hotaling, the journalist famous for getting Jimmy the Greek's career-ending remarks about black basketball players onto tape (the Greek had conjectured that they were better because back in the slave days, the "owner would breed his big black to his big woman"). In *The Great Black Jockeys*, Hotaling describes the cruelly bizarre scenarios that often developed in the Colonies, where the planters owned both horses and riders: slaves racing for their freedom, owners buying horses and jockeys on the same afternoon, slaves competing in races that might result in other slaves—even their own family members—being sold, depending on the outcome. Largely because of all this forced experience, blacks were considered the best riders until well after the Civil War. In the first Derby, held in 1875, thirteen of the fifteen jockeys, including the winning jockey, were black. (Ask any Southerner why lawn jockeys are black—we tend to have no idea.) The only black faces I have seen so far at the Derby were in the paddock, and belonged to rappers.

DARKNESS

It is worth considering the complete lyrics of the song itself, "My Olde Kentucky Home," one of Foster's most famous. They are not at all what you think. The "darkies" are not really "gay"—not even in the song, I mean—Foster is toying with you there, seeing if he can get you to take out your hankie. He composed the song during a party, a "gay ball" at an old Southern home, amid dancing belles and beaux. We must picture him there, jotting down the last verse on the back of some sheet music while he pretends to listen to the drunken son of a landowner talk about how *his* family's darkies never have no complaints:

> The head must bow and the back will have to bend,
> Wherever the darkey may go:
> A few more days, and the trouble all will end
> In the field where the sugar-canes grow.
> A few more days for to tote the weary load,
> No matter 'twill never be light,
> A few more days till we totter on the road,
> Then my old Kentucky Home, good-night!

"No matter 'twill never be light." Few lyrics, outside the early blues and British heavy metal, could match that one for sheer hopelessness. The Derby commissioners should make the crowd sing the whole thing, rather than bowdlerizing one line.

Several of Foster's songs were hits in his lifetime, and he was able to negotiate a lucrative royalties deal with a New York music publisher. But he was an alcoholic of dimensions seldom seen since the days of John Robert Shaw, and he drank himself into such chronic debt that he started selling off the rights to his compositions for a few dollars apiece, then spending the dollars on beer.

He died in a Bowery hotel in January of 1864, while the Civil War raged. He had been in bed for days with a fever, his wife and child having long since left him. In the middle of the night he rose to call a chambermaid for help, but he swooned, gouging his head on a washbasin as he fell. He was found hours later by George Cooper, one of the only friends he had left. Cooper described the scene:

> Steve never wore any night-clothes and he lay there
> on the floor, naked, and suffering horribly. He had

wonderful big brown eyes and they looked up at me with an appeal I can never forget. He whispered, "I'm done for," and begged for a drink. . . . We put his clothes on him and took him to the hospital.

Foster died three days later. History has recorded his possessions at time of death: in his tattered leather purse were thirty-eight cents and a scrap of paper on which he had written, in pencil, "Dear friends and gentle hearts."

DOWN THE STRETCH

Your experience of a horse race is strongly colored by where you choose to sit. Here, at the wire, I will see the field pass twice—once just out of the gate, and once as they hit the finish—and I will see nothing of the rest of the race. I cannot even see the gigantic electronic screens posted at each of the turns. From the press box (the opposite extreme), I could look through binoculars and watch the whole thing develop, see the moves, the jostling for position, who is using the whip and when. But I may never be back to the Kentucky Derby, and I want to taste the track off their hooves, to see their eyes.

When the gates fly open the horses are like a freak storm moving over the track together, their legs attended by a cloud of dust that they trail behind them, their jockeys' colors flashing kaleidoscopically in the sunlight. The loudness of their pounding takes me by surprise. It overwhelms even the crowd. I am so stunned by the sight of them that by the time I collect myself, they have disappeared around the turn. We who are sitting close to the wire stand there listening to the call, waiting for them to reappear.

As the race unfolds through the track announcer's sharp, metallic call, I notice that it is dominated by unfamiliar names, and one name in particular: War Emblem, who leads from the break. Our eyes strain in the sun to catch the field emerging around the final turn, and when it does, War Emblem is still in front. He comes across the wire having never lost the lead, the green-and-white silks of the Thoroughbred Corporation—of the Saudi flag—rustling on the jockey's back.

The crowd is strangely quiet. There is more clapping than cheering. There has been virtually no talk about this horse, and the great majority of bettors base their decisions on talk, which is why racetracks make money.

In the post-race interviews, Baffert and bin Salman are genuinely ecstatic. "That last hundred yards," Baffert says, "you wish it would last forever." The reporters are understandably gentle on the subject of the prince's being the first Arab owner ever to win the Derby, in this of all years, and not just an Arab but a Saudi, and not just a Saudi but a man with a "bin" in his name. The prince broaches the topic himself by saying that he has won this one not for himself but "for the Saudis, the great friends of the Americans," but when one brave scribe ventures something along the lines of "Don't you think this a bit weird?" bin Salman is quick to brush him off. "I am a businessman, not a politician," he says—a strange remark for a prince to make, but in this case an accurate one. "I leave these questions to our politicians and your politicians."

More interesting to the daily reporters is the question of whether bin Salman and Baffert have "bought the race." The story of their association with War Emblem is both wholly without romance and deeply American. Three weeks before the Derby, they realized they had no contenders. This was not an acceptable place to be for Bob Baffert, who had already won the race twice. Then one day, back in Riyadh, the prince was watching the Illinois Derby via satellite, and he saw something in the winning horse, which led from the wire and

- 161 -

took it going away. He called Baffert, who promptly acquired the colt for $900,000 from its original owner, a Chicago steel magnate named Russell Reineman (said Reineman later, of the decision to sell, "The steel business has been terrible lately"). Baffert liked War Emblem, despite the horse's being something of a head case (before what would have been its first race, in September of 2001, War Emblem threw his jockey and ran out of the paddock into a parking lot), so the trainer immediately started pointing him toward the Triple Crown. All in all, the story could not be more at odds with what horse racing fans and the people who write for them like to hear, the preferred version being, "We raised this colt from a yearling on our beautiful farm in the Bluegrass, saw its promise, believed, and here we are." (A week after the Derby, John T. Ward would sum up the racing community's disdain for the way Baffert had gone about winning: "How can I put this diplomatically?" he said during a conference call with reporters, "On Derby day, there didn't seem to be such an emotional outburst that there is sometimes." And John Clay, a sports columnist for the *Lexington Herald-Leader,* later wrote, "It was as if the Triple Crown had gone to the highest bidder.")

Bin Salman does not go for what I would consider the obvious response to this challenge, which would be to point out that Reineman and his trainer, Frank Springer, had not been planning to enter War Emblem in the Derby at all (the horse has bone chips and other "soundness issues"), meaning that none of us would have had the pleasure of seeing this animal run. Instead he goes for a more direct answer, and also probably a truer one. What he says makes me like him: "Everybody buys the Derby, because you have to buy a horse or raise a horse in order to win. . . . If you tell me [next year] who is going to win, I'll buy it again."

The interviews done, I walk up to the front of the press box and look out over the track. This is where my father sat twenty-nine years ago—off to the left is the turn where he would have seen Secretariat making his move. I should have looked for some of his old colleagues, to introduce myself, but everything has happened so fast. Now the sun is low. The last race of the day is over, and people are fleeing—yes, fleeing is the verb. Helicopters are circling above the infield. Whatever energy my three hours of sleep provided me with is forgotten, and I decide that I should take Trent's father up on the offer of a ride on the bus after all.

I make it through the crowds, over plastic beer cups and a tornado's worth of blown white paper, past a guy in a blue satin jacket who is sitting at the foot of a steel column, sobbing into his hands. Outside in the parking lot the dark-windowed limos carrying P. Diddy and Ivana and their set are already maneuvering through the mob, headed for the Governor's Ball. I call Trent on his cell phone, but he tells me the bus has already pulled out. I will have to get a cab, which seems like no big deal, I walk down the street that everyone else seems to be walking down, passing a little black kid in his front yard who is holding up a sign that says "Please wave if you are famous!" Up ahead is Taylor Boulevard, which I can see is busy with traffic. There I will hail a cab, or call to have one pick me up.

Three hours later I am sitting outside a Rally's restaurant on Taylor Boulevard, at a plastic table with an umbrella sprouting unsteadily from the center of it, getting cold. It is dark. Four cab companies have promised me that I would have a car within twenty minutes. Fourteen cabs have passed by my raised arm (I have nothing to do but write this stuff down). Out of boredom and a desire not to look like a vagrant, I have ordered three separate meals from Rally's, all of which are now ganging up on my intestines. I do not want to call Trent, because he lives far away and the traffic is awful.

If you are interested in seeing the other side of the Derby, in seeing all that is left behind after the 'N Sync guy and the Backstreet Boys guy have been spirited away, I urge you to sit for three hours at one of the outdoor tables at Rally's, on Taylor Boulevard, as the sun goes down across the street behind Edward's Olde Taylor Bar. And there you will see such sights as will give you pause. The people walking up and down this street are so drunk they seem blind, wandering in and out of houses (every household on the street is hosting a party) as if they were looking for home, down on all fours puking, hollering. Every woman who walks in front of Edward's gets harassed, and not construction-worker-whistling harassed, but scary harassed. The magic of Churchill Downs is only a few hundred yards away.

After a long while, and having run through all my ideas (calling to ask about getting a bus: no buses in that area; asking two cops for a ride: no way), I get up to go for a walk, not knowing what else to do. I head down Taylor toward the road that leads back to Churchill Downs. Along the way, two men spill out of a house and, though they have just noticed me, start coming at me very quickly. The one in the lead, who looks to be about fifty years old and is wearing a disheveled blue mechanic's outfit with a matching trucker's cap, falls into step beside me and says, "Hey, pal, nice suit."

I look down, I have had the good sense to take off my tie and stuff it into my pocket, but I am still wearing my prep-ass navy blazer. These three words actually speak themselves in my mind: *You are fucked.*

"Thank you," I say.

"I'm tough as a pellet," the man says. I have never heard the expression before, but that is what he says.

"I don't doubt it," I say.

"You better not," he says.

"I don't."

We have stopped walking now. There is an awkward pause. Up close, I can see that his face is nut brown, the color that comes from years of oil and sun and tobacco smoke. Silver hair curls out from under his cap at the edges. But his eyes are bright. "I'm Irish," he says, apropos of nothing except the fact that he is about to kick my ass.

"I am, too!" I say, thinking I see an opening.

But he spits back, "Bullshit!"

"No, I am," I say, and tell him my name.

Again, "Bullshit!"

"I'm from New Jersey," he says.

"Really?" I say, trying to keep my register low. "I'm from New York."

"BULLSHIT!"

At this point his friend catches up and reasonably assumes that the first man and I are hassling each other. The friend is wearing the same outfit, but he is shorter, and even a bit meaner. He looks remarkably like Popeye, down to the squint. He barges right up to me and puts a quivering fist in my face, so close I can smell the liquor he has spilled on his hand. "You better get out of here," he hollers. "You better get back to your *friends*." He says the word "friends" as if these were the most contemptible things a man could have. I look back at the house. People from the party are starting to come out onto the porch, waiting to see if there will be a pummeling they can help to finish. This can only get worse.

"I don't have any friends," I say, knowing, as these unintentionally pathetic words leave my mouth, what the response will be.

"*BULLSHIT!*"

"No, seriously. I'm just trying to get out of here."

At this point a very unexpected thing happens. The first man suddenly changes. His grimace goes soft. He turns away from me and looks up the road, toward Edward's. "Man," he says pleadingly, "can you help me find my car? I can't find my fucking car." His friend looks puzzled by this sudden swerve away from the unspoken but perfectly understood pummeling plan.

"I don't think I can help you," I say. "I'm sort of stuck myself. I've been waiting here for hours."

"Listen," he says. "If you find my car, we'll take you wherever you need to go. All you need to do is drop us off at the casino."

The casino he mentions is on a riverboat on the Ohio. I have read about it in the *Courier*. Its profits have been cutting into those of Churchill Downs, a thorn in the racetrack's side. I leave aside the complicated logic of his plan and say, "Look, I'm sorry. I really don't think I can help you. I just need to get out of here."

By this point I have recovered enough of my wits to get irritated, and it occurs to me that these men, despite their tree-trunk arms, are so plowed that I could possibly hit them both, hard, and be ten yards away before they decided to react. But the first man, the spokesman, surprises me once again. He accepts my regrets and changes tack, "Can you at *least* help us find the titty bar?" he whines.

"Its that way," his friend barks at him, pointing back toward Rally's, annoyed that the first man has asked some prep-ass jerk for help.

"No its not!" the first man shouts.

Sensing that we could at any moment revert back to an earlier, more belligerent line of conversation, and therefore eager to help, I look up and down the street. Then I realize that we have been standing in the very parking lot of the titty bar all along. Its bright yellow sign identifies it as none other than "Déjà Vu: Totally Nude Gentlemen's Club." The men look to me, and I point to the sign.

They are so pleased that I have found the titty bar for them that they do not even seem to feel foolish, though neither are they grateful. The shorter one pushes me hard on the chest, causing me to take a step backward, and says, "You better get out of here now. Get back to your *friends*." They wrap their arms around each other and practically skip through the entrance of the gentlemen's club.

My acquaintances gone, I give in. I pull out my fancy cell phone—can I look like more of an asshole?—and call Trent to beg for a ride. The first thing he says, when I climb into the car, is, "Man, I can't believe you spent three hours on Taylor Boulevard."

The next morning, the paperboy brings the *Courier-Journal*, post-Derby day edition. None of my beautiful colts of the year gone by, I reflect wistfully, has warranted a mention. Most of them did not even make it to the race, not Mayakovsky (scratched early) or Buddha (scratched late), not Officer, which I heard bin Salman describe at the yearling sale as the best two-year-old he had ever seen "in person or in the documentaries." It all makes no difference to the copydesk boys at the *Courier*, who go for ye olde historical echo: in tall bold lettets the headline reads IT'S WAR EMBLEM.

Now and then, in a work of military history, one reads a description of a battle somewhere and blinks at the number of horses killed. So far as I am aware, no one has ever put these descriptions together and made a book about the suffering of the warhorse in history. It would be difficult to read. They are so obedient: that is their problem. We can train them to such a degree of submission that they will not shrink from sights or sounds that make the average man loose in the bowels. Century after century, we have prosecuted our insane conflicts from atop their backs, resting on their sturdy necks when we grew weary, eating their flesh when we were starving, disemboweling them and crawling inside their bodies when we were freezing. Hardly a field diary from the nineteenth century is without a scene like that recorded in the *Journal* of Captain A. C. Mercer, Royal Horse Artillery, Waterloo: "One poor animal excited painful interest—he had lost, I believe, both his hind legs; and there he sat the long night through on his tail, looking about as if in expectation of coming aid, sending forth from time to time long and protracted melancholy neighing." Strangely, the two most tragic chapters in the horse's fate may be the First and Second World Wars, deep in the twilight of our long history of riding it into battle. There is an excellent book, entitled simply *Cavalry*, by a British historian named John Ellis, which follows the culture of mounted warfare up into the twentieth century. "Petulance" is the word Ellis uses in describing the ridiculous refusal on the part of the European aristocracy to give up on the horse as an effective tool in modern combat, to give up on a "fantasy world" of lancers and Hussars (the aristocracy's position in society, after all, had been linked to the horse for so long). Ellis describes scene after scene of carnage in World War I, when some well-bred French or English officer, a sentimental relic of the nineteenth century, shakes out his tussy-mussy and orders a mounted regiment into the fray. And they always obey, "only to be mown down by German machine guns."

The worst perpetuator of these lethal fantasies—one could make a case against him as a war criminal, for crimes against his own men—was British field marshal Douglas Haig, who was fighting to "save" the cavalry from obsolescence as early as 1908. "It is not the weapon carried," he said, "but the moral factor of an apparently irresistible force, in coming on at highest speed in spite of rifle fire, which affects the nerve and aim of the . . . rifleman." In July of 1916 he tested these "mystical drivellings," as Ellis describes them, by sending squadrons of the Twentieth Deccan Horse and the Seventh Dragoon Guards forward against heavily entrenched squadrons of German infantry. "As they came out of the cornfields in front of the wood," Ellis writes, "a German machine gun opened up." The result: "heavy losses."

In describing a particularly grotesque rout that occurred during the battle of Arras, in France, 1917, Ellis quotes an officer of the Highland Light Infantry, who was there:

> An excited shout was raised that our cavalry was coming up. Sure enough, away behind us, moving quickly in extended order down the slope . . . was line upon line of mounted men, covering the whole extent of the hill-side as far as we could see. . . . It may have been a fine sight, but it was a wicked waste of men and horses, for the enemy immediately opened on them a hurricane of every kind of missile he had . . . high-explosive, shrapnel, whizz-bangs, and a hail of bullets. . . . The horses seem to have suffered most, and for a while we put bullets into poor brutes that were aimlessly limping about on three legs, or else careering about madly in their agony; like one I saw that had the whole of its muzzle blown away.

Ellis sums it all up with a cold eloquence: "The horse did not belong in no-man's-land."

So many horses had died in World War I that some voiced fears for the global equine population: numbers had dipped low enough that a single epidemic might put the species to within range of extinction. Field Marshal Haig, not convinced by the tens of thousands of men he had watched ride to their deaths, was still arguing in 1926 for the "value" of the horse in war, writing that "as time goes on, you will find just as much use for the horse—the well-bred horse—as you ever have done in the past," but by the time World War II broke out, even the old fops had accepted the fact that tanks, planes, and machine guns made cavalry tactics untenable. The official line, taken by both the Allied and the Axis powers, was that the days of waging war on horseback were over. Only Poland, deeply attached to the romantic ideal of the dashing lancer and dependent on horses for transport (its relatively low industrial capacity left its tank corps outnumbered three-to-one by the Germans at the start of the war), never let go of its cavalry forces. Polish nobles had been breeding Arabs for warfare and show since adopting them from the Turks centuries before. There is a beautiful though spurious Polish film, *Lotna*, about a famous "swords against tanks" battle with German Panzers. Ellis tracks this legend down to the incident that inspired it, an engagement in southeast Poland, early in the war, when a cavalry brigade suddenly found itself alone in front of advancing German armor. Faced with no other option, the commander gave the order to charge. Ellis: "Not one of them even reached the tanks."

The sword, it seemed, would be hung above the mantel, and the charger turned out to graze. But history took yet another turn. Germany invaded Russia, and the Germans discovered that because of the terrain there, and because they found themselves up against Cossack troops who had never abandoned their mounts ("Proletarians, to Horse!" Trotsky had written to inflame them in 1919), cavalry units were again deemed necessary.

The result was a black period in the history of what Edwin Muir called our "longest archaic companionship" with the horse, nightmares of mass animal death and anguish. The human rights advocate and scholar Boria Sax, in a book entitled *Animals in the Third Reich* (2000), describes what happened in the Crimea on May 4, 1944, when the retreating German army realized that in order to escape from the Russians, they would have to leave their horses behind, which would mean letting them fall into the hands of the enemy. They decided to "liquidate" them instead. Thirty thousand horses were led to a precipice above the Bay of Severnaya. One by one, the vets of the Seventeenth Army shot the horses in the head and pushed them over the edge of the cliff, their bodies hurtling hundreds of feet into the bay, which began to fill up. At a certain point, the animals that had yet to be killed realized what was happening and became frightened. The decision was made to turn the machine guns on them. They were driven off the cliff, as if with a hose, until not one was left. Thirty thousand. "The routine resembled the mass executions of Jews or partisans," Sax writes, "who would also be shot in such a way as to make them fall into mass graves."

The Polish historian Janusz Piekalkiewicz, in his *Cavalry of World War II* (1979), describes a scene in language that cannot be paraphrased, only invoked. The setting is Lake Ladoga, in Finland, October of 1941:

> Two days after reaching the back of the lake, the Russians were not only surrounded by the Finns— but the forest was on fire as well. . . .
>
> The Finns closed off numerous escape routes and started shooting in the direction of the wall of fire with whatever weapons they could muster. The blaze spread rapidly, fanned by the north wind, and

thousands of horses, driven wild with pain, raced towards it, ignoring the rapid fire of the machine-gun batteries. Many of them galloped to and fro like giant torches, bellowing and shrieking in agony until they finally burned to death. Another few thousand raced in terror from the raging flames and hurtled towards the lake.

A great tide of horses poured out of the forest and plunged into the waters of Lake Ladoga. Moments later, the small, shallow bay was seething with animals scared out of their wits and seeking shelter from the blazing shore and the untold depths of the lake in these shallows. Soon, a cloud of mist swept over the swarm of hemmed-in animals, covering them with a coating of ice as the evening frost rapidly descended over their shivering mass.

The first Finnish scouts who made their way next morning through the burned forest and reached the shore of the bay were astonished by what they saw. "The lake was like an endless sheet of marble on which someone had placed hundreds and hundreds of horses' heads. They looked as if they had been disembodied by the sharp blow of an executioner's axe." Only the heads were visible, staring towards the bank. One could still see horror in their eyes.

ONCE MORE UNTO THE BREACH

PAUL WOLFOWITZ [Deputy Secretary of Defense]: If you would indulge me for a minute, actually, I have with me a dispatch that came from one of our Special Forces guys who is literally riding horseback with a sword with one of the Northern Alliance.

BOB SCHIEFFER [CBS newsanchor]: With a sword?

WOLFOWITZ: With a sword, with the Northern Alliance group of several hundred people who had nothing but horses and rifles. And he said, "I'm advising a man . . . how best to employ light infantry and horse cavalry in the attack against Taliban tanks, mortars, artillery, and machine guns," a tactic which I think became outdated with the invention of the Gatling gun. . . . It's, in a sense, the return of the horse cavalry, you might say, but no horse cavalry in history before this could call in airstrikes from long-range bombers.

SCHIEFFER: Do these people—do the people in the Special Forces know how to ride horses? I mean, there is a difference in jumping on a horse and hanging on and being able to ride. Are they trained to ride horses?

WOLFOWITZ: I can't say for sure, but apparently these guys were. They're trained in an extraordinary range of survival skills and local customs and language, and they're quite an amazing group.

—*Face the Nation*, November 18, 2001

Something beautiful happened in Nuremberg in the summer of 1650. The pan-continental Thirty Years War— which remains not only one of the bloodiest but also the least easily understood wars in all of history, in part because its causes were such a monstrous intertwining of religion, national self-interest, petty feudal grudges, and the greed of nationless mercenaries—had officially been concluded two years earlier with the Peace of Westphalia. But the implementation of the peace, and the demobilization of the European armies, had yet to be worked out. Germany, France, Spain, Sweden, and Denmark were still poised for a resumption of hostilities. So in 1649 a congress of the peace was convened in Nuremberg, with delegates from each of the former warring parties gathered to discuss the terms. It was presided over by Octavio Piccolomini, the Duke of Amalfi and the lieutenant general of the imperial armies, who had seen combat in every one of the war's thirty years. He survives in history primarily as the man who was both the student and the slayer of the great mercenary general Wallenstein. Piccolomini was one of a very few imperial officers to have survived the battle of Weisser Berg, near Prague, in 1620, and he had lived through the murder of his only son by Swedes in 1645. All his life had been spent participating in Europe's destruction of itself, and now he had come to Nuremberg, a city left relatively intact by the wars (though ten thousand of its citizens had starved to death during a siege), a city that thought of itself as the true capital of the Holy Roman Empire, to ensure an end to the slaughter.

At several points it seemed that the negotiations would fail, that the sides would go back to war. But finally, on June 27, an open letter from the emperor Ferdinand III announced the unanimous ratification of an enforceable treaty. The

Thirty Years War was over. Europe exploded in a weeks-long ceremony of fireworks, banquets, and theater. It was all recorded—down to the seating arrangements—in a strange and wonderful book, one of the strangest books ever created, the Swiss engraver Matthaeus Merian's *Theatrum Europaeum*, which was written in High German and appeared in twenty-one volumes between 1637 and 1738. One rarely finds a mention of it in English. It is essentially a daily chronicle of a hundred years' worth of events in Western Europe, and its span goes well beyond Merian's own life, which ended in 1650. It is hard to imagine whom it was published for, or why it was published at all.

I searched it out at the New York Public Library in the hopes of confirming an account I had happened across in a book titled *The Rocking Horse: A History of Moving Toy Horses*, by a British hobbyist named Patricia Mullins. I was curious about Kaspar Hauser's horses, where they might have come from, and there is a section on Germany in Mullins's book in which she mentions the "woodcarving districts surrounding Nuremberg . . . the centre of Germany's growing toy trade." In the context of that trade, Mullins includes an anecdote from the Nuremberg peace congress. The source is given as the *Theatrum Europaeum*.

The following Saturday, I humped the sixth volume of an early edition of Merian's opus back to a table in the reading room, undid the twine on its enormous cardboard slipcover, and began turning over its vast pages, eventually coming across an engraving of a fireworks display with the caption "Nürnberg 1650." I was looking for a single word, *Steckenreiter*, stick rider. On page 432, there it was. The paragraph in which the word appeared matched Mullins's story in every detail.

Near the end of the prolonged festival that followed the signing of the treaty in Nuremberg, on Sunday, July 7, the boys of the town, who had been largely excluded from the celebration, assembled outside the city walls. There were more than a thousand of them, and each was mounted on a hobbyhorse, a *Steckenpferd* such as the one we see a boy riding in Brueghel's great *Kinderspiele* (a knobby-kneed boy at the very bottom of the painting, his back turned to us, wearing a black cloak and a black floppy hat, which obscures his face, holding in his left hand a forked stick, his whip). At the appointed hour, the boys rode in from the perimeter of the city, a great army on their "cock horses," as the toys would have been called in England at the time, galloping along, waving their free hands above their heads. They were the Army of the End of the Thirty Years War. They rode straight to the residence of His Princely Grace Octavio Piccolomini, who greeted them with delight. When he asked them what they wanted, they said they had come for a souvenir of the peace. Piccolomini thought for a moment and told them to gather again the next Sunday, to ride before him just as they had done, and he would give them what they wanted.

The next day, he ordered a thousand silver coins to be minted. On one side of each coin was an imperial eagle, and inscribed beneath it were the words VIVAT FERDINAND III. ROM: IMP. VIVAT. On the other side were the image of a boy riding a hobbyhorse, a whip in his hand, and the motto FRIEDENS-GEDÄCHTNIS IN NÜRNBERG, "In Memory of the Peace of Nuremberg."

On Sunday, Piccolomini was waiting, as he had promised, for the return of the *Steckenpferdreiter*. Their leader came around the corner blowing a trumpet, and the *Theatrum Europaeum* says that when all of the boys had appeared, they were like "a moving sea." Piccolomini distributed the coins himself, putting one into each grubby fist. When it was over, he stood and watched the boys ride away, brandishing their coins, which flashed in the sunlight.

Encyclopaedia Britannica, 1911: "Piccolomini died on the 11th of August 1656. He left no children . . . and his titles and estates passed to his brother's son. With the death of the latter's nephew Octavio Aeneas Josef in 1757, the line became extinct."

LISTEN TO THIS

Inge Müller was a German socialist poet of the postwar years and the wife of the playwright Heiner Müller. She was twenty when Berlin fell to the Russians in 1945, and both of her parents were killed in one of the Allied bombing raids. Memories of what she had seen drove her to suicide in 1966. Three years before, she had written this poem, based on a factual incident. It is included in her collection *Wenn ich schon sterben muß*—"If I Must Die":

> FALADA 45
> A horse drug a cart
> Down a ruined street.
> The driver was dead in his seat.
> The cart was on fire.
> A man hollered, "Catch it!"
> And rushed from his house with a hatchet.
>
> Others crept forward
> From cellars, by ones

And twos. You could still hear the guns.
A woman said, "Listen,
We have to survive."
The horse was still alive.

Ignoring its screaming
They gorged on the meat.
A sudden explosion tore open the street
Killing three, so the rest
Staggered off with their share
To a house. Then the house wasn't there.

Word that the war was over came over the air.

Hippophagy: Ptolemy's word for the eating of horse flesh. It had been verboten in Germany for well over a thousand years when World War II started (though the infantry chefs of the Eastern front became expert at preparing the meat, when all other provisions were exhausted). In 731, when St. Boniface was appointed by Pope Gregory III to serve as apostle to Germany, he had an unusually hard time converting the pagans there. Foremost among their objections was that, under Christianity, they would no longer be allowed to honor the horse god, which they did by sacrificing and eating the animal's flesh in an annual rite. Afterward they would nail the horse's head to an ash in a sacred wood, where it was said to "give forth oracular responses." The pope instructed Boniface to persuade the people that the meat was unclean, writing:

You say that some eat the wild and very many the domestic horse. This, most holy brother, you must never allow to be done, but, with the assistance of Christ, prevent it by all means, and impose a suitable penance; for it is filthy and execrable.

By the turn of the millennium, the practice had been abolished in most of Europe. St. Olaf, in converting the Scandinavians to Christianity, "put to death or mutilated all who persisted in using that heathenish food," and Voltaire mentions that in Burgundy people were still being executed for eating horse as late as 1629. A movement to make it acceptable sprouted in England and France in the mid-eighteenth century, led by social reformers who went so far as to stage elaborate "horse dinners" in Paris and London, serving "chevaline" to hundreds of unsuspecting guests, but in many places, including Germany, the taboo held firm—not as a crime but as a social prejudice. Müller's terrified, starving Berliners are engaged in something that their countrymen would have recognized, with however much sympathy, as a violation of ancient Western codes. Others might have noticed, too, an enactment of something even more ancient.

In this respect (and others), Müller's horse is reminiscent of Picasso's in *Guernica*, its body twisted and wracked with the horrors of war, its mouth open and teeth out so that you can almost hear it screaming. Is it a symbol of suffering humanity? Or would it be more correct to say that the artist's very use of the horse symbol *is* humanity, going back tens of thousands of years to the limestone walls at Chauvet (we know that Picasso was an early student of the prehistoric paintings at Altamira, famously remarking, after seeing them by candlelight, "We have learned nothing")? Does *Guernica* say to us, "Look at what they did," or does it say, "This is what we do"? Both, probably, and only the horse can accept or bear that sort of metaphoric load. It had embodied Western progress for millennia; when that civilization broke down, it served equally well. The motif of its suffering, at our hands, spoke of something gone horribly wrong—of "a botched civilization."

To understand what happens to the horse in modern literature and art, one has to be listening carefully for transpondencies (a word that does not exist, taken from another, "transponder," which did not exist until 1945, when the U.S. Army coined it to describe a new invention, a kind of beacon that would receive a radio signal and automatically transmit a different, coded version of the same signal). The best known of these transmissions begins with the murderer Raskolnikov's dark, enigmatic dream in *Crime and Punishment.* In the dream he is a child, walking with his father in the marketplace of his hometown. They come upon a broken-down cart-horse, worked almost to death. A sadistic crowd has gathered around her (shades of the Passion, of Christ's collapse under the weight of the cross on his way to be crucified). "Fetch an axe to her!" one cries. "Finish her off." Which they proceed to do.

> But the poor boy, beside himself, made his way screaming through the crowd to the sorrel nag, put his arms round her bleeding dead head and kissed it, kissed the eyes and kissed the lips. . . . At that instant his father who had been running after him, snatched him up and carried him out of the crowd.

The scene forecasts Friedrich Nietzsche's mental collapse in the plaza in Turin, where he tried to come between an old cab-horse and the driver who was beating it to death. Nietzsche rushed forward and threw his arms around its head, whispering, in one version, the words "Mein Bruder" into its ear. The similarity between the two scenes is likely not coincidental. Nietzsche had read Dostoevsky closely—"I got my most precious psychological material from him," he once wrote. It is almost as if the Russian writer had shown him a way to go mad. Thirty years later, this signal was picked up again on an improvised stage in St. Moritz, Switzerland (the place, incidentally or not, where Nietzsche's mind had first begun to unravel). There, the great Russian dancer Vaslav Nijinsky stood before an audience of idle aristocrats and told them, "Now I will dance the war, the war which you did not prevent and are also responsible for." He danced "frightening things," by his own description. When he was finished, he placed his hands on his heart and spoke his last coherent words: "The little horse is tired." In his "mad diary," which he began keeping that day, we can see that he is thinking, in his way, about Nietzsche—whom he mentions more than once, comparing their madnesses—and that he is haunted by a certain familiar childhood memory:

> The draymen was driving his horse downhill and whipping it. The horse fell, and all its guts dropped out of its behind. I saw that horse and sobbed in my heart. I wanted to sob aloud, but I realized that people would take me for a crybaby, and therefore I wept inwardly. The horse was lying on its side and screaming with pain. Its scream was like a low moan. I wept. I felt.

In describing the horse's career as a symbol, the Lexington writer Guy Davenport makes the point that "all art is a dance of meaning from form to form." Inge Müller's poem is shot through with a grid of allusion that suggests how long the horse has been at the center of that dance, and how complex the patterns can become. Consider the title, "Falada 45." Hans Fallada (two l's) was a respected German novelist and a contemporary of Müller's. In 1938 he completed a book titled *Iron Gustav*, a fictionalized version of the life of Gustav Hartmann, "the last Berlin coachman," who, in the words of Fallada's biographer, Jenny Williams, "sprang to fame when he drove his coach and horse to Paris and back in 1928."

Goebbels was dissatisfied with the book, and ordered Fallada to extend the narrative through 1933, so that he could place the story within the context of Hitler's "reforms." When Fallada tried to beg off, saying that he didn't know enough about politics to give the requested material any authenticity, Goebbels not only withheld his *nihil obstat* but demanded, now, that Fallada complete the project according to the new specifications. The author—to the lasting detriment of his reputation in Germany—complied. When it was published in Germany, *Iron Gustav* ended with an old coachman expressing his admiration for National Socialism. And in 1947 Fallada, who had survived the war, killed himself with an overdose of morphine.

The coachman in Inge Müller's poem might be Iron Gustav himself, the spirit of old Berlin, "dead in his seat." His famous cart is pulled aimlessly through the wreckage, and his faithful horse is destroyed by those who do what they must to stay alive, no matter the depth of betrayal involved.

Adjust the dial on the transponder a bit, however, and you pick up a different, more staticky signal. Hans Fallada was not born with that name. He was born Rudolf Ditzen. He borrowed the pseudonym from a tale by the Brothers Grimm, "The Goose-Girl." The princess in that fable is betrothed to a foreign prince. Her mother sends her away with a waiting-maid and a magical talking horse named Falada, both of whom are to look after her. But the waiting-maid betrays her by stealing her identity. She marries the prince and consigns the true princess to looking after geese in the common. But she fears that the horse may speak and reveal the truth, so she asks the prince a favor, to "let the slaughterer cut off the head of the horse." This is done.

What follows is one of those inexplicable bits that make the Grimm Brothers' tales so powerfully weird. When the real princess hears that Falada has been beheaded, she gives the slaughterer a piece of gold and asks him to hang Falada's head on the gate under which she must pass on her way to the common. She speaks to the head each morning as she passes through. "Oh!" she says. "Falada, 'tis you who hang there," and Falada's reply is the same every time:

'Tis you; pass under, Princess Fair:
If your mother only knew,
Her heart would surely break in two.

One day the wise old king observes this little exchange, and suspects that the goose-girl is not what she seems. He prises the truth out of her, and order is restored, in classic Grimm fashion: the false maid is "put stark naked into a barrel lined with sharp nails, which [is] dragged by two white horses up and down the street till she is dead," and the true prince and princess rule over the kingdom, "in peace and happiness."

Müller's horse is the wandering ghost of Falada, but the random cruelty that afflicted the long-ago princess is everywhere now, with no justice in sight, and the magic of the fairy world has been reduced to the terrible disappearing act of the penultimate line, "Then the house wasn't there." Falada's prophetic speech—"If your mother only knew / Her heart would surely break in two"—has become *Das Pferdeschreien*, the horse screaming.

BACK ON TRACK

After the Kentucky Derby, I become one of a large group of people who subscribe to the theory that War Emblem—and/ or Victor Espinoza, his jockey—"stole" the race. A horse is said to "steal" a race when it comes out fast and sets a false pace. The other, stronger horses, stalking the lead horse, mistake its speed for the limit of its abilities, and so wait just off pace for it to tire out. But the horse is holding something back. And when the stalking horses begin to make their move, it unleashes its reserves, capitalizing on its lead to take the race. It is a legitimate tactic not entirely deserving of its pejorative name, but it is a ruse, one that often does not indicate which horse is actually the fastest in a field. It is my opinion, one I share with many people, that War Emblem will be a no-show in the Preakness and the Belmont Stakes—the two remaining legs of the Triple Crown—because the jockeys will have seen his tricks and will be sure to burn him out before he makes the homestretch.

I cannot make it to the Preakness, so with my girlfriend, Mariana, I decide to watch it at an Off-Track Betting shop in New York's Chinatown, off the Bowery (just a couple of blocks from the hotel where Stephen Foster met his end, as it happens). Inside every OTB is a fully functioning, self-contained culture, a yin and yang of cautious hope and stoical depression that swirls inside each head and circulates through the room itself. Such a serious atmosphere (I have hardly ever been anyplace with a woman when not a single man looked at her). One gets the feeling that many of these men have been here since the shop opened, and will leave only in the evening when it closes, and have been doing this every day for years. The men (all men) are Chinese and Hispanic, mostly. The atmosphere is devoid of festivity. Everyone is intent on his betting sheet, or on one of the TV monitors, or on one of the automated machines at which you can enter in your picks.

Here and there we see a "stooper," a man who does not have the money, or is too cheap, to bet, who walks around stooping to pick up discarded tickets, hoping that some greenhorn has failed to realize that when a horse he has bet to show ends up placing instead, for instance, he still wins money.

At the track, you can usually tell the difference between a hard-core gambler and a horse fan by whether or not a person yells the horse's name or its number during the race. Here it is all, "Six! Six! Six!" and some of the sheets used by the bettors to calculate odds, I notice, do not even include the names of the horses. These men are silently calculating elaborate mathematical equations, over and over, trying to convert their paychecks into something a little fatter. The bets tend to be small. When a race is over, one rarely hears a groan or a whoop. They turn away and go back to the counters.

We approach one of the machines and consult our *Daily Racing Form* for the numbers. A Chinese man with very thick spectacles is behind us the entire time, saying, "Okay, sir. Please, sir. Okay, sir." A race he wants to put money on is coming up. We finally figure out the machine, which spits out our slips with a whirr and a *thunk*.

Moments later the race begins. We cannot hear the call for all the chatter, but we see clearly enough what is happening. Unusually for War Emblem, he is not first out of the gate. Instead the lead is shared by a horse called Menacing Dennis and one of John T. Ward's, Booklet. I have money on the latter. But by the first turn, Booklet has dropped away, and it is War Emblem who shares the lead with Menacing Dennis. Then it is War Emblem alone, and I am shaking my head. As they head down the stretch (the Preakness is the shortest of the Triple Crown races—it happens almost comically fast, given how much anticipation it generates), I watch Proud Citizen, trained by the California-based trainer D. Wayne Lukas, come within a length of War Emblem. And I think, *This is it, they're calling his bluff*. But then something goes wrong. Espinoza gives his horse the whip, and instead of the nothing that is supposed to happen, War Emblem surges. He is the real thing, goddammit. He pulls away from Proud Citizen. Then in the final yards he gets another challenge, this time from a horse called Magic Weisner. (Magic *Weisner*?) And he is running even faster, pulling away from this one too. Suddenly he has won. Suddenly he has positioned himself to win the first Triple Crown in twenty-four years. And this time there is no question of "stealing." They came after him, but he was too good.

In the OTB, no one cares. They are already scanning the sheets for the next race, already lining up at the machines. Of course, I am forced again to admit: This is what it is all about. These men. The upturned proud and lonely faces of these men, cathode horses shining in their eyes, numbers dancing in their heads. We wad up our tickets and leave them in the trash can by the door.

The forbearance that the American sporting press showed Prince bin Salman at the Derby press conference (the man was, after all, in the midst of the greatest experience a Thoroughbred owner can have in his or her life) dissipated in the weeks following the race and disappeared entirely after the Preakness. The fact that a Saudi had won the Derby was hard enough to swallow, given our "new reality" post-9/11, but that he was poised to take the first Triple Crown in almost a quarter of a century—that was going too far.

Most of the articles written about War Emblem's owner struggled to be polite. Reporters called the Council on Foreign Relations and were told that the bin Salman family was relatively enlightened, within the political context of Saudi Arabia (i.e., they believe in a woman's right to drive). Those who wanted to probe a bit deeper restricted themselves to the prince's media company. The Saudi Research & Marketing Group publishes eighteen different newspapers, including some that are printed in London and then distributed in the Middle East, a system that allows them a little more latitude under the laws governing speech in Saudi Arabia. Their editorial content is a mixed bag. The *Baltimore Sun* reported that *Asharq Al-Awsat*, the most important of the papers, reprints Thomas Friedman's columns from *The New York Times* and uses the term "suicide bombers" rather than "martyrs" when reporting on events in Israel, which has earned it a liberal reputation. The *Arab News*, on the other hand, ran a column by David Duke arguing that the Jews were behind 9/11.

A few of the pieces about bin Salman that appeared in the States devolved into outright racism. *New York Newsday*, a paper that enjoys a large readership among track aficionados (William Nack got his start there), led the way with a laughably unfounded, unsourced, and unsubstantiated bit of innuendo about the prince: "As one person said, 'You've got to wonder what's under the rug.'"

Meanwhile, back in Louisville, the *Courier-Journal* interviewed Sandy Macleod, a security officer at Belmont Park. "I've never really trusted Arabs," said Macleod, "but after this . . . I'm not sure sending the Triple Crown to Saudi Arabia is good for the game" (this despite the fact that the prince's horse had drawn massive attention to a sport that needed it badly— very few Americans care about or even notice horse racing until a three-year-old has won both the Derby and the Preakness). It was *Newsday* writer Jimmy Breslin, however, who went lowest. Breslin actually attended the Derby, where he grudgingly entertained local yahoos with tales of terror. "Were you near the firemen?" one woman asked him. "I almost had to help a couple of them out," he replied. (*Almost!*) In Breslin's considered opinion it was "understood that these Saudis don't have the class of a goat. If this bin Salman had any, he would stay away [from Belmont Park] and not run his horse out of respect."*

Bin Salman did stay away from the Belmont Stakes. Various reasons were given: family commitments, business matters. Maybe he wanted to avoid the press corps, who would have done their homework since the Derby and learned that bin Salman's father, Prince Salman bin Abdul Aziz, the governor of Riyadh, was known to be a major financial backer of various Islamic charities that had funded, inadvertently or not, Middle Eastern terrorists (it has long been thought that the Saudis pay a kind of blood money to Al Qaeda, bribing the organization to keep the violence away from the kingdom itself, and in 1996 Mary Anne Weaver had written in *The Atlantic Monthly* that Prince

---

*A group calling itself The Sports Ethics Institute finally issued a bulletin asking, "What message does it send about respect, tolerance and journalistic objectivity when a sports journalist writes that he wouldn't bet that Saudi Prince Ahmed bin Salman, owner of winning race horse War Emblem, isn't a 'conscious, active [foe] of democracy,' isn't 'sympathetic toward repressive religionists so extreme that doing "God's work" would include . . . killing thousands,' and 'won't apply even a cent of their American winnings toward the enabling of suicidal, indiscriminate mass murderers'?"

Salman—the father—worked closely with Osama himself when the latter was just a *jihadi*). Most reporters assumed that in reality bin Salman's absence had to do with death threats, which is what NBC suggested on the day of the Belmont. But Richard Mulhull, the president of the Thoroughbred Corporation, told me some months later that the truth was much less exciting: the prince was in the hospital undergoing routine stomach surgery. He had asked his colleagues to keep this a secret, not wanting his health to detract attention away from his horse. (Today will be the prince's last chance to see War Emblem run. He will die back in Saudi Arabia on July 22, when a blood clot that has formed in his leg after the surgery comes loose and goes into his heart.)*

---

*A cousin of bin Salman's died early the next morning, in a car accident on the way to the prince's funeral, and a more distantly related prince was said to have died of thirst in the desert less than a week later—a cluster of sad coincidences that sparked talk of intrigue and foul play. But within a week, the talk had died down everywhere except in paranoid Internet "chat" forums.

Two years later, in September 2003, the rumors were unexpectedly revived when Gerald Posner, a respected journalist and judge (formerly known as a slayer of conspiracy theories), published a book titled *Why America Slept*, in which he suggested that bin Salman had been mixed up with Al Qaeda. Posner based this claim on information given him by two anonymous sources, one in the C.I.A. and one, as Posner had it, "in the Executive Branch." The sources told Posner that Abu Zubaydah, a high-ranking Al Qaeda operative captured in Pakistan in March of 2002, had been tricked by the C.I.A. into giving up the names of Saudi princes who were secretly funding bin Laden's network, and that Prince bin Salman was among those named (the captive supposedly spat out the prince's cellphone number from memory, claiming that bin Salman had known beforehand that an attack against the United States was planned for 9/11). The cousin who died in the car accident was also betrayed by Zubaydah, according to Posner's sources; so was the prince who died in the desert; and so was the Pakistani air marshal, Mushaf Ali Mir, who died some months later in a mysterious plane crash.

Posner discovered that all four of these men died not long after the C.I.A. gave a briefing on the Zubaydah transcript to the Saudi and Pakistani intelligence services. The author declared himself "all but convinced the deaths were planned"—presumably to silence the men Zubaydah had compromised before they could be questioned by the Americans. Unfortunately, none of the claims could be substantiated or disproved. Everyone who knew bin Salman, in the United States and in Saudi Arabia, dismissed Posner's account as ridiculous; but the idea that two independent government sources had concocted such an elaborate tale seemed equally far-fetched. The story was never pursued by the Washington press corps, and it froze where Posner had left it; as a bit of tantalizing—if potentially defamatory—innuendo.

There are 103,222 people at Belmont on the day of the race, a record crowd by thousands, at a time when Americans are supposed to be scared of large gatherings. There is a chance to see a horse win the Triple Crown, something you can tell your grandchildren about, and people want to be there, even if the horse *is* owned by a Middle Eastern dude.

I catch an early train from Penn Station, but the grandstand is already swarming when I arrive. Thousands are picnicking out back on the grass. Another day of perfect weather. The atmosphere is straight out of the nineteenth century—it feels as though a four-hour-long program of religious speakers could begin at any moment.

One of the first people I see is Kevin Richardson, from the Backstreet Boys, in a white suit, his goatee looking even more waxen and false, like hair you might draw with metal shavings and a magnetic pencil on one of those little toy faces. I did some research on him, after the Derby, and learned that his nicknames are Mr. Body Beautiful, Kev, Boo, Kevi, and Train. He grew up riding "horses and dirt bikes" in Lexington—the dirt-bike detail tells me that I can trust this information. He is my brother.

I ask eight different track employees where I can pick up my press credentials. One directs me to the "ID Office," where a heavyset, sluggish cop with blue-black circles under his eyes tells me that I am in the right place but that the guy who works there has gone out for a drink. While I wait for the guy I scan the dozens of track ID cards tacked to the walls, former employees mostly. Among the dour, let's-get-this-over-with expressions, one smiling face sticks out: it is Osama. They have given him his own card. Underneath his picture it says: "Manure Inspector."

Curiously, the Internet conspiracy theorists had already arrived at Posner's theory, within a week of bin Salman's death. On June 29, 2002, a poster at a Web site called Free Republic mused, "Wonder when the royal Saudi family will go after the killers?" To which a poster using the handle "Mamzelle" replied (on June 30): "If these three are somehow connected to Al Qaeda, maybe the Saudi family *are* the killers."

When people see a strong horse and a weak horse, by nature, they will like the strong horse.
—Osama bin Laden, videotape transcript,
December 13, 2001

MARGARET WARNER [PBS newsanchor]: Judith Miller, final comment from you on that point?

JUDITH MILLER [*New York Times* correspondent]: Well, I agree with [former CIA officer] Larry Johnson. I think it's made a tremendous difference to . . . as the Clinton administration used to call it, to drain the swamp. And as for the Arab street and the root causes, I think I will have to quote Osama bin Laden himself, "People prefer a strong horse." The United States is emerging as the strong horse.

LARRY JOHNSON: Well done.
—*NewsHour with Jim Lehrer*, December 27, 2001

THE RIDER IS LOST

Only reporters who write for dailies are allowed in the press box today, so I borrow a seat in the grandstand, high enough up that I can see the whole track through the binoculars. The gates shoot open for the fourth race, but about twenty seconds in, just as the field approaches the first turn, a horse goes down on the track, and then another horse. A sickened groan rises from the crowd. Immediately the accident begins to get replayed on the huge electronic screens, the same groan going up each time, with diminishing volume. A horse named Imadeed trips—it looks as if her front legs have simply given way—and another horse, Pleasant County, trips on her. Over and over they crash hideously in slow motion. One can see, in the replay, that Pleasant County is already dead. She falls on her head, and by the time her great body settles onto the track, her legs are already stiff. Imadeed staggers to her feet and begins to limp around. The jockeys weirdly mimic this scene—one hops up, but Pleasant County's rider stays down. The one who is able to stand runs over and helps the other jockey to his feet. A horse ambulance pulls up and a couple of men bring out the folding gray screen that means: *Dead horse* (the screen comes in specially handy when a horse has to be euthanized on the track—nothing makes a crowd feel less like betting money than watching an animal get spiked in the neck with a megadose of barbiturate). Imadeed is led, hobbling but alive, into another ambulance, and both vehicles tear away.

In *The Horse: The Most Abused Domestic Animal*, Greta Bunting writes about the dark trade in horseflesh that still goes on in this country: the slaughterhouses exporting meat to Belgium, Canada, Japan, and Iceland; the dread "killer buyers" haunting country auctions in their quest for cheap, broken-down nags they can sell to the slaughterhouses. Even champion racers have been sent to the knacker's yard. Fans of the sport were shocked in 1982 when it was reported that Exceller, who in '78 defeated two Triple Crown winners—Seattle Slew and Affirmed—had been sold into slaughter by his Swedish owner. When asked why, the man claimed he could simply no longer afford to keep him (though he had paid millions to obtain the horse in the first place). This fate also befell the 1986 Kentucky Derby winner, Ferdinand, who was similarly "disposed of" by his Japanese owner. Needless to say, if this could happen to a champion, it happens every day to less distinguished Thoroughbreds. Many people underestimate the cost involved in maintaining such an animal, and unless you are a prince or a sheikh or have otherwise acquired billions, it is easy to go from being one of the oft-romanticized "little guys" who bought a yearling on the cheap to being someone who is saddled with an unwise investment. Thoroughbreds are delicate and prone to all sorts of medical complications, and the high cost of treating them means that unless there is some financial incentive to keeping them alive, they are most often euthanized on the least excuse. There you have another problem, however, because it also costs a lot of money to bury an animal that weighs over a ton, so the "bone men"—procurers for the horse slaughterhouses and rendering plants—are often called in, happy to take a dead horse off someone's hands.

On-track breakdowns are a separate issue. A study commissioned by the animal-rights group Equine Advocates found that a third of all U.S. horses sent to the "processing plants" in a given year come from racetracks. Pretty much everyone who works in or around the Thoroughbred community agrees that "soundness"—the capacity of a horse to bear up under the pressures of racing—has become a real problem. In 1993 William Nack wrote an insightful article on this subject for *Sports Illustrated*, entitled "Breakdowns," in which he thoroughly pissed off many in the racing world by arguing that a lot of trainers are essentially riding their horses to death, "sending them out on the track with dangerous infirmities masked by narcotics and painkillers." A set group of performance-enhancing drugs was legalized in the 1970s, and all others were thereby made illegal, but track veterinarians can only police the use of drugs for which they can test, and as I learned at the Gluck Center in Lexington, trainers who want to use dope are usually one step ahead of the vets. Nack cited a 1992 study carried out by Julie Wilson at the University of Minnesota. Wilson found that a horse fatality occurs in one of every ninety-two races run on American tracks—ninety-two being roughly the number held in a single day—and that in one of every twenty-two races, a horse is injured badly enough that it cannot finish. Many of these horses will of course be euthanized quickly thereafter. "And that does not reflect the number of horses fatally injured in morning workouts."

Every expert you ask about the soundness issue will give you a different explanation. They are too inbred; they are getting too big (their average height has grown by two "hands"—or eight inches—over the past 250 years, a result of breeding for size, which has meant a narrowing of the legs that these animals can ill afford: their ankles, which contain twenty-two delicate bones, are already thinner than human ankles in spots); they are not allowed to spend any time gamboling with other horses in the field, an experience, some say, that used to toughen them up; there is more pressure on trainers to race them even when there may be doubts about their readiness; they are raced too young (Man o' War did not run in the Derby because his trainer believed that horses are not ready to compete so early in their three-year-old year).

The most convincing answer that I have come across is in good old R. W. Collins's *Race Horse Training*. Collins pins the blame on what was, at the time (he was writing in 1937), an innovation: winter racing, which began at Florida's Hialeah Park in 1931 and soon came to include a handful of California tracks. Before that, Collins writes,

> it was the well grounded custom of racing men either to turn out, or to winter at one of the Kentucky, Maryland, or even New York tracks, all their worthwhile horses. . . . It was generally considered either impossible, or very bad judgment to try to train a

horse the whole year around without a turn-out. The fall of the year usually found one's equine charges beginning to border on thinness, and the year's accumulations of bad legs and injuries were needing rest. . . . After a winter's repairs, or the cheering influence of the farm on a sound horse, or even the comparative rest of an idle winter at the track, the horses came out in the spring fat, almost fit, and mostly sound.

This is a theory one *never* hears at the track, and I have not come across it in any of the dozens of articles written about the soundness problem in the last ten years. The reason for that may be obvious: it comes uncomfortably close to the pocketbooks not only of the powerful interests behind the winter tracks but of the corporations that control year-round simulcast betting. Hundreds of millions of dollars are involved, and at this point it is unthinkable that Thoroughbred racing should become, once again, a seasonal sport, like basketball or football. Yet anyone who has tried to prehandicap the Derby based on two-year-old performances knows that it is futile: one can more or less count on at least half of the agreed-upon contenders not making it to the race in May, and the cause is always the same: winter injuries. "This *continuous racing*," Collins wrote sixty-six years ago, "is also the answer to the questions so often put to horsemen: Why are there so many bad horses now, so many cripples, and so many horses destroyed almost daily on the racing strips of America?"

It is said that the "bone men" will, if summoned, come directly to the track. With a somewhat morbid desire to find out whether this is true, I leave my seat and head for the stables, through a long, dim tunnel that smells of hay and horseshit (healthy horseshit actually smells good—it has a mulchy, woodsy odor lacking in gag factor). At the end of the tunnel I emerge into the light and see the wooden stables ranging away from me in rows, lined up along tree-lined streets. It is so quiet back here, so pastoral. I can still hear the loudspeaker back at the track, but it already seems to emanate from another world.

The security guards at the information booth, all of whom are in their forties or fifties and are already exhausted from what is for them the busiest day of the year, do not want to hear that I am looking for a dead horse. They stare at my shiny blue-and-orange press badge and shake their heads grimly. "I just want to find out what happened to her," I say through the window. "Can you tell me which barn her trainer is in?

One of them leans way back in his office chair and says to a guy in the far corner, "Do you know who trained that dead horse?"

"She's already gone," the other guy says.

"Really?" I say. "They already took her away?" I should have gone straight to the track vet, but even so I would probably not have made it in time.

"You can see the other horse," the guy says, by which he means the one who lived. "He's in Steve Young's barn. Number 23."

Steve Young is Imadeed's trainer. The grooms at barn 23 eye me suspiciously, which I understand—their boss does not need bad press about how his extremely expensive horse went down and caused the death of somebody else's extremely expensive horse. I try to make it clear that I am only curious. If I knew the Spanish, I would say, "Look, I'm just a hack!" But instead I ask, ungrammatically, about "*el caballo que se calle.*" They nod toward the one they are feeding. "*¿Es ella?*"

"Who are you?" one of them says, very pointedly in English.

"A journalist," I say. "*Por una revista.*"

"*Hable con Mr. Young,*" he says, and points me toward the other end of the barn.

I find Young in his office. He is kicked back in his chair, a remote control in his hand, watching television—live feed from the track. He jumps up when he sees me, looking younger than I had expected. His dark hair is mussed and his eyes are bright red and his speech is choked with saliva—he has either been drinking or crying. I suspect the latter.

The first thing he says, before I even ask a question, is, "We don't know yet."

"How bad is it?" I ask.

"As bad as it gets."

I gesture toward the horse the grooms had pointed out to me. "Is that her?"

"Yeah, that's her."

"She looks so good."

"She's content. But there's a contusion. We worry about infection."

Young looks completely despondent. I tell him how sorry I am, and he says nothing. Then, as I am walking away, he mutters, "I appreciate it." (The next day, the *Daily Racing Form* reports that Imadeed might be saved as a broodmare, but circulation never fully returns to her right leg, and she will be put down back in Kentucky on June 20.)

I start to walk deeper into the stable area, away from the track, and it only gets quieter and more bucolic as I go. Roosters, barn cats, pigeons roosting on bales of hay. And the horses, looking out from the gloomy shadows of their stalls, having already raced or about to do so, now and then looking up from their chewing to watch you pass, their bored eyes taking you in and then letting you go.

On the way to Baffert's barn—War Emblem's barn—I take a slight detour and pause for a minute in front of barn 5, where Secretariat was stabled. There is little activity now, but in '73 every person who had access or could get through security was here, wanting just to see him. From this barn, stall 7, he was led to what was probably the most remarkable horse race ever run. "Perfect achievements," wrote Kafka in "The Aeroplanes at Brescia," "cannot be appreciated." This one could.

Sham led the field going into the first turn. He was flying—everyone watching the race knew that he was going too fast. The strategy for Secretariat, for any horse, would have been to hang back and let Sham destroy himself, but Ronnie Turcotte decided to contest the pace. It was, to all appearances, an insane strategy. William Nack writes that up in the press box, turfwriters were hollering, "They're going too fast!" And there were shouts of "Suicidal!" in the crowd.

Secretariat caught him just after the first turn, and for the first half of the race it was a duel between the two rivals. Then, somewhere around the sixth furlong, Sham began to fall apart. He had been pushed too hard, and Laffitt Pincay pulled him off in distress. He was finished. Secretariat was alone, and Turcotte had done nothing but cluck to the horse.

This is when it happened, the thing, the unbelievable thing. Secretariat started going faster. At the first mile, he had shattered the record for the Belmont Stakes, and at a mile and an eighth he had tied the world record (remember that he was only three years old—horses get faster as they age, up to a point, most reaching their peak at four or five). Everyone—in the crowd, in the press box, in the box where the colt's owner and trainer were sitting—everyone was waiting for something to go wrong, because this was madness. Yet he kept opening lengths on the nearest horses, Twice a Prince and My Gallant. Nack, the master, writes:

> He is running easily. Nor is the form deteriorating. There remains the pendulumlike stride of the forelegs and the drive of the hindlegs, the pumping of the shoulders and the neck, the rise and dip of the head. He makes sense of all the mystical pageant rites of blood through which he evolved as a distillate, a climactic act. . . .

Turcotte, turning around, could hardly see the rest of the field. At a mile and three-eighths, Secretariat had beaten Man o' War's world record. He was, at that moment, almost certainly the fastest three-year-old that ever existed. And still he kept opening lengths. Twenty-nine, thirty. He was not lapping them, as my father remembered, but it would not have taken him long at that clip to do so.

He finished thirty-one lengths ahead of Twice a Prince. His time: 2:24. He had established the world record time—for a horse of any age—at twelve furlongs, beating the previous record by two and three-fifths seconds. Unprecedented. Unreal. People were crying uncontrollably. Reporters wanted to know what Turcotte had done, why had he so pressured the horse, when the race was clearly over? But Turcotte had never even showed his whip. He had hardly even touched the horse.

I came across a story about the '73 Belmont in the *Lexington Herald-Leader*. Jack Nicklaus, the golfer, was watching the race at home on television. As Secretariat pulled away from Sham, Nicklaus went down on all fours in front of the set, looking up in disbelief, pounding his fists into the floor and weeping, freaking out the people he had invited over to watch the race.

Nicklaus later told his story to the sports commentator Heywood Hale Broun, saying, "I don't know why I did that."

"You've spent your entire life searching for perfection," Broun replied. "And you finally saw it."

There is a passage on the tape that I noticed only after watching it dozens of times. It occurs near the end of the race. The cameraman has zoomed up pretty dose on Secretariat, leaving the lens just wide enough to capture the horse and a few feet of track. Then, about half a furlong before the wire (it is hard to tell), the camera inexplicably stops tracking the race and holds still. Secretariat rockets out of the frame, leaving the screen blank, or rather filled with empty track. I timed this emptiness—the space between Secretariat exiting and Twice a Prince entering the image—with my watch. It lasts seven seconds. And somehow each of these seconds says more about what made Secretariat great than any shot of him in motion could. In the history of profound absences—the gaps in Sappho's fragments, Christ's tomb, the black panels of Rothko's chapel—this is among the most beautiful.

Secretariat ran a few more races after the Belmont, winning all but one. His value as a stud was too great for his owners to risk seeing him injured on the track, so he was retired to Claiborne Farm, in Lexington. He stood there for many years, siring countless runners, but in 1989 he developed laminitis, a cruelly painful condition that affects the hooves, and he had to be euthanized. William Nack got a message that if he wanted to see his champion again, he had better come quick. Nack went, and wrote a piece about the experience for *Sports Illustrated*. While he was there, he interviewed Dr. Thomas Swerczex, the vet who performed the autopsy on Secretariat. This is what Swerczex told him:

> I'd seen and done thousands of autopsies on horses, and nothing I'd ever seen compared to it. The heart of the average horse weighs about nine pounds. This was almost twice the average size, and a third larger than any equine heart I'd ever seen. And it wasn't

pathologically enlarged. All the chambers and valves were normal. It was just larger.

LAST LEG

At Prince bin Salman's barn there is a crowd, but not a large one—turfwriters, mostly. It is getting extremely close to race time, and a sportscaster standing a few feet away from me says, for the rolling camera, "Baffert says he's not in ANY hurry. He'll be there on time." Baffert himself is standing just inside the barn, his arms draped over his young son's shoulders, looking back at us, inscrutable behind his dark glasses.

Just across the road, behind us, is the barn of D. Wayne Lukas, one of Baffert's rivals. Tension between the two trainers increased when Lukas made a point of saying to *The New York Times* that his horse, Proud Citizen, would wear a blanket reading "FDNY" before and after the race (no Arab owners here!). It seems that neither man wants to lead his horse out first.

Bob Costas zooms up in a golf cart and starts talking to Baffert. I had never known how small he was—almost small enough to be a jockey—and weirdly perfect in a George Stephanopoulos, doll-man way. I edge closer, to try to hear what Baffert is saying to Costas, but Costas is mostly talking to technical support back at the studio, one of those one-sided overheard conversations: "I . . . Thank you. You keep . . . You keep cutting out. . . . That's my *point.*"

Suddenly Lukas defers and decides to go first. We all turn to watch Proud Citizen being led toward the tunnel that connects to the paddock, his entourage flowing around him. Almost immediately Baffert starts out, too, having proved his point. He has War Emblem by the bridle, then passes the shank to a groom. This truly is a beautiful horse—not black in the way that Mayakovsky was black, not inky, but very dark brown, with a long proud face, and the white star.

We all fall into step, like a ragtag army, all of us careful to keep a few feet between us and the horse. It is weirdly silent. The only sound is the soft crunching of gravel. The thickness of history in the air is like the pressure of your own blood in your ears. Each of us is wondering if we are participating, however tangentially, in a Triple Crown. War Emblem is looking around, noticing the commotion. All his life, since he was sold as a yearling, it has been like this, strangers staring at him. Why are they here?

It is something to walk through the tunnel behind him, to try to keep your eyes on his dark head as it disappears and unexpectedly pops up again in the shadows, to see the dust swirling in the sunlight at the paddock end of the tunnel, where we are headed, and to hear the crowd around the paddock start to roar. To see the faces when he first steps forth, prancing now, into the light. This, too, we have to concede in fairness—it is also about this. About glory.

I did not expect to be back in the stable area for so long, and I have yet to place my bets, though I more or less emptied out my bank account this morning for that purpose. I rush out of the paddock and back up to the second floor, where, ever faithful, I bet the Sullivan System, decent money to place (in case you have forgotten) on every horse with odds between ten- and twenty-to-one. When I get to my seat, I have already missed the elaborate 9/11 mourning rite, during which (as I learned afterward) Proud Citizen bit two firemen.

This race does not feel like any of the races I have been to in the past year. There is something circulating through the crowd—I want to say that it is like goodwill. We are all waiting to see something beautiful, something which almost never happens, which almost never has a chance to happen, but which might happen today. In all the conversations I have

had and overheard since this morning, no one has expressed the slightest concern about the fact that War Emblem's owner is Saudi. No one cares. They know better. They know that a horse, unfortunately, has to be owned by somebody. NBC is talking about it, but nobody else is. It is just like the Clinton scandals. This total indifference to the counterfeit reality that columnists, pundits, and op-ed writers work daily to shove down our throats seems to me very American, and for the moment, I love my country.

People are shouting before the race even begins, coming out of their skins. But War Emblem stumbles at the very start (later, watching the replay back in the "auxiliary" press box, I see that he almost goes to the ground), and although he rallies, he never regains the lead. The race is won by another horse that no one has ever heard of, one with a beautiful name: Sarava. A colt called Medaglia d'Oro comes in second, at sixteen-to-one.

As at the Derby, the crowd is strangely muted after the

finish. First War Emblem shocked them into silence, now he has disappointed them into silence.

Funny. I did not think that I wanted this horse to win all that badly. His story was so crass. But when I finally drop the binoculars, my eyes are full of tears. It takes me a full beat to realize that I have just won five hundred dollars on Medaglia d'Oro.

A COLD EYE

At home in Manhattan it is morning, and the sun floats between buildings like a bubble of molten steel, though here in the Village there is only a glow, a brightening behind the blinds that seems tenuous, like a false dawn, as if any moment the light could think twice and just slip back, tidelike, into the ocean, and all would be darkness and waiting again. This is that single silent hour between the last cokehead finally kicked out of the bar, braying, not having been laid, and the first of the rumbling yawns of the shop-front gates being rolled up, over, and out of sight. It is fearfully still.

Once more I put on my headphones and click on the sorry little clips, and in my ears I hear the calls. Once more I close my eyes and watch him run: the Derby, the Preakness, the Belmont Stakes, 1973. I listen to Chick Anderson as he struggles and fails, in the human way, to describe perfection, to describe what no one had ever seen, and what no one there would ever see again.

And still the old question hangs over it all: Why? Why did he run as he did, with no one forcing him, or even urging him, with no one or thing to defeat anymore, with no punishment waiting for him if he slowed? For this morning, at least, at last, the answer is clear. It requires no faith. He ran that way, I know, because he could, and we cannot. One does not, if one is beauty, have to know what beauty is.

On a shelf in front of my desk, at eye level, sits a family photograph from my college graduation. My father stands beside me in the May sunlight, lifting a clear plastic cup of champagne. We are both wearing glasses, and the glint off the lenses hides our eyes, but I can tell that his smile is sincere. His hair, blown up from his high forehead by the wind, has gone bone white, though the mustache retains faint tinges of red. His face is a fatter, older version of mine, down to the jutting chin. This used to trouble me. I do not remember why.

He has been dead for three years. In dreams of him—I have them once a month or so—he is always dying, he is never well. Yet he is alive. He is off by himself in a little room, the door open so that we can see him, and the rest of us sit on couches, rubbing our hands. He gets younger as he gets thinner and closer to death. He is never angry or frightened in these dreams, only unhappy, maybe a little anxious, and on his face there is a vaguely regretful smile.

The thing that killed him, perversely, was something that could have killed a thirty-year-old jogging enthusiast. While in recovery from the second hernia-repair operation (a procedure he never should have agreed to so soon after the heart bypass, given all that his body had been through), a blood clot that had formed in his leg came loose and went into his lungs. They fought to save him for twelve hours. The surgeon wept, I was told.

I was traveling on the day he had the operation, which went according to plan. I called him that night, from the road, but he could hardly understand me through the drugs. He was mumbling incoherently. I remember sitting in the kitchen of this bed-and-breakfast in east Tennessee, with the phone in my hand, yelling "I love you" into the receiver, not knowing whether he could hear me. Finally I heard the nurse reach over and hang up the phone. I will never know whether the last words I said to him were the last words he heard me say.

Two days later, back in New York, I woke up to a telephone call from Riverside. A woman asked me if I was John Sullivan, and when I said yes, she told me that something had gone wrong. Earlier that morning the nurses had come into his room and turned my father over, to check one of his bandages, and he suddenly started gasping for air. Then he flat-lined. They had him "stabilized" now, she said, but I should get to the hospital immediately.

At LaGuardia, the departures screen said that the flight I had booked on two hours' notice was canceled. I pushed my way to the counter and explained my situation, but the best they could do for me was to put me on a flight that left later that afternoon. So I stood by the pay phone, calling, calling. They were still trying to save him. An hour went by. I called again, and my aunt Kathy, his little sister, said we had lost him. I hung up the phone. A little crowd of people there at the gate had heard enough of the different conversations to put together my story. They stared at me, and looked away

By the time I got to Riverside, late that night, everyone's tears were used up. It was a lobbyful of shock victims. My brother was on his way from Chicago, and my three sisters had been waiting on me to go in and see the body, so we walked in together, nervously holding one another's hands. He lay on the table, his poor tortured body covered in a sheet, my father. He was an otherworldly presence there in the harsh light. Nothing I recognized was left in the room. I kissed his forehead, recoiling from the coldness as from an electric shock. His strange, Hippocratic face.

That night, back at his bachelor apartment, I sat with my mother and sisters in silence. It had seemed for so long that something like this *would* happen—now that it had, it seemed untrue, another dream, I walked through the small, carpeted rooms, touching his things. The place had always depressed me, bur now I wanted to be here, to stay here, even. The smell of tobacco smoke clung to the furniture and the walls. On his bookshelf was a black-and-white photograph of the two of us in Ireland. An old man took it for us during a trip we made to the west in Cork County, where my father's grandparents had been born on a tenant farm at a place called Kilcomogue. We are sitting side by side on a low stone wall, and the sea fans out behind us, glittering like a sheet of foil. That morning we had been on Cape Clear Island, and had tried to walk out to the old castle there, about two miles from the harbor. But my father stopped when we were within sight of the place. He was panting, and said that he thought we had better forget it— even if he made the castle, we would never get back to the boat in time. I had never seen his body quit on him like that. On the way back, I had to stop every fifteen feet to let him catch up, which, little prick that I was, made me sigh dramatically with frustration.

The feeling that came over me in the apartment was so banal, so predictable. It was the feeling I had always told myself I would absolutely not feel when he died, but now it came on hard and unadulterated: guilt. I had been a bad son. How could I have let him live in this place, an apartment complex meant for college students who wanted rooms they could trash without worry, or immigrant families who themselves never stayed longer than a few months. When he moved there, it was an emergency measure. He wanted to let my mother get on with her life. We understood that he would stay only a year, until he could find a house. But after three, it became clear that this was probably the last address he would ever have, and I feared that he would die there, alone. Yet he never seemed to mind the place. When our family first moved to Columbus, in 1987, he went ahead of the rest of us, to start his job, and spent the months before we got there sharing a two-room basement dump with a Chinese graduate student who spoke no English. He was forty-five at the time, a man with a career and children. But that was his way: if he had his bookshelves and his Panasonic tape player and a box of Fig Newtons, he rarely seemed even to notice where he was. Still, I should have gone back to Columbus for a couple of weeks to help him find a house. With a little pressure, he could have been convinced.

And there were all the letters I had never answered. The unreturned phone calls. The Christmases on which we saw him for only a couple of hours, and those spent in a crappy restaurant somewhere. He used to send me a Cleveland Indians schedule at the start of each baseball season. It showed when the team would be at home, and when they were away, and on it he had penciled in telephone numbers for the hotels where he would be staying. I almost never called.

We were not estranged; in fact, we probably talked more often than most fathers and sons. It was just that I put him in the position of always being the one to make the effort. It was punishment—for his refusal to change his ways, for his fuck-ups, for the way he preferred being my friend to being my father, no matter how plainly I needed the latter, for the fact that you could never bring up his effect on the world around him, even on his own family, without driving him back into a hostile silence. I remember that in 1995 when my sister got accepted to the University of Arizona, where she wanted to study archaeology, she briefly considered not going, for fear that something would happen to my father while she was gone (she was the closest to him in the last years of his life). I took him to lunch one afternoon and explained to him what was going on, begging him to reassure my sister, to tell her not to be crazy. But he just shook his head with an embarrassed smile, as if I had said something gauche, and his silence seemed to imply that, out of affection for me, he would resist letting me know that I had overstepped my bounds. He never said a word to my sister.

He was at his worst when faced with the awkwardness of

another's disappointment or dissatisfaction. First he would blithely proceed as if it did not exist, and when this failed, he would withdraw. I wanted to let him win this game, to be the son who told himself, and everyone else, that the old man was all right, that his angels outnumbered his demons. He had worked hard to provide for us—now it was our job to be there for him, not to scold him.

But I found it impossible, in part because I felt intensely that old cliché, "If you loved us you'd want to live" (moral logic that is somehow too impeccable to work on earth), and in part because so much of what I wanted I thought I wanted *for his sake.* He was only forty-nine when he and my mother divorced, and after he moved out, he immediately began to let himself go. Even his smell changed. It had always been a mixture of tobacco and sweat and Old Spice, somehow pleasant and robust, but the longer he lived in that apartment, the staler it got, and when I hugged him, and breathed it in, it seemed unwell. The elephant in the room that was his health and his habits got uglier as it aged. It got bigger too, and in the end it threatened to squeeze me out of the room altogether. I could never compose my face carefully enough to hide the unhappiness I felt on seeing him, sitting there alone with the carton of cigarettes and the ice cream and the television and the sense of humor still maddeningly intact. Gallows humor, it had become. Here was this extraordinary man who had stopped fighting it, and chosen solitude—too soon. And who dismissed the idea of therapy on the tired grounds that he would never let "some New Age flake-o tell me what I've done wrong with my life." And who saw the complicated pain in his children's faces when they were with him, since he was too smart to miss it, yet remained, at some essential level, unmoved. And I loved him. Nor did I doubt, for even as long as it takes a synapse to fire, that he loved us, and would have done everything he could to make us happy if it had been within his power. It came down to weakness.

I always believed that I would one day get to tell him that what he was, even what he became, was enough for me. I wanted to say that it had been my mistake, the chill in our friendship, to tell him that if he was so intent on neglecting himself, I knew he had never neglected us, never hurt us, or had never meant to. But when the nurse hung up the phone that night in his hospital room and I heard the dial tone, the conversation between us, which I had always assumed—so foolishly—would go on and on, and allow for retraction, got cut off for good.

Late that night, in the room where I slept whenever I stayed with him, I sat down at his old desk, his father's desk. In the drawer were his "quitting journals," as he called them, special notebooks, set apart from the others, filled with his rapid, loopy script. He would start a clean one with each new attempt to kick cigarettes. I had glanced at them once or twice when he was alive. Now they belonged to me, along with all of his "creative work," under the terms of the will. They were largely self-excoriations, full of black thoughts, efforts to locate and take hold of his own willpower. How *badly* he wanted to change. Worse than any of us could have wanted that for him (there was a notecard on the table by the bed, written when he was going to a support group: "Reasons to quit: 1. It worries my children"). I flipped through one of the notebooks. He was writing about how embarrassed he was every morning when he would start to cough and could not stop, and he knew the neighbors could hear him through the thin walls. Turning the page, I found a one-sentence paragraph, set off by itself. When I read it, I knew that I would never look at the journals again. "If I should not wake up tomorrow," he had written, "know that my love is timeless and fond."

We had a Catholic service for him at the Milward Funeral Home in Lexington. His old friends were there, people he had not seen in years. I was thrown when three younger men, colleagues of his, came up to me and told me that my father had taught them to write. All I could say was, "Me too." This was something he would *never* have claimed for himself, that he had been a mentor to anyone; his sense was that he reeled off funny little pieces, and for some reason the newspaper, whichever one it was, paid him to do it.

In a little anteroom, the immediate family gathered just before the priest was to begin. We asked the funeral director to unseal the coffin so that we could look at him one last time, and he did, lifting it more slowly than necessary, to show that he understood the gravity of the moment. But the sight of my fathers face meant nothing to me. His mustache had been clipped to within the borders of his mouth. His hands were at his sides—whereas in life, when he was napping, he always folded them over his stomach. People say that it helps to see the corpse. But I think it is a flaw in nature that the body remains behind at all. We should disappear when we die.

The night before, back in Columbus, I had written my father's eulogy. Now I was standing in front of the people he had loved most in his life, trying to use the thing he had loved most—language—to get across some sense of the man. I was tempted, in the moment, to talk about his darker side, because I knew that my father liked people to think he was "zany," and part of me thought that I needed to defend against that, on his behalf, to flesh him out, to make them see him as I saw him. But a better instinct prevailed. What others saw after all, was real; the humor was never feigned. And if it persisted in spite of the sadness, there was something noble in that.

I told a story about a time he came to see me when I was in college, at Sewanee, in Tennessee. There is a restaurant called Pearl's on the edge of town. Back then, it was the only decent place to eat on the isolated mountaintop where the school is located, and you always took your parents there when they came to visit. My father and I had dinner at a table outside, on a gravel patio. We talked for a long time, and put away a couple of bottles of wine in the candlelight. He was animated, acting out stories, as he liked to do. Neither of us knew that as he leaned forward and wiggled and rocked back, his considerable weight was twisting the chairs hind legs deeper and deeper into the gravel.

When the check was finally paid, he moved to stand, and the chair went backward, taking him with it. It happened so slowly, a topple—the way cartoon characters fall after they have been knocked on the head—and what I tried to describe at the service was the expression on his face as he fell. He was smiling. His eyes were wide, and he had, somehow, a look of both surprise and almost excited expectation, as if he was cresting the hill on a roller coaster. It seemed to take hours for him to land flat on his back in the gravel, which he did with a thud, his arms outstretched. His glasses popped off his face and landed behind him.

I ran around the table, my face reddening with embarrassment. A crew of busboys and waiters joined me, no doubt fearing a lawsuit. People at the other tables turned to stare. My father's eyes were closed, and his body was shaking. We were all asking him, "Are you okay? Are you okay?" but there

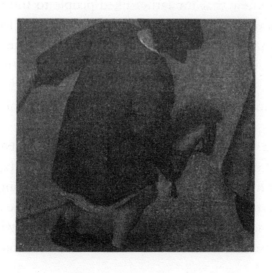

was no response. I knelt at his side, wondering why he did not even move to get up. It took me a second to realize it was because he was laughing too hard.

We had two wakes for him, one across town at his niece's place, for his brothers and sisters and all of my Sullivan cousins, and another that night at my grandmother's house, for the Milward side. Both were exceedingly Irish (the first authentically so, the second in spirit): loads of whiskey and jokes, with only the stray, sentimental tear, and everyone saying, over and over, that it was just as he would have wanted it. And it was, except that I had to keep stopping myself from saying, "Would he have wanted it quite this soon?"

Very late that night—it must have been early the next morning—my brother and I were in a hotel room that my grandmother had rented for those of our friends who had traveled to come. There were clothed and sleeping bodies draped like refugees across the beds and floor. It was quiet. The two of us sat up Indian-style, facing each other "with watery eyes, passing a bottle of Bourbon back and forth and whispering. We were going on about the Beach Boys, for some reason, and one of the last things I remember my brother saying, before I fell back against the bed, was that in his opinion the greatest single moment in all of popular music was the complete bar of vocal silence near the beginning of "Good Vibrations," after Brian Wilson sings "I" but before he sings, "I love the colorful clothes she wears." My brother was weaving as he counted out the four empty beats on the carpet. "It's like . . ." he said, "it's like the whole universe is in that silence."

Then we were silent, drinking. Before it went black, my mind was already driving through the dark, with headlight vision, leaving the parking lot, taking a left onto Richmond Road, following Richmond as it turned one-way and became, without any signage to mark the change, Main Street, which I knew was deserted, the stoplights flashing yellow, then across the bridge, to where the cemeteries were, left into Calvary, curving along the paths back to a corner where two hedges met, where my father's body was already under the ground. Is it cold there, even in summer?

My brother shook his head. He said, "I can't believe Dad's dead."

REMNANT

It took me over a year to believe that my father was dead. Not that I denied it or even actively disbelieved it; I simply had not yet learned that it was true. Proust wrote about this phenomenon. There is a scene, midway through *Remembrance of Things Past*, in which Marcel returns to the fictional seaside resort of Balbec. He had been there years before, with his grandmother, an almost angelically selfless woman who doted on him like a hen, and whom he loved. That first time, she had come to his room in her nightgown, having heard his "anxious sniffing" through the wall, and had helped him off with his boots, saying, "Let me! . . . It is such a joy for your Granny."

Now there is no one to notice his trouble. His grandmother is gone, and he is alone. Tired and ill, Marcel bends down to take off his own boots. "But no sooner had I touched the topmost button," he says,

> than my bosom swelled, filled with an unknown, a divine presence, I shook with sobs, tears streamed from my eyes . . . I had just perceived, in my memory, bending over my weariness, the tender, preoccupied, dejected face of my grandmother, as she had been on that first evening of our arrival, the face not of that grandmother whom I was astonished—and

reproached myself—to find that I regretted so little and who was no more of her than just her name, but of my own true grandmother, of whom, for the first time since that afternoon in the Champs-Elysées, on which she had had her stroke, I now recaptured, by an instinctive and complete act of recollection, the living reality. That reality has no existence for us, so long as it has not been created anew by our minds . . . and so, in my insane desire to fling myself into her arms, it was not until this moment, more than a year after her burial, because of that anachronism which so often prevents the calendar of facts from corresponding to that of our feelings, that I became conscious that she was dead.

That passage came to me two years ago. I was washing dishes in my apartment in New York when my mother called to tell me that the dog of my youth—a gigantic piebald semi-retarded mutt, half-Great Dane and half-Labrador, with paws the size of dessert plates and a ridiculous black mask across his eyes—had been, as she put it, "put down" at the age of fifteen. She had come downstairs to let him outside for his morning *devoir*, and he had been unable to stand. She looked into his eyes and for the first time, in his long senescence, saw pain. "I'm sorry," she said, "I wish I could have told you first. But . . . we owed it to him, you know."

We were always dog people. Tippy was the first—my brother's pet. She was about 75 percent black Lab, one of those preternaturally intelligent mongrels that can unlock doors and cabinets. At my birthday parties she used to herd children away from the street like a shepherd. My little sister and I got off the bus one day after school and found her dead in her favorite spot in the front yard, under a giant maple tree that covered our house in shadow. We frantically patted her head, calling her name, but a black fly landed on her lip, to no response, and we knew that something was off. We burst into the house, screaming for my father. Normally, when you woke him from a nap, he would emerge from the bedroom enraged, his hand raised in preparation for one of his mock slaps, which seemed like actual pain-inflicters until they got to about six inches of your arm, at which point they would sort of flutter out, ending in a tap—then he would stomp away. But something about the pitch of our voices warned him, and he came into the hallway with a dazed and worried look. There followed one of those irretrievably pure childhood moments, from before decorum and shame have tamed our responses: I ran to him, threw my arms around his waist, and, looking up, called out, "Why? Why?" My sister stood behind me, bawling, waiting her turn. For a second it looked as if my father were going to laugh, and it occurred to me that I was being comical, but his look dissolved into a smile, and he said, "Nobody knows. It just happens."

Within a month, we had bought another Lab-like female from a man in Louisville who had seven puppies to sell (my mother chose her). My father named her Ruggles, after his favorite film comedian, Charlie Ruggles, and gave her to my sister, who was still crying every night over the shock of that first death. Ruggles was sweet but stupid: her slobber defined her. She was extremely athletic, however—a real jumper, with powerful haunches—and when her first heat came on, we found it impossible to keep her gated. She would bound over the four-and-a-half-foot chain-link fence that surrounded our backyard, her fore- and back paws bunching together just at the crest of her arc, and touch down already running like mad. Every male dog in the neighborhood still in possession of his equipment, it seemed, had a go at her, and she turned up heavily pregnant.

Her seven puppies—when she had them at four o'clock in the morning, in a cut-out refrigerator box, on the fourth of July—were every size and color. In most cases, we could trace each one to a neighborhood stud. The last to be born was the biggest, and we recognized him immediately as the bastard son of a Harlequin Dane who lived on the other side of the hill from our house and stood almost to my shoulders. The son looked like a huge potato that had sprouted a head, white with black spots all over, and pads on his paws that were the exact pink of a brand-new pencil eraser. My father named him Remnant (because he was Ruggles's last puppy: "the end of the rug is the remnant"), and he was the opposite of the runt: when his mother rolled wearily onto her flank to offer her teats, he would casually push the others aside, swimming through them almost, until he had established himself at the center of the litter.

Six weeks later, when the time came to give them away we made up our minds that we would simply keep whichever one was left over, after the other six had been taken away The seventh would be my dog. But we noticed immediately that when the prospective owners would show up, and most of the pack would go running up to them, jumping up onto their legs, Remnant would sneak off and hide in a boxwood tree by the back door, as if he knew what was going on and wanted no part of it. So I asked my parents if I could keep him.

That little show of intelligence turned out to be a ruse, or more likely an illusion. He soon revealed himself to be every bit as stupid as his mother. I should say, though, that with Ruggles and Remnant both, we were never certain if they had been born brain-damaged, or if we had accidentally made them that way by allowing them to eat whatever they wanted. You could never keep food away from them. They could get things down from the top of the refrigerator, out from under the bed, from inside boxes and bags. They ate loaves of bread, a large bottle full of heartworm pills, a packet of raw hot dogs, Shakespeare (my sister's gerbil), carpeting, grass, bulbs from my mother's gardens, our scary and demented cat Skipper's turds, and, once, an entire unopened box of big chunky chocolate bars, the kind they make you sell to raise money for school-related causes. I remember the next night, when my father sent me into the backyard with a plastic bag to do "poo patrol," there was a full moon, and the many prodigious piles that mother and son had left during the day were all glinting in the silvery light: flecks of the foil wrappers that the chocolate bars had been wrapped in.

We loved our fat, stupid dogs, even when the neighbors complained about them and our friends made fun of them. My father had contempt for the whole Montessori philosophy of pet-rearing, with thousand-dollar bills from obedience school and harsh commands issued in public for the admiration of other owners. To him—and to the rest of us, by training— dogs were *meant* to be like Remnant and Ruggles, large idiotic creatures who ran around and did as they pleased until you screamed at them, who terrified strangers but would never hurt one, who gave and craved unconditional affection in out-sized doses, and who agreed to live with you until one of you died.

Remnant, who kept growing through even his second year and was, in the end, positively enormous, with a bark like a shotgun going off, seemed the archetype of the big dumb mutt, and my father especially loved him. Sometimes he would call me over to the window in the family room, to watch Remnant (who had become an even better jumper than his mother) getting ready to go over the fence. The dog would trot to the middle of the lawn and turn, gathering speed as he approached the obstacle, finally soaring into the air; he did all this in a manner somehow leisurely, with a lolling tongue. "He runs like a pony," my father said, shaking his head.

When we moved to Ohio, our house had an identical fence around the backyard, but the neighbors immediately let us know that they would not put up with our dogs getting loose. So we had to chain them, for the first time in their lives. Or rather, we had to chain Remnant—Ruggles was too fat by this time to make it over. My father, however, realized after a couple of months that if you simply shook the chain at Remnant, and made clinking sounds in the general area of his faded red collar, and said, "Now you're chained, Remmy," he would believe that he had been restrained and not even attempt the jump. For five years the chain sat coiled by the sliding patio door, never again used, totally effective. My father named it the Great Chain of Non-Being.

After my parents divorced, when my father would stop by the house to pick me and my sister up or to drop off some piece of legal paperwork, Remnant would hear his master's voice and come pounding down the stairs. There was something sad about their little reunions in the foyer; even Remnant, trembling with emotion, could sense it. He would turn and head back upstairs after only a minute or two, casting an uncertain glance at my mother, as if he had been caught doing something bad. And my father held back, too: he would only bend to pet the dog, not squat, as he used to do, till their faces were level. Their respective displays were muted; it was like two old friends saying hello in a courtroom or at a funeral.

It did not surprise me when Remnant outlived my father. I could never see the dog as old. Even after Ruggles died, when I would come home for Christmas or Easter to find him much reduced—with a dog-diaper on (at one point), and the black around his mouth gone gray, his hearing and eyesight lost (you had to stomp on the floor to get his attention, a summons that he responded to when he felt like it), his back legs trembling as he climbed the stairs, and then his refusal to climb the stairs at all—it seemed to me that this was just more of his goofiness. And, indeed, when my mother had a scare a full six months before the end (she heard him whimpering one night, and called the vet, who said it was "probably time"), she was at the point of loading him into the station wagon for his final voyage when he suddenly called on mysterious reserves and began to prance around, looking five years younger. "It's like when he was a puppy and people were coming to adopt them," my mother said. "He knows when somebody wants to take him away."

But the second time, he failed, and he had nothing left. He allowed himself to be carried by my mother and her new husband in a bed sheet to the backseat of the car. He was silent all the way to the vet. And my mother came home with his ashes (there were a lot of them) in a Tupperware container.

I was not prepared for my reaction to this news; the call, after all, was one that if anything I was surprised hadn't come much sooner. But when I pictured Remnant (I at first saw a Polaroid of myself holding him under the swing-set when he was small enough to fit in my hands, his black-and-white face still pinched and fetal), I thought suddenly of my father, fourteen months dead, who had loved and been loved by this dim-witted dog, and I saw the two of them rubbing their faces together furiously, as they loved equally to do, saw Remnant sitting impatiently by my father's desk while he wrote, the great tail going nonstop like a windshield-wiper, until my father would finally finish and rise and mount the steps, crying, "Does Remnant want a bone? Does he want a bone?" and I saw my father out driving in the car after Remnant had gotten away, which he did all the time in the days before the Chain, when the dog would turn up at a strip-mall somewhere, with some old lady cornered, and my father when he found him would always say, "It's all right, it's all right; he only wants to lick you," and I understood in an instant that Remnant's tremendous head, even at the end when he could neither hear nor see, had been a repository, a link, that he had preserved in the recesses of his memory these strands of my father's being, perhaps only a scent or a certain word, but I knew, too, that our being consists in these strands, as much as it does in our bodies, that we draw our existence from a kind a web that is constantly eaten at from the outside, yet never disappears, though we do; it was as though Remnant had come back to teach me how death does its work, and that life is this slow amassing of a company of shades who build up around us until we are suffered to join them ("The dead annex the quick as surely as the Kingdom of France annexes the Duchy of Orléans," said Beckett); I saw a black void moving forward into the future—the children my father would never meet—and I saw man following dog into the darkness, the dog, like us, unaware of his place in the chain, the man my father, for whom I had not really grieved, not yet, the reality of whose death had so far failed, like the news of a foreign catastrophe, to impinge on my deepest self, the fundamental datum of whose death I was now for the first time hearing about, learning about, for it was not until that moment, more than a year after his burial, because of that anachronism that so often prevents the calendar of facts from corresponding to that of out feelings, that I became conscious that he was dead. And I shook with sobs.

ONE YEAR LATER

June 2003. The last year has been a weird one for racing. Keeneland's July yearling sale was canceled due to the ravages of Mare Reproductive Loss Syndrome, a mysterious illness—now epidemic in the Bluegrass—that causes mares to abort their foals. Scientists at the Gluck Center think that the problem may be tent caterpillars, which grow on the cherry tree leaves that horses love to chew. When digested, the bugs produce small levels of cyanide. This is only a theory (pesticides may also be to blame), but central Kentucky owners are chopping down hundred-year-old cherry trees by the score.

We are at war again—not in Afghanistan this time (though we are still at war there, too), but in Iraq, the ancestral home of the Arabian horse. An article by Laura King in the *Los Angeles Times* says that at the Baghdad racetrack, the American Second Battalion, Seventieth Armored Regiment, is camped in the infield, and a three-year-old colt, considered "promising," has been wounded by shrapnel. An Iraqi groom interviewed by King says that the horses "neighed and reared when the bombs fell nearby, and I felt their fear. I tried to calm them so they would not hurt themselves."

Meanwhile, there has been rampant sketchiness at home. A group of former fraternity brothers almost succeeded in faking a Pick Six betting ticket at the Breeders' Cup, back in September, which would have won them millions. Instead they may go to prison for fraud (Joe Drape has written an award-winning series of articles on the case for *The New York Times*). A study commissioned by the New York attorney general's office found that the state's racetracks, especially Belmont, are hopelessly corrupt. Dan Barry, also writing in the *Times*, said that the report describes an organization—the New York Racing Association—"in which cash receipts are not counted at the end of the day; where the arrests of employees do not spur institutional reforms; and where the presence of bookmakers with organized-crime connections is barely noticed."

Prince bin Salman's brother has taken over the Thoroughbred Corporation, and has decided to scale back the operation. He tried to give War Emblem to the families of the 9/11 victims—"an extraordinary attempt," said the *London Times*, "to improve relations with the United States"—but the families refused. "I've heard this offer," said one Steve Push, whose wife was killed in the attacks, "and it's not even a start. . . . They need a new PR consultant." The horse was finally sold to the Japanese, as a stud, but he is "refusing to cover mares"—his sperm is active, in other words, but *he* is not, a condition one often sees in stallions that were doped during their racing careers (unsubstantiated rumor abounds).

Most upsetting of all, Bob Baffert is starring in a commercial for an obscure brand of blue jeans. In the ad, Baffert says that the jeans give him "support right where I need it most," at which point an unfortunate computerized 3-D graphic zooms in on the crotch.

None of these stories has earned a tenth as much ink as what is now known simply as "the photo." The story goes like this: the Kentucky Derby has been won, for the first time, by a horse bred in New York, Funny Cide (the creepy spelling of his name derives from his grandfather, a colt by Seattle Slew, whose owner decided to give his horse the charming name of Slewacide). As Funny Cide came across the line at the Derby, a photographer from Getty Images captured the Chilean jockey, José Santos, with his whip hand in the air.

When holding their whips, jockeys use a counterintuitive grip similar to the one jazz drummers use to hold their left stick, so that they can strike behind them simply by rotating their wrists, without having to bend their arms. When the hand is loosened, this grip leaves a little hollow between the index finger and thumb. A reporter from *The Miami Herald* examined one of these photographs and believed that he saw something in the hollow—something like a battery, which disreputable jockeys will occasionally use to jolt their horses in the home stretch. The *Herald* called up Santos, who speaks English with an extremely thick Chilean accent. Did he have anything in his hand during the Derby? "All I use," said Santos, "is a cue-ring to call the outriders." No one at the *Herald* had ever heard of a "cue-ring" ("outriders" is a term sometimes used to describe the people who bring the ponies to collect the Thoroughbreds after the race). The reporters called old, crusty horsemen, guys who had been around, and asked them, but all said that if there was such a thing as a "cue-ring," they had never heard of it, either.

Suddenly there was a full-on scandal. The six-o'-clock news picked it up: "Did the Derby winner cheat?" Newspapers blew up the photo so that readers could decide for themselves. The stewards met in Lexington to discuss the matter; they even flew in José Santos, whom they spent two hours grilling.

In the end, the story was a nonstory. The stewards said that when you blew up the photo a dozen times (more than anyone else had bothered to do, evidently), you could see quite clearly that the "dark thing" in the hollow of Santos's hand was the dark green silks of the jockey behind him and the strap of the jockey's goggles. When the *Herald* had called Santos in the first place, the jockey had said not that he carried "a cue-ring to call the outriders" but "a Q-Ray to cure my arthritis." A "cue-ring" does not exist, but if you type "Q-Ray" into the Internet, you get a site advertising homeopathic magnetic bracelets said to alleviate, among other things, the symptoms of arthritis (which many jockeys develop after starving and dehydrating themselves for years). The stewards apologized, the *Herald* apologized, Santos said that he wanted to get on with his life.

But then, in keeping with racing's desperation for stories with a little human bite, the nonstory became a *huge* story. Santos's reputation had been besmirched! He was a fine, upstanding man, a family man with a beautiful wife and a son who had a habit of weeping from sheer excess of filial piety. His career had been tough, "full of ups and downs," and he had only ever won one Triple Crown race, an upset at the Belmont back in 1999. Now they wanted to take his success away from him, those snotty bastards. In a "chat room" interview that appeared on the New York Racing Association's Web site, the very first question asked was:

> Do you think the bluebloods were in cahoots with the *Miami Herald*? Did the Kentucky personnel and politicians and stewards, and owners and breeders become so offended that one of theirs [i.e., Empire Maker] did not win the Derby? Is it possible?

Santos answered, "I doubt it." But the story was on. Empire Maket, the horse that had been favored to win the Derby, was bred and trained in Lexington, and he had been beaten by this interloper, this Yankee upstart, a horse with (as one heard over and over) "an unfashionable pedigree." A *Southern* paper had libeled him; and Santos had been forced to defend himself in *Lexington.* Not only that, but Funny Cide's owners were "little guys," a wacky band of businessmen from upstate New York who had pooled their money to buy the gelding. One of these amateurs, a very old guy, dressed like Willy Wonka, and they all tooled around in a school bus. In selecting a trainer for the horse, they had gone with Barclay Tagg, a soft-spoken man who looks uncannily like the actor Ed Harris, and who had never won a Triple Crown race before the Derby.

The story fell apart at every turn. Empire Maker was owned not by a Lexington blueblood but by a Saudi blueblood, Prince Khalid Abdullah. And Funny Cide's owners were of course quite well off (sorry, but you do not own and maintain Thoroughbreds unless you have a lot of money, and only in a sport rife with princes, sheikhs, and rappers could these men be considered "little guys." Upper-middle-class pre-retirees is more like it). The unfashionable pedigree? Seattle Slew won the Triple Crown in 1977; and Funny Cide's great-grandfather on the *other* side, the sire side, was Northern Dancer, who won the Derby and the Preakness in 1964 and went on to become one of the century's greatest "sires of sires," producing the colt Nijinsky, a horse the English think of the way we think of Secretariat. As for the whole New York angle—the city had been through hell after 9/11, New York needed this one, etc.—that dissolved upon closer inspection, too. Bobby Frankel, the person who trained the potential "snobby spoiler," Empire Maker—and who had *also* never won a Triple Crown race—was more of a New Yorker than any of the people attached to Funny Cide. He was born and raised in Brooklyn, and still had his city accent, whereas the

Funny Cide crew lived in a wide-lawned suburb somewhere upstate. One of them would call the others to cocktails every night with a bugle.

No matter: the line had been drawn in the dirt. When Santos and Funny Cide won the Preakness, the jockey flashed his open hand at the wire, as if flicking dishwater off his fingers, the message being, *No battery here.* And the next morning, the headlines were more or less the same from coast to coast: DISGRACED JOCKEY REDEEMED.

Now here we are again, at Belmont Park, and once again a horse is poised to win the Triple Crown. It has been precisely twenty-five years since Affirmed won in '78, ending the "decade of champions," as the 1970s are known. When Secretariat won in '73, it had likewise been twenty-five years since Citation in '48, and only the most jaded racing fan can resist the symmetry. This one has destiny written all over it. Even the rain that is falling seems only to say: The drought must end.

Triple Crowns come in spurts and do not reappear for long stretches. There were none in the 1920s, then suddenly three in the thirties. There were *four* in the forties, but none in the fifties or sixties. Then there were three again in the seventies, and there has not been one since. We are living in a different age, the age of the All but Triple Crown. Since 1919, when Sir Barton was the first horse to win the Kentucky Derby and the Preakness and the Belmont Stakes all together, seventeen horses have won the first two races only to lose the third, and more than half of these have come along just since 1979. There were three in the eighties, three in the nineties, and so far two in the still-young first decade of the century.

We are living, in other words, in the age of the heart-breaker. This probably has something to do with racing's decline in popularity during the last few decades. Who wants to get mixed up in a sport whose most famous, notable event—the running of a Belmont with Triple Crown potential—is one that we associate with having our hopes first wildly excited then swiftly crushed? And the trainers want a Crown, too. This is the only time their profession ascends to a degree of popularity or exposure enjoyed by the classic American sports on a daily basis, and the reason is that the public wants to see *somebody*, or in this case something, pull it off. The Super Bowl always has a victor; the World Series always has a victor; but the Triple Crown is unique in that the loser can end up being more or less alone in the spotlight. Sarava's winning of last year's Belmont survived for about twenty-four hours in the public consciousness, but War Emblem's loss of the Triple Crown, that was a story, and that *sucked*.

It is terrifically hard to win the Triple Crown. Larry Barrera, who was an assistant trainer when Affirmed won the last one, in 1978, told the *Racing Form*'s Jay Hovdey that when the horse "came into the winner's circle, and they threw the carnations on his shoulders, Affirmed went down to his knees. They buckled, he was that tired." These horses are young and inexperienced, and the three races are each very different; one is unusually short (the Preakness), one is unusually long (the Belmont). The fields go from being scandalously overcrowded, at the Derby, to nearly nonexistent at the Preakness, to full again at the Belmont, where the competition often includes fresh horses whose trainers have skipped the first two races, gunning for this one. That is one reason why the professional handicappers, and not just hacks like me, still shake their heads when they talk about Secretariat. For a horse must be a serious champion to win the Triple Crown—versatile, sound, unflappable, with stamina to match its speed and the underlying toughness to run three demanding races in one month—and Secretariat did not merely win the last race of the Triple Crown, he obliterated it. He was running another race, one that existed only in his head. The Belmont, at that point, was an afterthought.

On the train from Penn Station this morning, it seemed

that Mariana and I were the only people not festooned with silver-and-maroon I LOVE FUNNY CIDE buttons and NEW YORK LOVES FUNNY CIDE caps. Two very drunk men in the seats behind us had this conversation:

GUY: Funny Cide, my side, your side, I don't give a fuck which side. He's still gonna win.

OTHER GUY: Yeah, East Side, West Side . . .

GUY: Yeah.

OTHER GUY: But he's not going to win.

GUY [stunned]: Oh, yeah—he's not gonna win? Who the fuck's gonna win?

OTHER GUY: Empire Maker.

GUY: *Bullllllshiiiiiiiiit*. Listen. I open up the paper this morning, first thing I see is Jerry Bailey [Empire Maker's jockey] talkin' 'bout, "I wouldn't change seats with nobody for this race." You wouldn't, huh? You wouldn't change seats with the guy who's about to run for a five-million-dollar bonus [the amount Visa has said it will pay anyone who wins the Triple Crown]? *Bullllllllshiiiiiiit*.

OTHER GUY: Yeah.

The *Daily Racing Form* was warning us to be cautious—a majority of the handicappers were not predicting a Crown—but as the half-hour trip wore on, we found ourselves succumbing to the hype. And now, at the track, we are completely caught up. There is a level of excitement in the concourse and the stands that I have only read about in books. And even with the memory of last year's dream-crusher still fresh in my mind, I think, Who gives a damn if the drama is cooked up. Let him win. It has been twenty-five years. A story in Lexington's *Blood Horse* magazine says that Funny Cide's trainer and his assistant, Robin Smullen, received a surprise gift yesterday. A man approached them and gave them Secretariat's overgirth (the strap that goes over the saddle, securing it). "'His name is David,' Smullen said, who said she couldn't remember his last name. 'He gave us . . . loaned us . . . the overgirth. It's signed by [jockey] Ron Turcotte, [trainer] Lucien Lauren, and [owner] Penny Tweedy.'"

The Funny Cide crew have decided not to use the overgirth during the race. Smullen tells *The Blood Horse,* "We'll have it in the bag when we go over there."

At eleven o'clock, Mariana and I are standing at the cash machine behind a mustachioed man in a polo shirt who has already had more than a few. He wears a baseball bat and the skin on his face is tobacco-smoked. He is having trouble getting the machine to work, and he keeps turning around to apologize in a raspy voice to the line, which is now eleven people long. It is becoming clear to the rest of us that his account is maxed, but he refuses to accept this, smacking the side of the machine and saying to himself, "Is this thing working?" Finally he turns around and says, "It don't matter. I'm gonna hit the Pick Six." His friend, who is drunk enough to need to be leaning against a nearby pole, suddenly comes to life and says, "Hey, you're missing the Funny Cide crew! On the escalator!" He is pointing down the concourse. Both men start to jog in that direction, shouting, "Jack Knowlton! Jack Knowlton!" (Knowlton is one of the owners, the spokesman for the Funny Cide crew.) Sure enough, midway up the escalator, surrounded by a mob of photographers, are both Knowlton and the fruity old guy, who wears a lemon yellow jacket, a white bowler, and green-checkered pants. Both of them look a little scared and ignore the two men, who are running toward them now, proclaiming their love for the people's horse.

The undercard is under way, but the day is all about the big one: Santos's pretty wife and perpetually weeping son are spotted in the paddock! Santos wins the first race on another mount, a good omen! Bailey loses the third race, on a horse called Al Saqaar (hmm, sounds Arab), another good omen! By the time the special entertainment comes on after the fifth race—an obscure Broadway singer who stands under a green umbrella and does Billy Joel's "New York State of Mind," and who, as he croons along, never stops giving the sound guy the upward-jerking thumb motion that means, *Give me more monitor*—it is clear what today is all about: New York, baby. Funny Cide is the home team. The cops and firemen, our new heroes, are everywhere in their uniforms, along with more serious men, with humorless faces, who carry serious-looking machine guns. As the singer nears the end of the song, he plays with Billy Joel's original lyric, "Don't care if it's Chinatown or Riverside." Now it goes:

And it's fine with me, I've let it slide.
Don't care 'bout no other horse. It's Funny Cide.

When Jerry Bailey wins the tenth race, the one before the Belmont Stakes, the crowd boos him.

Mariana and I are asked to leave our seats in the grandstand (we have been sitting, unawares, in the section reserved for Visa bigwigs), and we take it as a sign that we should try to get up against the rail. If history is made today, we want to be as close as possible. The crowds along the way are a nightmare, ass-grabbing New Yorkers who are seven hours drunker than they were when we got here and who have lost enough money by now to be very upset. Mariana calls my attention to the tickets on the floor, saying, "Look how weird these bets are." I look down: pinwheels, superfectas, other exotics, all of them wrong. Wreckage for the stooper to pick through.

There is a disconcertingly large, implicitly hostile frat element. A girl screams, "Kiss my soggy ass!" I see a guy spitting on strangers from the top of a staircase. At the ramp down which the horses walk to reach the track, a man with a pony-tail, the sides of his head shaved clean, is screaming at the guy behind him. "*Don't—fucking—push me,*" he says, coughing out every word as if it were stuck in his throat. "*Don't— fucking—push me.*" While his head is turned, Empire Maker walks past.

At the rail, we can see nothing. There are too many umbrellas. The surface has now officially been declared "sloppy," and the track workers lift up their pants to run across it, their boots splashing in the mud. After ten minutes of trying to find a stable peephole, we decide to try to bluff our way into the photographers' pen (I am wearing a press badge, so it just might work). The race is minutes away, so we run, back through the concourse and down another ramp. The guy keeping watch over the entrance to the pen rolls his eyes when I give him the pleading look, but he lets us in— no doubt simply tired by now of turning people away—and we make ourselves small against the railing, trying to be as inoffensive as possible. One of the photographers drops a piece of equipment, and it instantly sticks an inch deep in the mud.

There is no better place to watch a race go off than from the "photogs' pen." Placed about ten yards in front of the gate (the spot on the track that will become the wire in a few minutes—the Belmont is a long, complete loop), the pen is designed so that the cameramen can get their "money shots," the ones that will be on the front page of the papers tomorrow, and it is recessed, so that your eyes are only about a foot off the ground. When the horses are loaded into the gate, we are looking up into their faces through the wire mesh, right into their eyes, which give away nothing.

When they break, the roar of the crowd comes crashing down on our backs, physical, with concussive force, as if a dam had broken. And the feeling—it is as if the bolting open of the doors were the click of a shutter, and you are suddenly frozen in a photograph of some historical moment. It is the seventies, and you are in *Life* magazine. Everyone around you, they must be in the photograph, too, because it is, for the moment, not conceivable that you are here, or that it is now. What might happen is too much, and it puts you at a distance. But I know that this has to do with me, too. What else have I been hoping to see for the last two years, after all, why else have I been following the two-year-olds, spending vacations hunched over out-of-print volumes of horse lore, studying the *Racing Form*, if not to see a horse do it again—be perfect, at least for May and June—or to know that one can.

Many of the articles, tomorrow, will report that Funny Cide breaks first, but this is not what happens. Empire Maker breaks first, then immediately downshifts, allowing Funny Cide and a few other horses to pass him. Thus Empire Maker instantly establishes himself in the stalking position, which is what I thought José Santos wanted to do. This is a long race, after all, and Funny Cide has so far proven nothing about his stamina.

They go past absolutely blasting mud, some of which lands on our shoulders. Their riders are clinging to their backs like monkeys, like mannequins, hunched in the position that Faulkner described, with greater accuracy than taste, as "excrescent and precarious." When they round the first turn, Funny Cide is in the lead, and the roar has only gotten louder. My sense of time goes into the same unreal suspension that you feel when you have just jumped off a waterfall. Things are happening too fast and in slow motion at the same time. And the track announcer says, "In the lead is *Funny Cide*."

They are in the backstretch, only the tops of their heads and the jockeys visible now, and Funny Cide still leads. This is all wrong. Mariana and I are having a weird unconscious exchange under our breath: "No *way* he has that much horse," I say. "Yes he does," she says.

They round the bend, and Santos has somehow held on. The horses have already run the length of the Derby, and Funny Cide is still in the lead by half a length, "You're right," I say. "I can't believe it." I think: He may do it. What may be the first Triple Crown winner in a quarter century is emerging from the bend, coming into the final turn, back into our sight. He has been ahead of the pack from the moment he passed us, over two minutes ago. Seconds are left.

But something is happening. He is tiring, running beyond his limits. His nostrils are blowing wide open with each outward snort, and his teeth are parted. Santos, sensing the pressure at his back, has gone to the whip too soon, is using it too urgently, rocking with the horse's head as if he could force it on like a bicycle that is rolling to a stop.

As they clear the turn, Empire Maker is mid-move. And there is an instant, a scene that suddenly freezes and expands, in which Funny Cide looks to be fighting him off. But Empire Maker is strong. He is coming on cold and mad and feary, looking as though he could run forever. Yet with only the homestretch left to go, Funny Cide has it by a head. The announcer is screaming, knowing that he must compete with the crowd. All Funny Cide has to do is stay in front for two more furlongs, to find something, in his worn-out muscles, that he can use. He has already run so far.

They are neck and neck. And Santos is raising the whip so high before he brings it down with a smack. I can see the horse's eyes again, and I know that he knows that this is a race. He knows what it means to win, to surpass. The fields of praise are open before him. Every bit of his strength he has given away to his rider, yet somehow he wants to give more, to run harder, to pull away from the pounding behind him, the sound of the others, who want him to lose.

If he failed in his mission, this story will end here.

SOURCES

This book is meant to be as much a tour (albeit at times a cursory one) through the literature of the horse as through the culture of Thoroughbred ownership and racing, so it makes little sense here to include any "notes toward further reading": the book itself can be read as a series of such notes. Sources are given mainly as a guide to readers who want a fuller understanding of individual topics addressed in the various sections.

Be warned, however, that to become interested in "horse books" is to fall down an especially deep rabbit hole. Few subjects have been written about as often or, as I have found to my envy and delight during the past three years, as well. I eventually stopped counting the number of times I thought to myself, "Somebody should do a book just about this" (about, say, the history of the early black American jockeys, or some other obscure theme I congratulated myself on having discovered), only to learn, the next time I went to the library, that somebody *had* done a book, and that it was first-rate. But this is the fun.

It perhaps goes without saying that in a few places.—most notably in "ICON," the section concerning the physical evolution of the horse and the history of its meaning in human culture—I have reduced to a sentence or a paragraph material that fills not only entire books but entire libraries; and by the same token I have, out of mercy for both myself and the reader, often been emphatic and self-assured about subjects that are in fact passionately debated by the experts (David Anthony's theories regarding the advent of riding, for instance). I did this also in hopes that the amateur spirit presiding over this book—and which the book is in some ways *about*, if I have succeeded—will be unlikely to inspire in novices undue faith in my opinions.

And finally, if any of my fellow Kentuckians are among those reading this, please write to your senators and congressmen asking that they do all they can to bring *A Narrative of the Life & Travels of John Robert Shaw, the Well-Digger, Now Resident in Lexington, Kentucky, Written by Himself, 1807*, back into print. Let not the man have been blasted in vain—whilst ramming.

THE KID

Sullivan, Mike. "Out of the Shadows Comes the Kid with His Mission." *Louisville Courier-Journal & Times*, May 6, 1973.

———. "Sham ran perfectly, but 'just got tired.'" *Louisville Courier-Journal & Times*, May 6, 1973.

THE CHILD OF EUROPE

Herzog, Werner. *The Enigma of Kaspar Hauser*. DVD director's commentary. New York: Criterion Collection, 2002.

Kitchen, Martin. *Kaspar Hauser: Europe's Child*. New York: Palgrave, 2001.

Newton, Michael. *Savage Girls and Wild Boys*. New York: St. Martin's Press, 2001.

EIN REITER WILL ICH WERDEN

Hillenbrand, Laura. *Seabiscuit*. New York: Random House, 2001.

BEAUTY

Keylor, William R. "A Re-evaluation of the Versailles Peace." *Relevance*, vol. 5, no. 3 (Fall 1996).

Boemeke, Manfred F. "Woodrow Wilson's Image of Germany, the War-Guilt Question, and the Treaty of Versailles." In *The Treaty of Versailles: A Reassessment after 75 Years*, edited by Boemeke, Gerald D. Feldman, and Elisabeth Glaser. Boston: Cambridge University Press, 1998.

Nack, William. *Secretariat: The Making of a Champion*. Cambridge, Mass.: Da Capo Press, 1975.

EIGHTEEN HORSES IN ONE LINE

Kuhnert, Max. *Will We See Tomorrow?* South Yorkshire: Leo Cooper, 1993.

TRIALS

Filson, John. *The Discovery, Settlement and Present State of Kentucke*. New York: Corinth Books, 1962.

Haywood, John. *The Natural and Aboriginal History of Tennessee.* Knoxville, Tn.: F. M. Hill-Books, 1973.

Shaw, John Robert. *A Narrative of the Life and Travels of John Robert Shaw, the Well-Digger, Now Resident in Lexington, Kentucky, Written by Himself, 1807.* Louisville, Ky.: George Fowler, 1930.

Thackeray, William Makepeace. *The Paris Sketch Book; The Irish Sketch Book; and, Notes of a Journey from Cornhill to Grand Cairo.* London and New York: T. Nelson, 1907.

"EIGHTEEN STRAIGHT WHISKIES"

Sinclair, Andrew. *Dylan the Bard; The Life of Dylan Thomas.* New York: St. Martin's Press, 1999.

HIS BIRTH UNKNOWN

Anonymous (The South Carolina Jockey Club). *The History of the Turf in South Carolina.* Charleston: Russell and Jones, 1857.

Clark, Thomas D. *Kentucky: Land of Contrast.* New York: Harper & Row, 1968.

Conn, George H. *The Arabian Horse in America.* Woodstock, Vt.: Countryman Press, 1957.

Dohner, Janet Vorwald. *The Encyclopedia of Historic and Endangered Livestock and Poultry Breeds.* New Haven: Yale University Press, 2001.

Doughty, Charles M. *Travels in Arabia Deserta.* New York: Random House, 1937.

Harrison, Lowell H. *The Civil War in Kentucky.* Lexington: University Press of Kentucky, 1975.

Hollingsworth, Kent. *The Kentucky Thoroughbred.* Lexington: University Press of Kentucky, 1976.

Hotaling, Edward. *The Great Black Jockeys: The Lives and Times of the Men Who Dominated America's First National Sport.* Rocklin, Calif: Forum, 1999.

Lancaster, Clay. *Vestiges of the Venerable City: A Chronicle of Lexington, Kentucky.* Lexington: Lexington-Fayette County Historic Commission, 1978.

Macdonald, Margaret Taylor. *The Milward Family of Lexington, Kentucky, 1803–1969.* Dallas: Margaret Taylor Macdonald, 1970.

Mastin, Bettye Lee. *Lexington, 1779: Pioneer Kentucky.* Lexington: Lexington-Fayette County Historic Commission, 1979.

Morland, T. Hornby. *The Genealogy of the English Race Horse.* London: J. Barfield, 1810.

O'Hare, John Richard. *The Socio-Economic Aspects of Horse Racing.* Washington, D.C.: Catholic University of America Press, 1945.

Porter, Roy, ed. *The Cambridge Illustrated History of Medicine.* Cambridge, England: Cambridge University Press, 1996.

Rancke, George Washington. *The History of Lexington, Kentucky: Its Annals and Recent Progress.* Bowie, Md.: Heritage Books, 1989.

Renau, Lynn S. *Jockeys, Belles and Bluegrass Kings.* Louisville: Herr House Press, 1995.

Weatherby, James. *An Introduction to a General Stud Book.* London: J. Weatherby, 1791.

Wentworth, Lady. *Thoroughbred Racing Stock and Its Ancestors.* London: G. Allen & Unwin, 1938.

Whyte, James Christie. *History of the British Turf, From the Earliest Period to the Present Day.* London: Henry Colburn, 1840.

MORNING WORKS

Adams, Henry. *The Education of Henry Adams.* Boston: Houghton Mifflin, 2000.

Collins, Robert W. *Race Horse Training.* Lexington: Blood-Horse, 1938.

Keeneland: Reflections on a Thoroughbred Tradition. Lexington: Keeneland Association and Harmony House Publishers, 2000.

Lawrence, D. H. *Apocalypse.* London: Penguin Books, 1995.

Palmer, Joe H. *This Was Racing.* New York: A. S. Barnes, 1953.

AMONG THE YEARLINGS

Budiansky, Stephen. *The Nature of Horses: Exploring Equine Evolution, Intelligence, and Behavior.* New York: Free Press, 1997.

Clark, Thomas D. *Kentucky: Land of Contrast.* New York: Harper & Row, 1968.

BLOOD

Adami, George. "The Second International Congress of Eugenics: The True Aristocracy," *Scientific Monthly*, vol. 13, no. 5 (Nov. 1921).

Allen, Garland. "DNA and Human Behavior Genetics: Implications for the Criminal Justice System." In *The Technology of Justice: The Use of DNA in the Criminal Justice System*, edited by D. Lazer and M. S. Smith. Cambridge: MIT Press, 2004.

Conley, Kevin. *Stud: Adventures in Breeding.* New York: Bloomsbury, 2002.

Davenport, Charles Benedict. *Heredity in Relation to Eugenics.* New York: Henry Holt, 1913.

Galton, Sir Francis. *Inquiries into Human Faculty and Its Development.* New York: E. P. Dutton, 1908.

Hitler, Adolf. *Mein Kampf.* New York: Reynal & Hitchcock, 1939.

Springfield, Rollo. *The Horse and His Rider: or, Sketches and Anecdotes of the Noble Quadruped and of Equestrian Nations.* New York: Wiley & Putnam, 1847.

Stokes, W. E. D. *The Right to Be Well Born; or, Horse Breeding in Its Relation to Eugenics.* New York: C. J. O'Brien, 1917.

Thurtle, Phillip. "Beaufort's Bastards: Information Processing and Industrial Breeding." In *In Vivo: Embodying Information*, edited by Phillip Thurtle and Robert Mitchell. Seattle: University of Washington Press, forthcoming.

Tucker, William H. *The Funding of Scientific Racism: Wickliffe Draper and the Pioneer Fund.* Chicago: University of Illinois Press, 2002.

A CERTAIN MYSTICAL QUALITY

Vernon, Arthur. *The History and Romance of the Horse.* New York: Dover Publications, 1946.

ICON

Adorno, Rolena, and Patrick Charles Pautz, eds. *The Narrative of Cabeza de Vaca.* Lincoln: University of Nebraska Press, 2003.

Alford, Violet. *The Hobby Horse and Other Animal Masks.* London: Merlin Press, 1978.

Andrews, Charles M. *Colonial Folkways.* New Haven: Yale University Press, 1920.

Bahn, Paul G. *Journey Through the Ice Age.* Berkeley: University of California Press, 1988.

Bell, John. *A Journey from St. Petersburg to Peking, 1719–22.* New York: Barnes & Noble, 1966.

Cawte, E. C. *Ritual Animal Disguise.* Cambridge, England: D. S. Brewer, 1978.

Chauvet, Jean-Marie, Eliette Brunel Deschamps, and Christian Hillaire. *Dawn of Art: The Chauvet Cave.* New York: Harry N. Abrams, 1996.

Cornwall, I. W. *Prehistoric Animals and Their Hunters.* London: Faber and Faber, 1968.

Crowell, Ann. *Dawn Horse to Derby Winner: The Evolution of the Horse.* New York: Praeger Publishers, 1973.

Dent, Anthony. *Horses in Shakespeare's England.* London: J. A. Allen, 1987.

Doughty, Charles M. *Travels in Arabia Deserta.* New York: Random House, 1937.

Ewers, John C. *The Horse in Blackfoot Indian Culture.* Washington, D.C.: Smithsonian Institution Press, 1955.

Graham, R. B. Cunninghame. *The Horses of the Conquest.* Norman: University of Oklahoma Press, 1949.

Hayes, M. Horace. *Points of the Horse: A Treatise on the Conformation, Movements, Breeds, and Evolution of the Horse.* New York: Arco Publishing Company, 1969.

Henry, Marguerite. *King of the Wind.* New York: Rand McNally, 1948.

Howey, M. Oldfield. *The Horse in Magic and Myth.* New York: Castle Books, 1958.

Hudson, Charles. *Knights of Spain, Warriors of the Sun.* Athens: University of Georgia Press, 1997.

———. *The Southeastern Indians.* Knoxville: University of Tennessee Press, 1976.

Morison, Samuel Eliot. *The European Discovery of America.* New York: Oxford University Press, 1974.

Olsen, Sandra L., ed. *Horses Through Time.* Boulder, Colo.: Roberts Rinehart Publishers for Carnegie Museum of Natural History, 2000.

Prescott, William H. *The History of the Conquest of Mexico.* Chicago: University of Chicago Press, 1966.

Wright, Louis B. *The Cultural Life of the American Colonies, 1607–1763.* New York: Harper & Brothers, 1957.

FIRST FRIDAY IN MAY

Dickens, Charles. *American Notes.* New York: Modern Library, 1996.

Hersh, Marcus. "The Making of a Star, Race by Race." *Daily Racing Form,* June 7, 2002.

Milligan, Harold Vincent. *Stephen Collins Foster: A Biography of America's Folk-Song Composer.* New York: G. Schirmer, 1920.

Moore, Harry T., ed. *The Collected Letters of D. H. Lawrence, vol. 2.* New York: Viking Press, 1962.

LISTEN TO THIS

Acocella, Joan, ed. *The Diary of Vaslav Nijinsky.* New York: Farrar, Straus and Giroux, 1999.

Bicknell, A. S. *Hippophagy: The Horse as Food for Man.* London: William Ridgeway, 1868.

Buckle, Richard. *Nijinsky.* London: Weidenfeld & Nicolson, 1971.

Chamberlain, Lesley. *Nietzsche in Turin*. London: Quartet Books, 1996.

Davenport, Guy. *Every Force Evolves a Form*. San Francisco: North Point Press, 1987.

Fallada, Hans. *Iron Gustav*. London: Wyman & Sons, 1940.

Ostwald, Peter. *Vaslav Nijinsky: A Leap into Madness*. New York: Carol Publishing Group, 1991.

Williams, Jenny. *More Lives Than One: A Biography of Hans Fallada*. London: Libris, 1998.

WAR

Brereton, J. M. *The Horse in War*. New York: Arco Publishing Company, 1976.

Ellis, John. *Cavalry: The History of Mounted Warfare*. Vancouver, B.C.: Westbridge Books, 1978.

Piekalkiewicz, Janusz. *The Cavalry of World War II*. London: Orbis Publishing., 1979.

Sax, Boria. *Animals in the Third Reich: Pets, Scapegoats, and the Holocaust*. New York: Continuum, 2000.

PEACE

Encyclopaedia Britannica. "Piccolomini, Prince Octavio." Edinburgh and London: A. & C. Black, 1911.

Merian, Matthaeus, et al. *Theatrum Europaeum*, vol. 6. Gedruckt zu Franckfurt: Bey Wolffgang Hoffmann, 1637–1738.

Mullins, Patricia. *The Rocking Horse: A History of Moving Toy Horses*. London: New Cavendish Books, 1992.

THE PRINCE

Anonymous. "By All Accounts, This Is One Prince of a Fellow." *The Louisville Courier-Journal*, June 5, 2002.

Breslin, Jimmy. "No Apology After Big Win." *New York Newsday*, May 7, 2002.

Moran, Paul. "Prince: Man of Mystery." *New York Newsday*, June 3, 2002.

Morgan, Jon. "Prince's Crowning Moment Could Bring Backlash." *The Baltimore Sun*, June 8, 2002.

The Sports Ethics Institute. June 10, 2002. www.sportsethicsinstitute. org/respect_tolerance.htm

Weaver, Mary Anne. "Blowback." *The Atlantic Monthly*, May 1996.

THE RIDER IS LOST

Bunting, Greta. *The Horse: The Most Abused Domestic Animal.* St. Petersburg, Fla.: G. Bunting, 1997.

Finley, Bill. "1986 Derby Winner Was Slaughtered, Magazine Reports." *The New York Times*, July 23, 2003.

Nack, William. *My Turf: Horses, Boxers, Blood Money and the Sporting Life.* Cambridge, Mass.: Da Capo Press, 2003.

LARGER

Nack, William. "Pure Heart." *Sports Illustrated,* June 4, 1990.

——. *Secretariat: The Making of a Champion.* Cambridge, Mass.: Da Capo Press, 1975

Surface, Bill. *The Track: A Day in the Life of Belmont Park.* New York: Macmillan, 1976.

ONE YEAR LATER

Drape, Joe. "Bettor Said to Have Frat Ties to Fired Worker." *The New York Times*, Nov. 1,2002.

Faulkner, William. "Kentucky: May: Saturday." *Sports Illustrated*, May 16, 1955.

King, Laura. "Racetrack Survives War and Vandals." *Los Angeles Times*, May 28, 2003.

ACKNOWLEDGMENTS

This book has been so long in the works, and has passed through so many different forms, that I have probably forgotten more people to whom I owe thanks than I will remember. The whole idea—of "doing something on horses"—grew out of a fireside conversation with Guy Davenport about the long history of the talking horse as a literary motif, and his advice (as well as his ability to point one toward obscure sources) has been indispensable. To those at *Harper's Magazine* who helped me shape the excerpt that appeared there—Lewis Lapham, Ellen Rosenbush, Roger Hodge, Virginia Heffernan, Naomi Kirsten, and especially Ben Metcalf—I am grateful. Stacey Clarkson, the art director of *Harper's,* put her organizational talents and her painter's eye to work in helping me track down the images in this book. I appreciate the National Thoroughbred Racing Association's allowing generous press access to a reporter with dubious intent and credentials. The parts of this book that are set in and around Lexington, Kentucky, would have been much harder to write without the hospitality of my friends and family there: my grandmother, Jane Milward; my uncle John and aunt Luanne Milward; my uncle Greg and aunt Mimi Milward; and my friends Chris and Becky Johnson. All of them gave me places to work, fed me, and tried to explain to me three years ago why it was that a horse not yet a year old could be called a "yearling." My uncle John in particular answered no end of stupid questions. Needless to say, no one in my family is in the least responsible for any seemingly unflattering things I may have said about Kentucky; indeed, on more than one occasion they have asked me not to say them. My sisters Lisa and Michelle both helped me find necessary things among my father's papers, and are lovely people. My uncle Jerry Sullivan was as excellent a source as he is a human being. Maria and Amos Johnson, as well as Benicia Hernandez, gave me a patio on which to work during a tense phase in the book's completion. Several friends have done me the invaluable and much-appreciated favor of simply listening to me read drafts over dinner or the telephone, and of laughing in the right places, out of pity or not, I do not care: Ben McGowan, Jack Hitt, Kevin Baker, Wyatt Mason, Beth Sullivan, Worth Wagers, Mark Richard, Sanford McGee, Amy Hughes, Silas Davenport. Bill Nack, out of sheer kindness, alerted me to the presence of several ghastly factual errors. My mother, Elizabeth Terry, caught a few instances in which I had tinkered with the truth, possibly in order to minimize my own guilt over having caused certain family disasters. I love her. Jin Auh, my agent, understood this project in all its strangeness from the start, was as excellent a critic as she was a representative, and has my thanks. Lorin Stein at FSG is the sort of book editor writers are told, when they move to New York, no longer exists—uncomfortably perceptive, unforgiving when called for, and patient when it took me a while to see his point. I am deeply thankful for his editing, encouragement, and humor (Annie Wedekind at FSG also offered a number of sensitive criticisms, all of which turned out to be useful). For help with the UK edition (including the help of causing it to exist) I'd like to thank Matt Phillips, Kris Potter, Phil Brown, Fiona Murphy and everyone else at Yellow Jersey Press—also Tracy Bohan at Wylie, a stellar agent and person. Lastly, I thank Mariana Chloe Johnson, who on a perfect fall day at Keeneland consistently outbet two self-styled horsemen by picking the ones with names she liked. Without her this book would have been less readable, the years it covers less bearable. *Gracia' por todo y "ma' pa'lla," mi alma.*

INDEX

New York Racing Association, 223, 225
Nicklaus, Jack, 200
Nietzsche, Friedrich, 181–82
Nijinsky, Vaslav, 181–82
Nijinsky (horse), 226
North, the, 145–46
Northern Alliance (in Afghanistan), on horseback, 173
Northern Dancer, 226
Nuremberg, Germany, 22–23, 175–77

Officer, 97, 167
Off-Track Betting (OTB), New York, 185–87
Olaf, St., 180
Olsen, Sandra L., 127
Other Paper (Columbus, Ohio), 18
Oxley, John, 71

Pakistan, 190n
Palmer, Joe H., 29
Palmer, Robert, 114
parents with bad habits, 9–10
Patchen Wilkes Stock Farm, 91
Paterson, Ann, 129
Peace of Westphalia, 175
Peru, 137
Petén Itza, Mexico, 135–37
Peter Volo, 91
"Phantom Flight" of September 13, 2001, 121–23
photographers, track, 232
Picasso, Pablo, 180
Piccolomini, Octavio, 175–78
Piekalkiewicz, Janusz, 171
Pincay, Laffitt, 20–21, 199
Pioneer Fund, 89
Pizarro, Francisco, 133
plague, 42–43
Pleasant County, 193, 197
Poe, David, 44
Poe, Edgar Allan, 44
Poland, 170
Ponies, 132

PortaBubble, 15
Posner, Gerald, 190–91n
Powell Walton Milward company, 45
Preakness, 185–88, 227
pregnancy testing, 55
prehistoric times, 127–29, 143
Prohibition, 70
Protestants, 101
Proud Citizen, 186, 202, 203
Proust, Marcel, 215–16
Przewalski horses, 131–32
Ptolemy, 179
Puritans, 141
Push, Steve, 223

Q-Ray affair, 225
quarter horses, 49, 96
Quinlan, Michael, 147
Quinn, Arthur Hobson, 44

racetracks: corruption at, 223; early, 58
Ranck, George W., 43
Ray, Joseph, 33n
Raytheon Corporation, 121
Reed, Billy, 21
Reese, Mark, 12
Reese, Pee Wee, 12–13
Reineman, Russell, 162
Remnant (author's dog), 218–22
Revolutionary War, 35
Rice, Pat, 129
Richardson, Kevin, 151, 191
riding, prehistoric origin of, 128, 143
Rig Veda, 139
Riverside Methodist Hospital, Columbus, Ohio, 3, 6, 16, 207
Riwoche horse, 132
Rockefeller, John D., Sr., 89
Rome, Italy, 138
Rose, Pete, 17
Ruggles (author's dog), 217–20
Rusbridge, Jack, 122n
Russia, 170–71

sacrifice of horses, 139, 142, 179

Weston, Stephen, 54
westward expansion, 35
Whisperer, the, 99
Whyte, James C., 51
wild horses, 49, 81, 132–33
Wilson, Julie, 195
Wimmer, Chris, 108–09, 112, 113
winter racing, 195–96
Wolfe, Thomas, 112
Wolfowitz, Paul, 173
"work" (horses), 75–76, 79
World War I, 31, 168–70

World War II, 90, 100–1, 170–73,
    178–79
Wrigglesworth Arabian, 53

yearlings, sale of, 82–87, 93–99,
    119–21, 222
Young, Steve, 197–8

Zad-el-Rakib, 52
Zeyd, the Bedouin, 51–52
Zoeller, Fuzzy, 146
Zubaydah, Abu, 190n

ILLUSTRATION CREDITS

2   "Hobbyhorse race, England, 1937." Copyright © Hulton-Deutsch Collection/CORBIS.

12   "Figure 42" from *The Horse: Structure and Movement*, by R. H. Smythe, copyright © 1967. J. A. Allen and Co., London. Courtesy of Robert Hale Limited, London.

21   *Travoys Arriving with Wounded at a Dressing Station, Smol, Macedonia, 1916*, by Stanley Spencer (1891–1959). Courtesy of the Imperial War Museum, London/Bridgeman Art Library.

27   "Anatomy Lecture, May 1942." Copyright © CORBIS.

32   *Shire Horse, "Elephant"*, by an unnamed artist, reproduced in *The Great Horse* by Gilbey, circa 1792. Courtesy of the Mary Evans Picture Library.

39   *Sleeping Stable Boy and Witch*, by Hans Baldung, circa 1534. Courtesy of Öffentliche Kunstsammlung Basel, Kupferstichkabinett.

48   "Figure 41" from *The Horse: Structure and Movement*, by R. H. Smythe, copyright © 1967. J. A. Allen and Co., London. Courtesy of Robert Hale Limited, London.

52   *Measured Drawing of a Horse Facing Left*, by Andrea Del Verrocchio (1435–1488). Copyright © Metropolitan Museum of Art, New York, Frederick C. Hewitt Fund, 1917 (17.76.5).

63   *Study for a Sculpture of a Horse*, by Leonardo da Vinci (1452–1519). Courtesy of Biblioteca Nacional, Madrid/Bridgeman Art Library.